A BED for the NIGHT

A BED
for the NIGHT

The Story of the Wheeling Bellboy

E. M. STATLER

and His Remarkable Hotels

by RUFUS JARMAN

HARPER & BROTHERS, PUBLISHERS, NEW YORK

Contents

A BED for the NIGHT

I

The Old Man

In 1950 the hotel industry decided to honor the person who had contributed most to the science of innkeeping during the past half century. In that period the lowly taverns had developed into public palaces, and the homely calling of serving food and drink, making beds, and sweeping floors had assumed the dignity of Big Business. The industry didn't have to look far before deciding that the only candidate for the title of "Hotel Man of the Half Century" was the late E. M. Statler.

Largely to make this official, *The Southern Hotel Journal* held a contest by asking four prominent hotel executives to nominate a candidate each. All four named E. M. Statler. Then a hundred other hotel operators were asked to vote either for the nominee or write in their own choice. All but two of them stuck with Statler.

"The Hotel Man of the Half Century," who has been dead since 1928, did not look much like the general conception of a hotel tycoon, which is sleek and suave. He was rugged and plain, with a wide, homely mouth and a lock of hair that fell over his forehead. He wore old fedora hats, and his secretary always had to remind him to buy a new suit of clothes. Even after he had become a successful hotel mogul, he dressed himself in three-dollar shoes, eighteen-dollar suits, carried an Ingersoll watch, and wore one pair of twenty-five-cent cufflinks for twenty years. Statler looked more like the late Will Rogers than like Adolphe Menjou.

By the same token, Statler's contributions to the science of hotel-keeping were simple, practical and typically American. The Waldorf-Astoria in New York introduced most of the flossier points of elaborate hotel service in this country, to appeal to the new-rich American millionaires who were its best customers. These patrons were fast acquiring finicky tastes and a quick-grown culture, based largely upon extravagance and display. So the Waldorf catered to them by starting such practices as having smartly groomed assistant managers on the floor at all times to see to their minor wants—a sensible service that is now followed, to some degree at least, by all large hotels.

The original Waldorf was the first hotel to put gentlewomen on all the guest floors to serve as floor clerks, and it introduced room service in America. It originated the supercourtesy practice of sending elaborate gifts of fruit, flowers, candy and liquors to prominent guests, with the compliments of the management. The Waldorf was first of the fashionable hotels to abolish the "ladies entrance." It was first to allow gentlemen to smoke in the dining rooms, and first in America to hire expensive orchestras to play for the entertainment of guests while dining. It was the first hotel to provide plushy apartments for permanent residences of wealthy guests, and even first to use velvet ropes to keep back the crowds at the entrances of its fine restaurants.

Statler, who probably never laid eyes on a millionaire before he reached his maturity, learned the hotel business by looking after the realistic wants of commercial drummers and touring theatrical troupes. He was, therefore, more interested in basic comforts in his hotels than in fancy trimmings.

"A shoe salesman and a traveling prince," he once said, "want essentially the same things when they are on the road—namely, good food and a comfortable bed—and that is what I propose to give them."

Once when a young executive at his Pennsylvania Hotel in New York complained that Statler wasn't giving some of the fine touches of service that a few of the fancy luxury hotels on the East Side were dispensing, the old man said: "Look. If I wanted to, I could run a so-called luxury hotel or a resort hotel that would beat any damn thing those frizzly-headed foreigners are doing, but I just don't operate in that field. To hell with it; I'm not interested in it. All I want to do is to have more comforts and conveniences and serve better food than any of them have or do, and mine will be at a price ordinary people can afford."

And so, Statler's first permanent hotel, the old Buffalo Statler, which opened in 1907, didn't have as many tailcoats and champagne buckets as the old Waldorf-Astoria, but it did have a bath with every guest room—which neither the Waldorf nor any other hotel in the world had at the time. To advertise it, Statler coined a slogan that was later to be copied widely by hotels throughout America: "A Room and a Bath for a Dollar and a Half."

Statler was the first hotel builder to install circulating ice water in every guest room. He was inspired to do this, he said in later years, by his experiences as a bellhop at the old McLure House, in Wheeling, West Virginia. There he was interminably hustling pitchers of cracked ice to the thirsty drummers on the upper floors.

While serving as night clerk there, Statler observed that guests sometimes had difficulty locating the keyholes in their doors, particularly when they returned to the hotel in a merry mood. So, when he built his hotels, he had keyholes placed above the doorknobs, rather than at the customary location underneath. This simple idea has prevented untold profanity, pandemonium and confusion among guests returning late from the local bars and fleshpots.

Until Statler came along, the more modest hotels provided only a few hooks on the walls where guests could hang their extra clothing, if any; the plush houses had wardrobe chests. Statler was the first to build a closet in every room, and he put an electric light in every closet—a convenience that some builders haven't gotten around to yet. Out of deference to women with drooping petticoats, he put a full-length mirror in every room. He originated a lock plunger with a button indicator that was installed in every door so that housemaids could tell whether or not a guest was in his room without disturbing him. And he put a pincushion, with sewing equipment, in every room, for which ten million guests with missing buttons have called him blessed.

Statler began the practice of delivering free morning newspapers under each guest's door. To allow this, all Statler doors stop five-eighths of an inch above the floor. The company last year delivered 3,000,000 newspapers, costing $150,000, to guests by this route. The Boston Statler was the world's first hotel with a free radio in every room. The Statlers still provide free radios in every room of all their hotels, although most hotels have now abandoned, or never did adopt, this practice.

Statler coined the phrase, "The customer is always right," and he went ahead to make it stick with a policy of refusing to keep any employee who couldn't please his guests. "Nobody has a right to insult one of my guests but me," he used to say, "and I won't." Statler was the first hotel man to provide for the drummer, the theatrical trouper and the ordinary American on the road the type of services, dignities and comforts—as real, if less fancy—that the wealthy classes were accorded in the plushy hotels of London, Paris, the Riviera and New York.

When Mr. Statler entered the hotel business, the industry was just beginning to emerge from the homely crudities of the tavern stage. It had not been many years since some hotels had punished guests for nonpayment of their bills by cutting off their trousers at the knees, and making them stand in the lobby with a sign around their necks that said: DEADBEAT. In some New England hotels, guests who used cuss words in the house were either fined or made to accompany the proprietor and his family to church services.

Even in Statler's time, the What Cheer, a 600-room hotel in San Francisco, still had among its printed house rules requests for guests to refrain from spitting on the carpets, lying in bed with their boots on, or driving nails into the furniture. This hotel had a strict policy of examining all guests suspected of having lice. If they were found to be inhabited, the hotel paid for the delousing.

Most of the better hotels had not more than one bath and toilet "down the hall" on each floor. Rooms were equipped with bowls, pitchers and slop jars. In pretentious hotels, this crockery was adorned with garlands of flora. Bathtubs in the one bathroom per floor were usually built on a sort of throne, and encased in wooden paneling. Usually a charge of twenty-five cents was made for enough hot water for a bath.

Nine-tenths of hotels were American plan. Food was unlimited, cheap and good. Rates in the best hotels were $1.25 a day for room and meals. Smoking was not permitted in the dining room; cigarettes were taboo; more wine and beer were sold than hard liquor; bars allowed no women; and the cocktail lounge and the beauty parlor were unknown. Hot water for shaving and ice water for drinking were at push-button call. Cigars were twenty-five cents a dozen. Rooms were heated with stoves or open fireplaces. There were usually signs to remind guests not to blow out the gas jets, and no proprietor called his house really full until all the double beds were fully occupied, often by bedmates who were complete strangers.

The old-fashioned day book was used instead of cards for registering guests, and there was a superstition among room clerks that if the register were closed, through some accident, business would be bad for the rest of the day. Most of the hotels' bookkeeping consisted of jotting down opposite the guest's name in the registration ledger whatever had been charged against his account.

During the latter decades of the nineteenth century some hotels began to benefit from scientific discovery. The old Hotel Everett, run by Samuel H. Everett, at 8940 Chatham Street, Park Row, New York, became, in 1890, the first hotel to be lighted electrically. The Everett had 101 incandescent bulbs in its dining room, lobby and reading room. The first dishwashing machines were installed in 1884. The first hotel barber shop (with 250 silver dollars imbedded in its floor) was put in the Palmer House in 1870. The first hotel passenger elevator was installed in 1854; that was in the old Fifth Avenue Hotel in New York.

But, in spite of these advances, most hotels remained stark in appearance and bare of luxuries. A great many hotels that were famous for tables groaning under loads of fowl and game had bleak, cold bedrooms upstairs, with blackened fireplaces, narrow windows and bare wooden floors. Even lobbies and public rooms, which were regarded as splendid in those days, had a certain raw-boned but overdressed look. And the service, while it might have been willing and enthusiastic, was also apt to be unskilled and bumpkinish.

Hotel living in America never became a thing to be envied until the big palaces, like the old Waldorf, were built with new American fortunes, and managed by Europeans who knew the secrets of service. It was E. M. Statler's notion that he could provide all these essential comforts in a simpler way, without the great array of flunkies and valets with which the European-managed hotels were staffed. He had to do this by designing hotels in which smaller staffs could dispense service conveniently. That is what he gradually did for his own houses, and they were to become the model for most of the larger hotels built in this country since.

Statler's formula for hotel building was to put the guest rooms in the center of the building—between the top and bottom, that is—with sample rooms where traveling men could display their goods on the top floor, isolated from the regular guests. Public spaces were on the first two or three floors. It was his idea to concentrate the functions spaces—ballrooms and private dining rooms —on the floor above the lobby to give private dinners and banquets semiprivacy, and prevent these functions from interfering with the normal flow of traffic on the lobby floor.

Statler had the idea of a three-sided kitchen on the same floor with his principal dining rooms. Earlier practice in hotel building was to put the kitchen in the basement, because basement space was less valuable and a nice view was not necessary from the kitchen windows. But Statler preferred to figure out a good place for his kitchen first, and build the dining rooms around it. A kitchen immediately adjoining a dining room, he felt, cut down the number of employees needed, and allowed more people to be served in less time.

One side of his kitchen served the main dining room. Another side served the café or coffee shop, while the third side served room service. Statler designed his batteries of service elevators leading directly from the heart of his plant—the kitchens, laundry and engineering departments—like a big artery to feed the upper floors. He surrounded his elevator shafts with wide service stairways, with a roomy service lobby on each floor. And he was one of the first hotel builders, perhaps the first, to close off these service shafts from the rest of the house as a protection against fire.

Old-time hotel men, both within and without the Statler organization, agree that the Old Man knew more about hotel blueprints than any architect. When one of his hotels was being built, he was forever scrambling out on the bare steel beams with a level and slide rule to see how well the builders were following the plans. One time, when his Detroit house was going up, Statler, climbing about on the framework, detected with his naked eye a line of windows in the court that were being built slightly out of line.

When the Boston house was nearing completion, Statler, who was sixty-five at the time, went up with several of his executives to inspect the building. When about half of the house had been viewed, the group suddenly discovered that the Old Man was no longer with them. They started a frenzied search, and finally found him lying in a dry bathtub, scowling at the ceiling. Statler said the ceiling was not smooth enough to suit him, and all the bathrooms with ceilings as rough as that one would have to be redone. Guests, he said, are most conscious of a rough ceiling when they are lying in the tub.

Statler was the first hotel operator to introduce standardization into the purchase of his supplies and materials. As soon as he had two hotels to work with, he began purchasing all his silver of the same pattern, with a simple S monogram. That way he could buy in great quantities at lower prices. The company nowadays owns its own silver pattern and most of the tools and dies for making the Statler style tableware. By owning its design and dies, the Statler Company, when it purchases silver, can bargain with several manufacturers to get the best price.

The Statler Company also owns its own design for china, which has recently been standardized to only two patterns for all the chain's hotels. It used to be when a new dining room was created —maybe a Chinese room—a new design of china had to be created to fit the decor. This was so expensive that the Statler people abandoned it. Nowadays, instead of designing new china to suit a new room, Statler's interior decorators are required to put in no colors that will clash with the china patterns. The company decided to cut its china patterns down to a simple floral design for ordinary use and a blue-and-gold service for fancy occasions, after learning through surveys that guests almost never notice details of a china pattern, unless it contains something that offends their artistic sensibilities.

It used to be the custom of old-time hotels to dazzle their guests with great displays of variegated glass, china and silver. Statler cut down on what he regarded as senseless paraphernalia by eliminating seventy per cent of the odd goblets and tumblers. He reduced cutlery to one size each in a dinner fork, steel knife, butter knife and teaspoon. He believed that most people are embarrassed by an array of silver that they are not sure how to use properly.

The Old Man went even further, and standardized furniture. Hotels, when he began operating, had various odd sizes and shapes of beds. Statler reduced them, in his hotels, to two varieties—a standard double bed and a standard single bed. This made it possible for him to save not only by buying beds in quantities, but springs, mattresses and linens as well.

He even rebelled against the tradition of the three-inch hem that marks the top of a bed sheet from the bottom, which generally has a one-inch hem. To Statler, all this meant was that a maid would lose time in making a bed, if she happened to throw the sheet on the bed with the bottom of the sheet at the head of the bed. So he had the hems made the same width at both the top and bottom of all his sheets.

Furthermore, he had the hems for double beds made two inches wide at top and bottom and those for single beds made one inch wide. This enabled a housemaid to glance at a folded sheet and know immediately whether it was for a single or a double bed. Statler was also the first hotel operator to build a linen chute opening from each floor, and emptying into the laundry.

The Old Man believed in testing everything he bought in bed linens to find out what manufacturer's products stood up best under wear and tear of laundering. He made his tests simply by running towels and sheets of several manufacturers through the laundry over and over until they began to fray. All other conditions being equal, Statler bought the brand that wore longest.

The company still buys its linens that way. According to R. M. Schildman, assistant vice president in charge of such things, each of the 195,000 face towels the company buys in a year will take 540 launderings before it begins to show signs of wear. Each of 165,000 sheets can be washed approximately 460 times before it begins to fray. The 125,000 pillow cases will take 425 washings, the 125,000 bath towels 325, and the 40,000 table cloths 300 washings. Another policy of the company is to buy all of its supplies a year or so before it actually needs them, so it can take advantage of the best market conditions at its leisure.

Another of Mr. Statler's originations was an interesting system of five types of keys for guest-room doors. The simplest of these is the key given to the guest, which unlocks only his room. Next is the housemaid's key, which unlocks all the doors in her block, usually sixteen. The floor clerk's key unlocks all the doors on one floor, and the manager's pass key works on all the doors in the house. Then there is a key called the "special emergency," which is kept in the hotel safe and unlocks all doors, even when they are locked from the inside with the key in the lock. This type is necessary when a guest dies or becomes critically ill. It is also useful for locking out guests for nonpayment of bills and other breaches of hotel etiquette, for when a door is locked with a special emergency key, it cannot be unlocked with a regular room key.

While the special emergency key is one of the handiest of gadgets around a hotel, its use sometimes results in interesting complications. Several years ago a gifted ventriloquist, who was stopping at the Detroit Statler, undertook to amuse himself one day by shouting loudly for help. He made his voice sound as though it were coming from one of a number of rooms other than his own. The management, which was not aware that a ventriloquist was among its guests, was deeply alarmed. An assistant manager and a couple of house officers were sent to investigate.

They could find nobody in distress. In fact, most of the rooms on that floor and on several floors above and below it were vacant. They had been reserved for some delegates to a convention, who were due to arrive later in the day. So, after unlocking all the rooms on the several floors from which the cries might have come, looking through them and finding nothing wrong, the assistant manager and his men relocked all the doors, and went away.

Now, once in a while the front office staff of one of the Statlers will go in training to try to break the existing record within the organization for rooming the largest number of people in the shortest time. An endeavor of this sort usually is undertaken when a large number of delegates to a convention are expected to arrive at the same time by special train. The Detroit house was preparing

for just such a try on the day the frisky ventriloquist had been vocal-
izing on the upper floors.

Several hundred of the convention delegates, who were to occupy
the rooms that had been examined earlier for a person in distress,
were arriving en masse on a special train from the East. The Detroit
hotel staff intended to use them in shattering a rooming speed
record that had recently been set by the Washington house when
some conventioning osteopaths had arrived there in a body.

The Detroit management had drilled its bellmen carefully, and
inspired them with do-or-die pep talks. Similar attention had been
given to elevator operators, room and information clerks and to
members of the housekeeping staff. Printed instructions on how to
operate with maximum efficiency and a minimum of lost motion
had been passed out, and a few of the younger bellmen had even
been engaging in some road work during their off hours.

And so, when the trainload of delegates hit the lobby late in the
afternoon, the staff was ready, filled with quiet confidence, in a
splendid state of physical training and with morale high. A special
staff saw to bringing in and sorting the baggage, as the arrivals
were formed efficiently into lines at the room clerks' windows,
where registration proceeded like clockwork, as the saying goes.
The key clerks passed the keys to eager bellmen with the quick
sureness of marathon runners handling their batons. The mail clerks
riffled through the stacks of letters being held for the delegates,
like card sharpers dealing a cold deck. And in next to no time, the
first wave of delegates, acompanied by straining bellmen bristling
with baggage, were aboard the waiting elevators, which whisked
them aloft at a speed of three hundred feet per minute.

It was an excellent start, and chances looked good to beat the
Washington record. But just as the front-office leaders were beginning to congratulate one another, events took an unexpected
turn. None of the bellmen were returning to the lobby to take up
the second wave of delegates. A frenzied assistant manager plunged
into an elevator, and was shot upward.

As he emerged on the floor where the first of the delegates had
gone, a scene of confusion met his eyes. Baggage was strewn about
the corridors, like the castoff gear of a retreating army. Sweating
bellmen cursed over keys that wouldn't open the doors, and cries

of dismay and chagrin resounded from the delegates, who were impatient to get into their rooms and start on the whisky. It was a rout, and the well-laid plans for setting a new speed record died right there on the ninth floor.

It was not until the matter was reviewed at the staff meeting next day that the reason for the debacle became clear to everyone. The assistant manager and the two house officers, after their unsuccessful search for the elusive voice of the ventriloquist, had relocked all those doors with the special emergency key.

Mr. Statler had been dead a good many years when these events transpired at Detroit. Else he would probably have arrived unexpectedly in the midst of the confusion to provide additional embarrassment for the management. For, according to old-timers in the organization, he had a knack for showing up when things went cockeyed. Some old employees claim he attracted slip-ups in service the way certain persons are prone to accidents.

Once he was inspecting the elevator service in his New York house by riding the cars incognito. On one nonstop trip down in a loaded car, the operator, a merry and uninhibited youth, switched off the lights as the car sped past the floors, and sang out: "Hold onto your hats, folks; we're going through a tunnel." Mr. Statler hadn't gotten over that by the time of his death.

He was once inspecting his Cleveland house, which had been shined, scrubbed, vacuumed and polished for the occasion. In one room—just one—he pulled up the spread, and looked under the bed. There was a trayful of dirty dishes. After Mr. Statler had gone to sleep that night, the red-faced management looked under every other bed in the hotel. There were no dirty dishes under any of the rest of them. In fact nothing whatever that shouldn't have been there.

Then there was one unforgettable night at his New York hotel, where he lived, when the old man awakened with a great yearning for an apple, and couldn't get one. This became known when a minor executive of the company was on his way to his room, at about three o'clock in the morning, and chanced to encounter Mr. Statler. The old man was wearing his faded brown bathrobe, and was striding up and down the corridor in front of his suite in a state of obvious agitation. He stopped his minor executive, and made the following disclosures:

He said he had awakened a short time before, with his desire for an apple. Secure in the knowledge that he, as one of the world's leading hotel operators, owned thousands of apples, he had put on his bathrobe, and gone down to the steward's department. All the apples had been locked up for the night. The only people around were some watchmen, who laughed merrily when he told them he was Mr. Statler, and wanted an apple. They said it was ridiculous to suppose that Mr. Statler would be wandering around the kitchen with a disreputable old bathrobe like that, and if he didn't go on about his business, they would throw him out.

"Now, George," the old man said, looking his executive squarely in the eye, "it is true, is it not, that I own and operate a number of large and prosperous hotels?" The young man said yes it was. "And these hotels are well stocked with foods, including apples?" The executive said that was so. "Well, does it not seem that since I own all these hotels and all these apples, I ought to be able to get an apple to eat when I am hungry?"

With that, Mr. Statler turned on his heel, and went into his suite, closing the door firmly behind him. The minor executive dashed downstairs and alerted everyone on duty, including the scrub-women. It was hard at first for the staff to comprehend that Mr. Statler was very hungry for an apple, and they had let him down. But once this fact had seeped into their minds, according to one man who was there, "all hell broke loose, and everybody tried to get into the act."

The doors of the storerooms were swung open, and the most luscious of all the fruits were brought forth. The silver vaults were broached, and out came the gleaming trays. The finest of the crystal glasses were assembled and critically inspected. So was the gold service, the snowiest of linen and napery and the fine steel-bladed knives. A bouquet of roses was produced from somewhere, and some tapers in heavy silver candelabra were made ready for lighting.

There followed a great scrubbing, buffing, polishing and shining until the trays and the platters and the knives and the crystal and the candelabra and the fruit shone with a royal sheen. And so, as the dawn broke over Manhattan, a procession advanced upon the apartments of Mr. Statler bearing a lordly mound of fruit and an array of eating equipment, the like of which is generally associated with the exotic courts of princes of the mysterious East.

Mr. Statler looked at all sadly. "All I wanted," he said finally, "was an apple. I just wanted to peel it with this old pocketknife that I have carried for years, and have used many times to cut my chewing tobacco. I was looking forward to eating an apple that way, but now I've lost my appetite."

2

The Daring Young Man
from Wheeling

In making his signature, Mr. Statler always used his initials, E. M., never his full given name. A number of his admirers have suggested that, since he had to sign it millions of times to things like checks, letters and souvenir menus, Statler employed the shortest form possible because he was a slave to efficiency. It shouldn't take a sensible person long to figure that any normal man with the given name of Ellsworth Milton would have used his initials, whether he was inclined toward efficiency or not. He probably just did it that way to preserve his dignity and self-respect.

His mother, a Scotch-Irish woman, gave her third son his first name in honor of a Union Army colonel who had been shot and killed while pulling down a Confederate flag from a building in Virginia—a somewhat ridiculous thing to do, on its face. But the boy had been born near the scene of and about the time of the Battle of Gettysburg, and the mother was obviously carried away by patriotism. The Milton part of his name was in honor of the blind poet.

The Statler family's economic status was low, but they ranked high spiritually and morally. The head of the family was pastor of a German Reform congregation in Somerset County, Pennsylvania, whose members were as poor as he was. Once in a while he tried to make extra money by farming futilely and by manufacturing matches by hand, which he peddled from farm to farm at five cents a package. But a man couldn't make a living that way, even in the good old days.

At least, that is the conclusion Elder Statler came to in 1869, when Ellsworth was six. He decided to move west, where the railroads were offering land almost free to people who would move out there and farm it. It is possible also that his decision was influenced by his desire to ride on a train. Elder Statler had long been an admirer of the iron horse, but had never had enough money to ride on one. He did once express his railroading leanings by writing a religious hymn, "The Spiritual Railway," which is still to be found in some old hymnbooks.

After a long train ride, which was exhilarating to the old man, but exasperating to the rest of the family, they wound up at Bridgeport, Ohio, across the Ohio River from Wheeling, West Virginia. They built there a one-and-a-half-story building to serve as a combination residence and store, as the old gentleman was tired of both preaching and farming. Three years later, a great economic opportunity arrived in that section with the building of the La Belle Glassworks in Kirkwood, Ohio, across the creek from Bridgeport. Naturally, all the Statler boys would work there who were old enough, including Ellsworth. He was nine at the time.

His job was known as "teasing the glory hole." This meant dumping wheelbarrowfuls of coke into a small furnace, in which glass was softened before going to the finishers, who made it into goblets and jugs. Ellsworth and the other boys of the community got fifty cents for a twelve-hour day, but it was stimulating work. When an exhausted boy fell asleep on his feet, he was stimulated by a bubble of molten glass flicked upon his bare skin by one of the finishers. It was a career comparable with some of the more appalling experiences of the less fortunate characters of Dickens. The boys, at a tender age, learned a great deal about fighting, stabbing, garroting, cursing, chewing tobacco and drinking whisky, which they stole from barrels that had been shipped there for filling the

Christmas demijohns the plant turned out. In view of these experiences in his early youth, it is remarkable that Statler, in his
later years, did not adopt some lusty profession such as piracy.

As it turned out, he passed up piracy, and entered the hotel business. This may have resulted from the view out of the window of
the Statler attic, where Ellsworth and his brothers slept in double-
decked bunks. Visible through the river mists was the Wheeling
skyline, dominated by the distant silhouette of the McLure House.
The McLure was an old-fashioned hotel, a rendezvous of the
Wheeling sporting set, haven for drummers and wandering theatrical stock companies and a center of all that was gay, colorful
and daring from a nineteenth-century Midwestern small-city point
of view. At least to the miserable "glory hole teaser" across the
river, he said years later, it represented the acme of things splendid
and desirable. So in 1876, when he was thirteen, Ellsworth gave
up his job at the glassworks (which now paid him ninety cents a
day) and became a bellboy at the McLure House for six dollars a
month, plus his board, a place to sleep and whatever he could pick
up in tips.

When Ellsworth was fifteen his father died. Ellsworth had become head bellboy at the McLure by this time, and was walking
along Market Street one evening a few days after the funeral,
meditating upon his new responsibilities of helping to care for the
family, when he observed some lurid banners set up at the entrance
of the Opera House. These proclaimed that Professor O. S. Fowler,
formerly of New York and currently with headquarters in Boston
(Lock Box 1501) was giving exhibitions of phrenology inside absolutely free to the public.

The posters further described Professor Fowler as being an
authority on "love, courtship and married life," "the rearing of children in a manner that renders the most hateful perfectly lovely,"
and: "NONE EVER NEED SPECTACLES. They cost and injure. FOWLER'S
JOURNAL NUMBER TWO shows how to see, to read perfectly up to
ninety WITHOUT SPECS . . . and even how to lay them off. WORTH
THOUSANDS—Also how to cure rheumatism, brain fever, etc. PRICE
25¢."

Ellsworth was not concerned about love, marriage, child care or
how to see without specs, but the Professor's phrenological talents

did interest him, and he went in to observe a demonstration. As he entered, Professor Fowler had a grip on the head of an abashed local citizen, who sat with downcast eyes and an expression of embarrassment as the Professor explored his skull. Ellsworth, who was acquainted with the victim, was surprised at the accuracy of the Professor's diagnosis. So, later that night, he returned as a private patient to get the Professor's de luxe, written diagnosis of his own character. Statler kept this scientific document—entitled "Phrenological Character of Ellsworth M. Statler"—the rest of his life. He would get it out and study it every now and then. The Professor had found, in part, as follows:

You, Sir, have one natural genius, namely mechanical. . . . You are not at all brilliant. . . . Show off to poor advantage. . . . Are a miserable talker, so that your ideas lose most of their force by your awkward expression of them. . . . You will pass along through life without being especially noted for anything. . . . Your caution greatly exceeds your enterprise. . . . You underrate your capacities. You often feel unworthy, inferior, insignificant. . . . You would do all right for farming. . . . Could do passably well at storekeeping, only you would be too loath to venture. . . . You should get your living from something sure, for you could not dare to run any risk. . . . You're smarter than any who know you think you are or than you consider yourself . . . Let this examination encourage you. Follow your own judgment every time. Act on it, whereas you generally act from your fears. . . . Attempt two or three times more, and you will accomplish it. . . . Yours is a good head.

It is possible that, without this phrenological diagnosis, Statler might have gone through life, as the Professor said, "without being especially noted for anything." It is true that the phrenologist completely misinterpreted most of Statler's traits, as they eventually turned out; but it may have been that Statler tried so hard to be unlike the "cautious, inferior, insignificant" creature the report described that he deliberately made himself into the most daringly successful venturer that the hotel industry ever saw. The fact that Statler kept the report the rest of his life certainly indicates that it had some sort of influence upon him.

Ellsworth wanted no part of either farming or storekeeping, which the report had mentioned as possible careers. He'd seen his father fail to get ahead at both. He did try the mechanical leaning, of which the Professor had spoken, by going to work that summer in his uncle's blacksmith shop at Boardman, Ohio, while the Mc-Lure House was closed for remodeling. He tried to make a wagon while working for his uncle, but it wasn't a very good wagon. So he quickly abandoned a mechanical career when the McLure House reopened, and returned there as night clerk.

In his new position, guests relied on Statler as an authority on all sorts of things from the tenderest barber in town to the most eloquent preacher to the most reliable sporting house. It was up to him to keep the bellboys on the ball, and he did that so relentlessly that they nicknamed him "The Colonel." At night he was in sole charge of the sleeping hotel. He put to bed the last reveler, and waked up the early risers who had to catch the daylight train. It was his job to drag out of bed the drowsy waiters, maids and the boys who fired the furnace, and get them busy putting the hotel to life.

The McLure lobby provided a fine example of the atmosphere old timers speak about when they reminisce about the good, gay old days. It had marble floors and lots of brass spittoons, heavy oak chairs and tables, against a background of Victorian ginger-bread, with a few stuffed fish on the walls along with some mounted heads of bison and mountain sheep. The baseball scores were posted in the lobby, and the atmosphere was charged with knowing talk about all sorts of sports, including cockfighting, prize fighting, gambling and the steamboat races that sometimes roared past Wheeling on the Ohio.

The place was inhabited by drummers wearing brown dicers and smoking Henry Clay cigars. Frequently there were brides and grooms, the former properly demure in the traditional gray travel-ing suit of that period, the latter resplendent and uncomfortable in frock coats, white neckties and tight brown gloves. Bellhops rushed up and down the stairs carrying cracked ice and seltzer to the gay bloods with hangovers—quartered, for the sake of con-venience, on the second floor.

Late in the evening, when the theater had let out, casts of stock companies that played the Wheeling Opera House—occasionally including such luminaries as Mary Anderson and John McCullough —would gather around the lobby stove. Then the local amateurs rallied anxiously around to regale the professionals with recitations of "Thy Sentinel Am I" or "Ostler Joe." They performed to an obligata of rattling dice and clicking dominoes from the adjoining bar.

After two years as night clerk, Ellsworth moved to Akron as clerk at the Buchtel Hotel; but he soon returned to the McLure when a chance opened for him to become day clerk there and lease the McLure's billiard room. Until then, the McLure's billiard room had been an unprofitable adjunct to the bar. Billiard rooms generally, as all respectable people knew, were low places, patronized by n'er-do-wells, with cigar and whisky breaths and no ambition whatever. Statler's mother told him that he would do better "to think of Heavenly things."

What Statler was thinking about was how to lure more drummers into the place. Providence quickly provided him with a lure in the person of his younger brother, Osceola, who had developed an amazing and unexpected talent for billiards. Osceola, who was still a boy in short pants, would stand beside the tables, idly knocking balls across the green baize. Some drummer, noticing his creditable shots, would condescend to take him on with the understanding that if the boy lost, the house paid for the game. Whereupon, Osceola would trounce the man miserably.

Osceola's fame quickly spread about town. There is nothing a small city loves better than some local champion, who can be expected to defeat all comers from out of town. The younger the local pride is, the better. It became a fashionable thing for people to come down to see the little Statler boy perform, with the benefit of a handicap, against professionals like Frank Schafer, Sr. Getting into the swing of the thing, Ellsworth became a billiard impresario, and would rent the Opera House for professional exhibitions.

Railroad men got special rates at the McLure—a bed and meals for thirty-five cents each. They used to hang about Statler's billiard room a lot, shaking dice while waiting for their trains. Statler learned from them that railroad mileage tickets in 1,000-mile units could be purchased for two cents a mile, and retailed, legally, at two and a half cents a mile, which was cheaper than they could be bought at the station. Statler then became a railroad-ticket broker. He built a ticket booth, adorned with cherrywood paneling, near the entrance of his billiard room, and dealt in excursion tickets to places like Atlantic City or Hot Springs. He also sold short-haul tickets, and travelers would bring him unused parts of tickets, which he would buy and resell.

Meanwhile, as hotel clerk, he was learning more all the time about the hotel business. The two Norton Brothers, who owned the McLure, mentioned one day that keeping the hotel's accounts was a tiresome bore. The day clerk took over that job. On the other hand, he annoyed the owners continually by asserting that the meals served in the dining room were unappetizing. He said the owners would realize that fact if they would eat there, instead of dining on specially prepared meals, served in their rooms. He was further concerned about various inconsistencies of policy—room rates, for instance. Rates were two or three dollars a day, depending on the size of the room, with meals included, and double rates for double occupancy. What bothered Statler was that, under this system, a man could take a two-dollar-a-day room, and his wife could take a three-dollar-a-day room for a total of five dollars a day, whereas it would cost them six dollars a day if they shared one of the three-dollar rooms.

Things like that would set him talking about the policies he would adopt some day when he owned a big hotel. "People don't want frills," he used to tell a friend of his named Herman Stoetzer. "They want a certain number of definite comforts—good beds, decent food and cleanliness. The rest is just cake icing."

Meanwhile, Statler had experimented further with his mechanical talents, of which Professor Fowler had spoken, by inventing a refrigerating device that carried bottles of ale on an endless chain. The bottles were kept cool within the ice chest until a customer deposited a coin in a slot, which tripped the mechanism, and released one of the bottles. This device was welcomed by some houses of ill repute that operated in the area, since an ordinance had been passed prohibiting such places from selling liquor and beer, which they had been in the habit of dispensing along with their other wares. The ordinance, however, did not cover the dispensing of ale by mechanical means.

Thus, the more advanced of the bordellos adopted this mechanism with alacrity until it was discovered that the device could be beaten with coins attached to horse-tail hairs. The coins were inserted far enough to trip the mechanism, then withdrawn. Yet, these creations of Statler's were apparently the forerunners of cold-drink dispensing machines that are now in wide use in stores and filling stations.

About this time Wheeling's sport-minded citizens became interested in the game of bowling. Some of them formed a bowling club, raised $1,500 by selling stock at ten dollars a share, and leased the Musee, an unsuccessful vaudeville house near the McLure Hotel. They built four alleys there, but limited players to members of the club. The club was soon showing signs of going broke. Then Statler decided bowling had a great future in Wheeling. He bought up fifty-one per cent of the shares at nine dollars each, and dissolved the club. Then he borrowed $3,000, and built four more alleys, and installed eight pool and billiard tables. He rented two rooms in the front of the building to a barber and a tobacconist.

Statler then organized a city-wide bowling tournament with a grand prize of $300 for the winning team. This stimulated the interest in bowling to proportions of near-hysteria. A large portion of the citizens who were sound of wind and limb organized into teams, and strove mightily for the treasure. Crowds of spectators flooded all the benches to cheer on this or that team by blowing fox-horns and ringing bells. The young bowling tsar approved of this enthusiasm, but worried because these hundreds of spectators came and went without contributing financially to his enterprise. He did try charging ten cents admission, but that cut the crowds so drastically that he quickly abandoned this policy.

Then one evening at dinner, Statler began to inquire of his mother about the costs of the food she was serving at home. He spent most of the meal writing this information in his notebook. The next morning he informed the tobacconist in one of the Musee's store spaces that he was going to need that space for an eating establishment. Within a few weeks, Statler had opened there The Pie House. It was only a lunchroom, eighteen by sixteen feet in size, but it soon became known as the place to eat in Wheeling.

For one thing, Statler, who always had a horror of the second rate, had equipped the place with egg-shell china and quadruple-plated table silver. Such luxuries were almost unknown at the time in Wheeling's public eating places. Local gourmands generally employed a direct manner of eating, with reckless abandon and a noticeable absence of etiquette, when wielding the old bone-handled forks and heavy crockery mugs that characterized other local hash houses. But they quickly began to respond to Statler's fine china and tableware by deporting themselves at table with delicacy and éclat. Such niceties as the crooked little finger held beneath the handle of the coffee cup began to be observed at The Pie House. Some diners went so far as to use napkins tucked under their chins, and to wield their toothpicks with commendable elegance.

Among Statler's culinary introductions to Wheeling was the minced ham and the minced chicken sandwich. Up to then, the local idea of a sandwich had been two slices of thick dry bread surrounding a chunk of ham or beef. Statler arranged with a butcher to grind his meat, fat and all, into a spicy paste, which was spread liberally upon thin slices of bread. The French had been celebrated for years for creating *pâtés* somewhat along these lines, but the idea was new in Wheeling and highly popular.

Statler used the best coffee he could get, not only for pleasing his customers' taste, but for attracting them. It was his idea to produce such delicious aromas from the boiling coffee that bowlers and spectators would find it difficult to pass The Pie House without stopping in for refreshments. The place did such rushing business that the pin boys, who set 'em up in the alleys, had to spend all their spare time turning cranks on ice-cream freezers. However, the *pièce de résistance,* from which the restaurant derived its name, were the lemon meringue, fruit and custard pies served there. These were turned out by the women folks at the Statler home.

So it developed that the Statler family became involved with most of the better-known places of relaxation and refreshment in the Wheeling of that era. Ellsworth's brother, Osceola, was running the billiard room at the McLure House, having been made a partner in that enterprise. Another brother, Bill, had charge of the Musee, and his mother and sister, Alabama, were turning out pies. As for Ellsworth, he was enjoying an income of $10,000 a year, which made him affluent indeed.

Supported by these tangible evidences of his ability, Statler's dreams of owning and operating a large hotel had solidified into a definite purpose—he announced that one day he would own and run a 1,000-room hotel in New York City. This was probably the biggest thing that he could conceive in his world. He got even more than that when he eventually reached New York, but he had to follow a roundabout progress to get there. In the words of a standard vaudeville line of those days, he had to go "by way of Buffalo."

3

Welcome to California

Mr. Statler's empire reached a climax on July 5, 1950, a full twenty-two years after his death. On that day, ground was broken at Wiltshire Boulevard and Figueroa Street for constructing a combined Statler hotel and office building. The ground-breaking for any large hotel has always been an occasion for resounding civic hosannas. But at the Los Angeles Statler's commencement, these outpourings of lofty sentiment were particularly lush.

Weatherwise, July 5, 1950 was a day that might have been ordered by the Los Angeles Chamber of Commerce. The sun shone brightly from a sky of deep blue. A crisp breeze whipped the flags and snapped the bunting that adorned the three-acre building site. Behemoth steam shovels stood waiting to begin excavating the foundation as soon as the first ceremonial spadeful of California soil was removed. Almost everybody who was anybody in Los Angeles civic life had been invited to the ceremonies, and almost all had come—more than 750 of them.

The mayor, of course, was present. So was the governor, the heads of most of the city's large business enterprises and banks, the president of the Chamber of Commerce and his merry men, representatives of organized labor, old Los Angeles families, local hotel executives and, naturally, all the high brass of the Hotels

Statler Company, Inc. The movie colony was well represented—officially in the person of Miss Celeste Holm. And there was, of course, the usual strong representation of sidewalk superintendents and curious spectators.

The ceremony reached its climax when the mayor placed a gilded shovel into the hands of Statler's president, Arthur F. Douglas, who then strode resolutely into the center of the distinguished circle. Above and around him there was a great grinding of newsreel cameras and popping of photographers' flash bulbs. Newspaper reporters scribbled furiously, recording the scene for posterity. Nearby could be heard the muffled voices of radio announcers describing the occasion as Mr. Douglas carefully poised the shovel, and prepared to plunge it into the warm breast of the golden state.

At this point, a small man in nondescript attire succeeded in forcing his way through the inner ring of spectators, and reached the side of the Statler president. He was clutching an oblong folded paper, and he addressed the hotel company president, with an interrogatory inflection: "Mr. Douglas?"

"Yes," responded the-center-of-all-eyes-at-the-moment, checking uncertainly his motion with the spade.

"I have something for you," the little man said. He thrust the paper into Douglas' hand, and vanished into the crowd.

Thinking he had been handed some last-minute instruction of utmost importance, Douglas opened the paper. A magnificent scowl convulsed his features, and he shoved the paper into the hands of the person nearest him. Then he quickly proceeded to spade up a gilded shovelful of Southern California's sandy loam. And so, construction of the largest hotel since the gold-drenched days of the 'Twenties was officially under way.

Meanwhile, the man who had received the fateful paper—Howard F. Dugan, Statler vice-president in charge of sales and advertising—was obviously embarrassed to find such a thing in his hands. After glancing at its contents, he began juggling it like a hot potato he would like to throw away. Then he started to conceal it in his pocket. It was too late. Some newspapermen, having observed the electrifying effects of the document, asked to have a look. Remembering one of the basic Statler tenets—"never try to conceal anything from the press"—Dugan showed them the paper.

"To the Sheriff of Los Angeles County," it read, "his Deputy or either Constable of the Town of Los Angeles within said County: GREETINGS. By authority of the State of California, you are hereby commanded . . . ."

The document, which was indeed a summons and complaint, went on to recite how a certain Witherspoon Frisby, as he will be called here, had been mortified, embarrassed and humiliated while a guest in the Hotel Statler in New York. The credit manager of that hotel had attached the baggage of the plaintiff, the complaint alleged, when said plaintiff had undertaken to pay for his board and lodging in that hotel with a bank check that the aforementioned credit manager contended—falsely and without justification—was fraudulent and unsupported by funds in bank. The said Frisby was hereby suing the Hotels Statler Company, Inc., in the amount of $25,000 for the humiliation, loss of sleep, general decay of health and mental anguish caused to him by this highhanded and completely unjustifiable behavior . . . .

"Well there," remarked Vice-President Dugan some minutes later as he recovered from the experience with the help of a martini, "is the hotel business for you . . . .

"While the flags are flying over the front entrance, and the band is playing in the lobby and the mayor is orating in the grand ballroom, there is always some character in a room on the fifteenth floor getting ready to go to sleep smoking a cigarette and set the mattress on fire, or slip you a bum check, or skip without paying his bill, and then sue the devil out of you for doing it . . . ."

Aside from this remarkable timing in the service of a legal paper, the ground-breaking for the Los Angeles Statler was a matter of some interest to the average American, and of considerable importance to the hotel industry. It is doubtful, however, if any average citizen or many average hotel men realized this. But the fact is that the degree of success of the Los Angeles Statler over the next few years may determine, in great part, the pattern of large American hotels of the future. Not just Statler hotels—*any* large hotels. Here are the reasons why:

The hotel business is America's seventh largest industry. The Hotel Red Book's 1951-52 edition lists in the United States 15,327 hotels, with an estimated total value of six billion dollars. More than two million guests can be accommodated in their 1,440,000 rooms on a given night, and a total of 258,600,000 room guests were entertained in American hotels in 1950.

Yet, during 1950, the American hotel industry didn't spend a penny building a single new hotel, nor did it in 1949. This is aside from the Los Angeles Statler, of course, and a few resort hotels and motels. (The resort hotel business is so widely different from regular hotel operations that it constitutes almost a separate industry.)

The hotel industry has become perhaps the most timorous, cautious and generally tenderfooted of all large industries in matters of expansion, or even in replacing its aging properties. From the early 1930's, depression years, until construction of the Los Angeles Statler, only three largish hotels were built in this country, and one of those, the Terrace Plaza in Cincinnati, has less than 500 rooms.

Another of the three is the 850-room Shamrock, at Houston, but this was built more as a monument to Texas oil and to its proprietor, Glenn McCarthy, than as an investment.

Besides Statler, the two most important hotel chains are the Hilton Hotels Corporation and the Sheraton Corporation of America. Neither of these has built a new hotel since the 1920's. Their holdings are almost entirely in hotels that were built by somebody else. The Sheraton Corporation is essentially a real-estate concern trading in hotel properties. The Hilton Corporation is the result of the promotional genius of Conrad N. Hilton in acquiring some of the most famous hotels in the country. But Hilton hotels are completely unrelated in either policy or atmosphere, ranging as they do from the imposing Waldorf-Astoria and the stately, but aging, Plaza in New York to the stampeding melee of the Stevens in Chicago, recently renamed the Conrad Hilton.

The simple facts are that between the completion of the Waldorf-Astoria in 1931 and the commencement of the Los Angeles Statler in 1950, only one important commercial hotel was built, strictly as a hotel operational investment, that has had any real bearing on the future of the industry. That is the house completed in Washington, D. C., by the Statler Company in January, 1943.

When the Washington Statler was being built there was doubt within the Statler organization itself that it was a wise thing to do, although the company's prospectus indicated it ought to make a profit of at least $150,000 a year. As it turned out, the Washington Statler has made over $1,000,000 profit each year since it was completed. Profits some years have been as high as $1,500,000, after all taxes, which makes it the most profitable hotel operation of its size in America. The main reason for the Washington Statler's great success—aside from providing high standards of comforts, service and food—is that it is new and different.

In spite of the sparkling success of the Washington Statler, there were many people in the hotel industry who believed, when the Los Angeles Statler was begun, that nobody could build a large, luxurious hotel in these costly times and hope to break even. Wages for hotel employees had almost doubled in the seven years since the Washington Statler opened. Building costs had shot up further than that.

When the depression of the 1930's struck, four out of every five American hotels went bankrupt, and they were built when wages and building costs were much lower than when the Washington house was started. There were four large hotel chains in the country when the depression began, and only one of them—Statler—survived.

Thus, if anybody but Statler had been undertaking the big house on the West Coast, most of the hotel industry would probably have regarded it as a fool project of somebody with more money than good sense. But since it was a Statler project, the industry was ready to be convinced that hotel building in these times is possible. The industry knows that the Statler Company does not build hotels for glamour or glory. It expects to make money running them—and before it moves a shovel of dirt, Statler has figured out ahead of time the profit it can anticipate.

Besides its reputation as a smart builder of hotels, the Statler Company is regarded by most hotel men as the smartest operator in that industry. In 1949, a normal year for these times, its seven hotels made a profit, after all taxes, of $4,134,717, or 9.6 per cent on a $42,858,916 gross. This was slightly higher in actual money than the profit of Statler's chief rival, the Hilton Hotels Corporation with its thirteen hotels. But, room for room, for every sixty-five cents profit Hilton was making, Statler was making a dollar.

One way the company manages to get so much gross return from its hotels is by knowing exactly who its guests are, and gearing operations to fit the guests. Statler knows, for example, that of its three to four million guests a year, fifty-three per cent are in the upper-middle economic stratum, and forty per cent are in the high economic reaches. It knows that two-thirds of its guests are between thirty and fifty years old, that twenty-five per cent of them are salesmen, twenty per cent are business executives and nineteen per cent are professional people. About eighty per cent of Statler's guests are men, and of the women guests, ninety per cent are housewives accompanying their husbands. Of women traveling without male escorts, twenty-nine per cent are professional women, mainly schoolteachers; seventeen per cent are housewives; six per cent are owners of businesses, and the rest are government employees, retired and so on.

The Statler Company knows that three-fourths of its guests are on business trips; their average length of stay is two and two-tenths days. While they are guests, eighty per cent will eat breakfast in the hotel; forty-five per cent will eat luncheon there, and sixty-one per cent will have dinner in the house. The company has determined that these percentages are about as good as a hotel can hope for. However, when the percentages of guests taking their meals in the house begin to drop, the company investigates to learn why. If necessary, it may make changes in the kitchen, or the food, or the menus, or dining-room decorations or in the advertising to get the people back to the Statler table.

An experimental kitchen was set up at the firm's executive offices in New York a dozen years ago. Its function is to get down on paper scientifically some culinary process that a chef has been doing all his life by instinct. Frequently the business of transferring a cook's art to hard, written data takes months of experiments in the kitchen. During its existence, the experimental kitchen has perfected and standardized about 1,500 recipes, which the company requires all its kitchens to follow.

When the experimental kitchen was begun, the company put a graduate home economist in each of the kitchens around the chain to direct recipe standardization, and to supervise the making of pantry dishes, such as cold sandwiches and cold salads. These home economists were women, of all things, which was a historic move in itself. It was probably the first time a woman had ever had a more dignified job than peeling potatoes in a large hotel kitchen. But Statler put them there because the company felt that women had a way with dainty salads.

Even though the chefs had never thought a woman's place was in the kitchen, they and the female kitchen executives have gotten along very well together, outside of several early skirmishes. Occasionally they even work together in developing some new dish. The company feels that some of its new dishes have had considerable influence upon American eating habits, which might well be, since Statler hotels serve over fourteen million meals a year.

One Statler culinary creation, ice-cream pie, has had a tremendous impact upon many Americans, among them Senator John W. Bricker, of Ohio, who became acquainted with this dessert when he was campaigning for the Vice-Presidency in 1944. Senator Bricker was so overwhelmed that the Boston Statler packed ice-cream pies in dry ice, and shipped them to him to sustain and cheer him along his campaign route. The Senator enjoyed ice-cream pie, particularly, at breakfast.

The Statler people delve constantly into science and mathematics to keep their food and other costs as low as is compatible with high standards. The company tests every type of supplies it buys in quantities, to see what brand performs best. Such testing ranges from the toy balloons that the headwaiter gives children in the dining room to the roast beef the children's parents are eating.

Each hotel steward is required to go to the market personally; he can't order by telephone, except in emergencies. He picks out the portions he wants of meat and other foods, and stamps them with a company stamp. When the foods are delivered to the hotel, they are not accepted unless they bear the stamp.

The company does a real job of research when it buys cured meats in large quantities, such as hams. After passing the steward's tests for flavor—the company's chief taster of such things, including whisky, is John H. Rudd, who has been employed at this pleasant work for more than thirty years—the meats are turned over to the experimental kitchen. Sample hams of the same size and weight, but from different purveyors, are cooked in a test stove equipped with devices to measure weight and bulk shrinkage. The amount of meat lost in cooking may vary as much as half a pound between two otherwise similar types of hams.

Statler efficiency takes notice of the leftovers from all these meals their hotels serve. The company sells its garbage to hog growers and, at higher prices, disposes of lemon, orange and grapefruit rinds to candy manufacturers. (Incidentally, the company uses only juices freshly squeezed by a hand-operated squeezer, in spite of its scientific attitude on practically everything. The experimental kitchen has tested many, but found no mechanical squeezer it believes to be as good as the old-fashioned method.)

In a recent normal year, Statler guests used 4,310,000 cakes of soap. The company conserves the remnants by melting them and pressing them into bars for use by employees and in the laundry. Each hotel accumulates millions of empty bottles in a year. These are ground up daily, and sold to glass manufacturers. During one ordinary year, guests used, or took away, 4,195,000 sheets of stationery and 3,070,000 envelopes. The Statler Company cuts expenses here by maintaining in Buffalo its own printing plant. During one average year, the Statler hotels gave away nine million books of matches. The company sees to it that its matches achieve the maximum in advertising potentialities by designing the covers with bold red and white diagonal stripes. Most people can easily distinguish a package of Statler matches at fifty paces.

The company gives much study to saving steps so that the minimum number of employees can accomplish a maximum of results. Statler studies in this field range from the best way bellboys can balance baggage, or how a maid can make a bed more effectively, all the way to designing kitchens that save trouble for the cooks and serve the maximum number of diners in the minimum time with minimum effort to all concerned.

Statler pays eighty per cent of its employees, who are union members, standard union wages, as other first-class hotels do. Its nonunion employees and department heads receive higher than average wages, and Statler's services to guests are far above those of the average hotel. Yet, Statler spends a lower percentage of its income on wages—because of its scientific approach to getting work done—than the average large hotel.

In spite of all its know-how and the scientific approach, the Statler Company makes mistakes now and then. It is probably a result of misjudgment of the general hotel picture, at about the time the war ended, that the company does not now own the Palmer House in Chicago, one of the world's most profitable hotels. In fact, Statler has no hotel in the Windy City, which strikes some people as peculiar because Statler is a famous convention host, and Chicago loves conventions.

The Statler Company wanted to build a new hotel there immediately after the war, and selected a site adjacent to the Chicago Tribune tower. Statler was dickering with the Wrigley Estate about buying the land when Colonel Robert R. McCormick, publisher of the *Tribune*, heard about it. The Colonel apparently did not want any hotel blocking the public's view of his newspaper plant, so he bought the property out from under Statler.

The company then considered buying the 3,000-room Stevens, but decided it was too far south from the Loop. Then Statler almost did buy the Palmer House, but decided against that, too. Later, Conrad N. Hilton bought the Palmer House for about $17,000,000, and that hotel, which has done tremendous business, has been the mainstay ever since of the Hilton empire.

The reason Statler declined to buy the big inn in the Loop— hindsight indicates this was a mistake—was that Statler engineers thought it would cost too much to "Statlerize" the house. This meant spending maybe three-quarters of a million dollars installing circulating ice water, which Statler hotels have in all bathrooms. It meant putting a radio in every room, and planing off the bottom of each guest-room door so that a morning newspaper could be slid underneath. All these are Statler *must* services.

Furthermore, the company would have had to spend a lot remodeling the back-of-the-house departments, such as the laundry, linen rooms, kitchens, pantries and storerooms. Statler refuses to allow its employees to work in just anybody's back-of-the-house. These departments have to be designed so employees can work according to Statler techniques. Any other method, the company feels, would not only be less efficient, but would probably cause unrest to the soul of Mr. Statler.

Sometimes the Statler people err in a lighter vein, and commit what amounts to a social error. Something of the sort occurred on the day General Eisenhower returned to Washington at the end of the war, and was being feted by the Washington Board of Trade at a luncheon in the Statler there.

The General was to be met before the luncheon by some Board of Trade leaders in a small room in which a bar had been set up. The Statler manager, Herbert C. Blunck, who was not exactly sure what the hero would want to drink, had the bar stocked with every known stimulant—whisky, brandies, gins, cordials, wines, beer, rums, liquors and even vodka and a jug of moonshine corn. Then, confident that he could produce any desired refreshment, Blunck asked the General what his pleasure might be.

"A Coke," said General Eisenhower. And, of course, there wasn't a Coke in the place.

The late President Roosevelt and Winston Churchill received friends a number of times during the war in the Washington Statler's suite 1240, a lush apartment with wall-high windows, a marble fireplace and an ornate grand piano. It was designed originally as the Washington home of Mr. and Mrs. Jesse Jones, but they never moved in. The place was too flashy to suit Mrs. Jones. In the same suite, John L. Lewis and the coal-mine operators glowered at one another across a green felt table during the winter of the great coal commotion.

The lost-and-found department at the Detroit Statler has on several occasions recovered false teeth that Ty Cobb has left behind, while the string ensemble there used to keep in practice on hillbilly ballads and folk music for the entertainment of the late Henry Ford. Mr. Ford, who enjoyed this music, used to dine regularly with Mrs. Ford in the Detroit Statler's Terrace Room.

Regular Statler patrons include: Harold Stassen, James C. Petrillo, Bing Crosby, Bob Hope, Jack Benny, Charles Luckman and Charles Wilson, Rosalind Russell and Ingrid Bergman, Governors Folsom of Alabama and Williams of Michigan, Admirals Halsey and Nimitz, General Omar Bradley and Colonel Charles A. Lind-

bergh. During the 1948 Presidential campaign, candidates Truman
and Dewey once inhabited the same suite on the same day in the
Boston Statler. Mr. Dewey checked in a couple of hours or so after
the President had checked out.

The Statler hotels, however, have never made a big play for
prominent people, and are not particularly noted as hangouts for
celebrities. Essentially, the Statlers are the great temples of the
upper-middle classes, the business executive, the high-bracket salesman and the conventioning Rotarian. The Statlers are noted principally for being clean, attractive, efficient and as generally satisfactory (and typically American) as well-kept plumbing.

As Jimmy McCabe, long-time general manager of the New York
Statler, once observed: "If I had some of those long-haired, foreign-
looking, suave, sleek guys for assistant managers bowing and scraping and monsieuring and modomming around my hotel, the way
they do in some of those fashionable joints over on the East Side,
somebody would be busting them on the nose every other hour."

Perhaps the most unpredictable phase of all hotel operations is
the business of reserving rooms. Whether a guest decides to come or
go, or how long he stays often depends upon the mere matter of
human whim. This makes things like forecasting the weather simple
by comparison. Yet, Statler has undertaken to reduce even that
nebulous thing to an exact science.

If a hotel doesn't make enough reservations, it is apt to be left
with vacant rooms, which is just that much revenue gone forever.
If it accepts too many reservations, the hotel "goes overboard,"
meaning it has more guests with reservations than rooms available,
and the hotel man's version of the old proverb is: "Hell hath no
fury like a man with a reservation who is told there are no rooms."

Strictly speaking, hotels do not "reserve" rooms. What they do is
promise to provide a certain type of room on a certain night. When
confirming a reservation, the management does not lock a room and
let it remain vacant pending the guest's arrival maybe six weeks
hence. Some people think that is the procedure, for they will demand to know weeks ahead of time what number their room will be.

One day in 1950 the Cleveland Statler received this telegram
from a gentleman in Baltimore: "Please reserve one room for tonight. Same room I occupied on October 20, 1916."

Actually, the room department often does not know longer than a minute or so before it gives the key to a guest with a reservation what room he is going to get. The question of how many rooms will be available for people with reservations depends upon how many guests will check out. The hotel has to estimate how many guests will leave and how many will arrive on a certain date to know how many rooms it should reserve. The trick is in making the estimate correctly.

The New York Statler, which has had as many as 3,420 registered guests on a single night, has a front-office manager named Marco Armani, who worked out a formula that is supposed to solve this problem. "Armani's Law" has been adopted by the company in all of its houses, making certain allowances for the customs of various sections. Given a full house of guests and barring unforeseen conditions, the formula—which is based upon years of experience and is said to be accurate within seven per cent—works like this:

If on a Sunday, 300 guests have indicated they will check out, seventy per cent more will actually leave than have said they would. Hence, there will be 510 rooms made available instead of 300. But the greater the number who have said they will leave, the smaller becomes the percentages that can be added. Thus, when 400 say they will check out, an additional fifty per cent may be added. When 500 say they will check out, 700 will leave; 600 indicated check outs means 780; and so on.

These percentages vary with the days of the week. On Wednesdays, they work out about the same as on Sundays, but on Mondays the percentages that can be added to the indicated check-outs are much lower than on Sunday or Wednesday.

Besides this, anywhere from twenty to thirty per cent of those who have made reservations will fail to show, and will not notify the hotel that they are not coming. The fail-to-show percentages also vary with days of the week, seasons of the year and conditions of the weather. Wrestling around with problems like these is what makes stomach ulcers and high blood pressure occupational diseases of the hotel business.

During one recent normal year, the New York Statler went "overboard" eighteen times, under the Armani system of figuring reservations, but it hit the room situation on the nose 154 nights—selling every room in the house, with nobody left over with reservations that could not be honored.

When a Statler hotel does go overboard, it can almost always get whoever is left out a room in another hotel. The company will pay his cab fare there, and send along a bellboy to handle his bags. When Statler cannot get a room in another hotel for a guest, it is generally because of unusual weather conditions, such as happened several years ago when a blizzard struck Detroit.

A crowd of guests with confirmed reservations arrived that night, but most of the guests in residence, who had planned to leave, didn't because of the weather. The same situation prevailed in the city's other hotels. So the Detroit Statler found itself late that evening with eighty people who had reservations and no place to put them.

Some twenty-five miles from Detroit is the town of Mt. Clemens, Michigan, noted for its health-giving spas with summer hotels attached. Most of these are closed in winter, but that night the Statler people got the owner of the Colonial Hotel at Mt. Clemens out of bed, and persuaded him to open his summer hotel for just that winter night. The hotel reached the executive vice-president of the Greyhound Bus Lines by long-distance telephone, and managed to charter two large buses.

Meanwhile, the owner of the Colonial, his wife and all their friends and relatives he could round up on short notice were stripping covers from the furniture, making beds and building fires. The Statler guests arrived presently on the buses, and bedded down for the night while the blizzard shook the shutters.

Statler has a number of patrons who are nonconformists. They refuse to make reservations. They will blow into town unannounced, point out that they are old customers, and demand that the hotel take care of them. At the other extreme are people who want a low-priced room for one night, but will write the hotel weeks in advance, and set forth an imposing list of requirements. These letters often run to great length, and contain abundant unnecessary information. Among these was a communication the Cleveland Statler received from a gentlewoman who lived in a small Ohio town. A small portion of what she had to say follows:

For myself I would like your $4.50 room, which includes tub bath. And since I am coming with a gentleman friend, I would very much prefer the rooms to be on different floors and, if possible, in different sections of the hotel.

My friend, Mr. Blank, is a very fine gentleman of the best type. A farmer, but a very high class one and very refined. Mr. Blank is from Blank, Ohio, and he drives a new Oldsmobile, which he is very proud of. And so am I. So we both want to feel that every attention will be given it in every way, and no scratches or anything put on the car while it is in the care of your garage. . . .

We will leave here early Monday morning, and should arrive in Cleveland in the latter part of the afternoon, I do not like to drive too fast. We will take Route Four from here to Sandusky, and in from there we will take Route Two, along the lake shore. We expect to enjoy the view very much as we ride. . . .

For myself, I am especially desirous of having a room in a cool, quiet, undisturbed section of the hotel. I know the Statler is right down town, but noise bothers me terribly. It doesn't bother Mr. Blank particularly, because he doesn't hear very well. I am sure that the $4 room you select for him will be acceptable, as he is not as particular as I am. But, of course, you know women are more particular than men. Ha!

One could go on quoting goofy letters that hotels receive from prospective and former guests for the rest of this book. But the idea to be conveyed here is that the Hotels Statler have tried to reduce the hotel business—one of the least predictable of all lines of endeavor, based as it is upon human foibles—to as nearly a scientific operation as possible, while maintaining about their houses a pleasant and hospitable atmosphere. Most of Statler's steady patrons are amazingly loyal because, when they walk into a Statler hotel in a city they have never visited before, they know what they are going to find. They know what services will be offered, how comfortable the bed will be, and a new Statler guest in St. Louis will know ahead of time how the custard pie will taste, having eaten pie just like it at the Statler in Boston.

There are some people, including rival hotel men, who criticize the Statler Company for being "too standardized." The time is probably near when such criticisms will be about as silly as criticizing the Ford Motor Company because all Ford cars look alike. The time is practically here—brought on by inevitable economic conditions—when any hotel has got to standardize and simplify, if it expects to provide a high degree of comforts, services, good food and decent buildings for its guests, and not go broke trying to do it.

The time is definitely here when any company that undertakes to erect an important hotel building has got to know something about hotelkeeping *and* how to build a hotel. The latter is a matter about which most of the hotel industry knows very little. That is why it is the Statler Company, and not somebody else, that has built the big new hotel in Los Angeles and has planned others at a time when most of the industry had felt that constructing fine, large hotels could not be practical.

American hotelkeeping in large houses today is based more upon the tenets of the late E. M. Statler than those of any other man. There are a great many competent hotel men in the country, who have learned these tenets well. But very few of them know much about hotel construction. At least, they have never had much say when it came to building a hotel. This may be a reason why so many hotels went broke during the 1930's.

In the past, hotel construction, outside of the Statler Company, was left pretty much to firms of architects, who knew a lot about building post offices, and to financiers, who were authorities on coupons instead of kitchens. But most of these hotel investors were frightened out of the field when all those hotels went broke during the depression.

The Statler Company is the only firm of hotel operators that has given much study to—or that has been in position to know much about—hotel construction. What this company is able to devise will probably be the answer to what type of larger hotels it will be possible to build and operate profitably, now that gold mines are getting scarce and taxes plentiful.

And it was for this reason—and not the service of an embarrassing legal paper in the midst of the ceremonies—that made the groundbreaking for the Los Angeles Statler in the summer of 1950 important to the hotel industry at large, and of great interests to hotel men everywhere who are concerned with the future.

4

The Manager Is a Pal of Mine

Throughout literature, managers of hotels have seldom been pictured as men of distinction. Until recent times, most of the world's story, poetry and song portrayed the innkeeper, at his best, as an honest, good-natured fellow, though shiftless and unreliable. At his worst, he was a hideous creature indeed—loutish, greasy, fat, often hiding evil intentions toward his guests behind a hypocritical smirk.

The pattern of the good hotel manager, in literature, was set in the fictional personage of a jolly innkeeper named Boniface in Farquhar's *The Beaux' Stratagem*. The hotel industry itself cheerfully accepted this personification, and for a good many years, hotelkeepers referred to themselves as "Bonifaces." The reason literature portrays so many unattractive hotelkeepers is the low esteem in which inns and taverns of yore were held by respectable people. The keepers of these places were regarded as encouragers and perpetrators of such pastimes as drinking, gaming and running around with wild women.

Fortunately, the dignity and prestige of the hotelkeeper has increased immensely in the community during the past fifty or sixty years. Some hotel managers have even turned to literature themselves, notably the late Frank Case, who wrote a couple of books of reminiscences about his Algonquin Hotel in New York. The late Lucius Boomer, chairman of the board of the Waldorf-Astoria, once did a standard text on hotel management. In a great many cities and towns, the hotel manager is now regarded as one of the most erudite and sophisticated of local authorities on matters social, artistic and cultural.

He frequently is not actually qualified as expert on these things, but the atmosphere in which he is believed to operate gives people that impression. The hotel in many small communities has now become the most impressive building in town, with the possible exceptions of the courthouse and the First Methodist Church. In contrast to the old inns and taverns that smelled of stale beer, the local hotel nowadays smells like Air Wick, and has become the community center for all sorts of onward and upward projects. The Community Chest drives usually emanate from there; so do the campaigns of the Red Cross. Local society disports in the hotel at charity balls and debutante parties, and eminent visitors are entertained there. The Rotary and Kiwanis Clubs have luncheons there, and the local hotel's furnishings often set the standards of luxury in the minds of three-quarters of the people in town.

The big hotels in large cities radiate somewhat the same atmosphere, only perhaps more so. Fully nine-tenths of the population of New York would prefer being asked to dine at a large hotel to receiving an invitation to the Metropolitan Opera or to Carnegie Hall. Probably as many persons visiting New York for the first time are as interested in seeing the Waldorf-Astoria as the Statue of Liberty. Out-of-towners who come to the city once or twice a year usually try to stay at the same hotel, and when they get home, they will speak to their friends about this hotel in an intimate and possessive way. Such hotels have come to represent the focal point of the excitement and satisfaction these people derive from visiting a city larger than their own.

It is human nature to fasten upon some particular person as being responsible for these things, and the person these people most frequently select as their contact with the big city is the manager of the hotel. Now, most of these people have never met, or even seen, the manager of the hotel where they customarily stop, but, in time, some of them come to imagine a long-time acquaintance with him, particularly when they have not received recognition in the hotel they believe they deserve. When the hotel is full and a man is told he can't get a room, he will often declare in a loud voice: "I'll speak to my old friend, Barlow Williams, your manager, and he'll straighten this out damn quick." The manager, whose name may be Bartlett Wilson, is sometimes standing within a few paces of such scenes, but seldom makes his presence known.

Some people expect their fancied acquaintance with the manager of a large hotel to elevate their prestige in many places outside of the hotel itself. Not long ago, the manager's office at the Cleveland Statler received a telephone call from the head of a local institution for the mentally deranged, who asked if a patient who had recently escaped, was registered in that hotel. After checking and finding that he was not, the hotel manager's secretary inquired why the institution had thought their man might be at the Statler. "We thought it was a natural place for him to go," the superintendent explained. "In all the years this patient has been with us, he has always said that the manager of the Statler was a close friend of his."

Occasionally, for some nefarious purpose or other, a character will register into a hotel as the manager of some other hotel in a distant city. Raymond McSoley, manager of the Cleveland Statler, was awakened from a sound sleep in his own suite shortly before dawn one morning by his night manager calling on the telephone. The night man said he was sorry to disturb Mr. McSoley but was happy to hear his voice, as he had just been informed by long distance from Erie, Pennsylvania, that McSoley was in jail there on charges of being drunk and disorderly. The man there had been removed to the Erie station house from the Lawrence, a prominent hotel in that city where he had indulged in some picturesque conduct.

McSoley, a sober, law-abiding citizen and the soul of propriety, immediately telephoned the manager of the Lawrence, first, to inform him that it was not really he who had been disturbing the peace in Erie, and, second, to learn what had happened in his

name. He was told that the man they had, who did not look particularly like a hotel manager, had registered the previous evening,
and repaired forthwith to the bar. Some sort of women's convention
was being held in the Erie hotel, and when the supposed McSoley
emerged from the bar an hour or so later, immensely refreshed, he
began to pursue various matronly ladies about the hotel in a manner
the management judged to be carnal.

In deference to a brother manager, the management of the Hotel
Lawrence desisted from interfering with his activities longer than
it would have ordinarily, but finally the situation reached such a
crisis that police had to be summoned. By this time several stately
ladies had been pinched severely upon their backsides, in some
cases for the first time in twenty or thirty years, and while most of
them were not exactly terrified, they were excited to a dangerous
point.

It developed that the man was an unemployed plumber from
Lorain, Ohio. He told police he had heard that when the manager
of one hotel was the guest of another hotel he never had to pay for
anything. He said he had used McSoley's name because the Statler
manager was an old friend of his—which was not true—and he had
always considered the Cleveland Statler a fine, respectable hotel of
the type he would like to manage if he ever got into the hotel business. The man admitted further that he had been attempting to
seduce the conventioning ladies with offers of free hospitality at the
Cleveland Statler. McSoley and his men kept an eye open for several
months after that in fear that some middle-aged ladies from the
Erie vicinity might show up to accept this offer, but none ever did.

Because people who are looking for the manager often have some
utterly ridiculous purpose in mind, Statler managers remain in the
background much of the time. Their assistants and secretaries screen
the demands to see the manager, and sidetrack most of them. Otherwise, most of his time would be occupied with senseless and inter-
minable conversations. However, when an extremely important guest
is arriving, the manager is required to be down at his front door
to greet the VIP in the hospitable tradition of the old innkeepers.

These occasions are high points in any hotel manager's career,
and he generally sees to it that a photographer is somewhere in the
offing to snap a picture of him greeting the duke or the visiting am-

bassador. Among Statler managers, Herbert C. Blunck, of the Washington house, has the most occasions to greet prominent guests. When the President arrives to attend a banquet or to address a meeting at the Statler, his entourage draws up at the front entrance, a clipped lawn with wide steps fronting on Sixteenth Street. Blunck, who is tall, good-looking and urbane, hovers just within the glass doors to shake the President's hand, and escort him to the Presidential Ballroom. The time of the President's arrival is never announced, but there are usually a few goggle-eyed guests standing around when he arrives, and soon everybody knows he is in the hotel. This gives most guests a tingling feeling of excitement and of being in the presence of big events. It is good for the prestige of both the hotel and the manager.

If the President is coming privately to visit some friends at the Statler, Blunck meets him at a side door, and almost nobody, not even most of the employees, knows the President is in the house. It was during such a visit that Blunck experienced one of the most unsettling episodes of his career—the result of some misplaced Statler efficiency. At the time, the hotel had a drive going on to save electrical current, and the house electricians had been instructed to cut off the generators of all elevators at midnight, except the two that operated all night. Mr. Truman had arrived in the hotel early to visit friends, and left for the White House just after midnight, or approximately one minute after the elevator generators had been shut off.

Manager Blunck was in the corridor beside a special elevator that was waiting to take the President down. It had come up before the generators had been stopped. The President entered this elevator, followed by Blunck; the operator pushed buttons, but nothing happened. The doors wouldn't close; the car wouldn't move. What complicated things further was that none of the other cars was allowed to stop on this floor, for security reasons, until after the President had departed.

Meanwhile, the Secret Service men downstairs, who had been informed some minutes before that the President was on his way down, became alarmed when he didn't arrive. The whole security caravan that moves with the President waited tensely while the Chief Executive of the United States remained stuck in an elevator.

At last, Blunck managed to summon another car, which got the President down before the Secret Service did anything drastic.

Obviously, the manager of a hotel can't stand around the entrance waiting to greet all his good patrons, but the Statler managers try to make up for this by dispensing "Statler Service" to all their valued customers and to others whose cause seems to merit extraordinary attention. "Statler Service" is a policy of trying to provide a guest whatever he asks, no matter how weird.

Several years ago, an international group of European intelligentsia, which was traveling about the United States observing things and being feted in a number of cities, was scheduled to arrive at the Buffalo Statler to spend the night and attend a reception and dinner. The person in charge, however, telephoned from Rochester the evening before they were to get to Buffalo, and asked for assistance in getting the group in sartorial shape for the dinner. It seemed that, because of their nightly appearances on the creamed-chicken-green-peas-and-mashed-potatoes circuit, all of the groups' formal equipment was unfit for wear again without a going-over by the laundry and dry cleaners. There wouldn't be time for that between their arrival in Buffalo and the reception.

A blizzard was howling down out of Canada that night, but Theodore Krueger, manager of the Buffalo Statler, sent a truck out into the storm to Rochester, where the soiled evening things were picked up. The truck was delayed by snowdrifts on the way back, but it arrived in Buffalo early the next morning, and the laundry and dry cleaners got busy. The suits were cleaned and pressed, and the shirt fronts were properly stiff, white and uncomfortable by the time the group was ready to sit down to dinner that night.

When J. C. Meacham was manager of the Detroit Statler, he received a letter from a steady patron living in a small Midwestern city, who said that while he and his wife were in Detroit a few days before, she had bought a new girdle. However, as women sometimes do, she had underestimated her size. The husband said he was mailing Meacham the girdle, under separate cover, and asked that he exchange it for a size larger. His wife couldn't remember the name of the store where she'd bought it, but was able to describe it accurately enough for one of the Detroit hotel's bellboys to locate the place, and exchange the garment.

Another time, a woman telephoned Meacham from Grand Rapids, and explained that her husband was in Detroit. She wanted to get word to him that his father had suffered a paralytic stroke, and tell him to come home at once. She said she didn't know where in Detroit to find her husband during the day, but she had planned originally to come to the city to meet him that evening at the Washington Boulevard entrance of the Statler, where he could be located at 7:30 P.M., if the hotel couldn't reach him earlier.

Meacham called in some bellboys, and told them to circulate through downtown Detroit paging the man, whose name was Joel Saunders. Now, Detroit is the fifth largest city in America, but it does not take long for word to get around town that Mr. Joel Saunders is wanted at the Statler Hotel when uniformed bellboys are on the streets yelling for him. Within a half hour, Mr. Saunders heard that his name was being shouted about town, checked with the hotel, and was on his way back to Grand Rapids.

One night, a young couple was arrested for some traffic infraction while driving through a small town about fifty miles from Boston, and fined twenty-five dollars, or three days in jail. They didn't have twenty-five dollars with them, and the magistrate refused to take a check. Since they always stopped at the Statler when they were in Boston, they telephoned the manager of that hotel, Donald B. Stanbro, and explained their trouble. Stanbro called a house detective and sent him to the rescue by automobile with twenty-five dollars to pay the fine.

And there was the time in Cleveland when the mother of a girl who was having her coming-out party at the Statler that evening telephoned the manager in a state of rare distress. It seemed that the girl's party dress had been finished just in time that afternoon, but the people who owned the shop had absent-mindedly locked up for the night without delivering it. The shop's owner had left on a trip to New York. The only other person with a key was his chief fitter, and he had gone to a theater—nobody knew what theater.

The hotel's problem here was to get the girl's dress somehow and prevent the downfall of her social career. Just why this became the hotel's responsibility is vague, but managers come to accept such things. What he did was to put a couple of telephone operators to calling every theater in Cleveland. They explained the girl's plight to each theater manager, and asked him to have the chief fitter paged. In case he was located, he was to be asked to come at once to the shop with key in hand.

Meanwhile, a hotel officer, a sister of the man who owned the shop and a policeman went to the store intending to break in and get the dress, provided the man with the key was not found in time. He was located before the group had to break in, and the young lady's entry into society was saved.

The Statler Company generally creates its managers from within the organization by promotions. By the time he is given a hotel to manage, a man is expected to know all the workings of the hotel and how to handle any crisis, from a complaint that the shrimp sauce is too tart to a strike of elevator operators. All these executive duties prevent the manager from devoting his full time to being the genial host, in the old-time manner, but the company insists on its managers getting into the local social and civic picture at every opportunity. Several years ago Howard F. Dugan, now a vice-president of the company, was elected president of the Cleveland Rotary Club, second largest Rotary group in the world, when he was the Statler manager there. Another outstanding example was when Thomas F. Troy, manager of the then Statler-operated Hotel William Penn in Pittsburgh was in 1951 elected president of the Pittsburgh Chamber of Commerce. Manager Stanbro, of the Boston house, scored recently when the Boston city fathers named a street for him.

Back when E. M. Statler was building hotels, it wasn't as necessary to watch pennies in order to make money as now. When he opened a new house, he always tried to get the most popular hotel man in the area as its first manager, regardless of his executive ability. Probably the most colorful of his old managers, was Bradbury F. Cushing, the first manager of the Boston Statler.

Mr. Cushing was not the executive type. He never soiled his desk with a paper of any kind. If anyone asked him even the time of day, he'd say, "See Bert," referring to his executive assistant who is now manager, Bert Stanbro, a bear for details. Cushing knew more people throughout New England than any other hotel man, but he was not acquainted with a fraction of the people who claimed to know him, as was constantly evident around the lobby.

It was Mr. Cushing's wont to stand in the lobby, immaculate in his morning coat and white carnation, smoking his cigar. If he decided he wasn't working at the time and didn't want to be bothered, he put on his hat—a signal with which assistant managers and room clerks were all acquainted.

Frequently, as he stood observing the comings and goings of his guests, rocking gently upon the balls of his feet, savoring his cigar, the voice of some irate person would be heard rising from the direction of the room desk: "Just wait until I tell my friend, Brad Cushing, about this. . . ." Mr. Cushing would gaze with mild interest through his cigar smoke in the direction of this outburst. If he did not know the annoyed party, which he usually didn't, he would shrug his shoulders, and the room clerk would continue to take no outward notice of the manager's proximity.

However, when Cushing didn't know a man's name he suspected that he ought to know, he knew how to overwhelm this party with an outpouring of flapdoodle and polite double-talk that would convince him that Cushing was intensely interested in every detail of his life and had thought of him every day for many years. This gift is as valuable among hotel managers as absolute pitch is to a musician.

It is a custom among hotel managers to compliment the rooms and often the food to managers and owners of other hotels who come as guests to their houses. On almost any night in the New York Statler there will be twenty-five or thirty rooms so complimented, mostly to visiting hotel men from small cities. This hospitality works in favor of the small hotel men, who love to visit big cities. It isn't very beneficial to the big hotel managers, who seldom spend a night in Pottsville or Chambersburg. The large hotel operators extend this courtesy graciously, but it did annoy Cushing when some small hotel man from the wilds of Maine would arrive at his hotel and complain to an assistant manager that the suite he got was not elaborate enough.

"Is his room complimented?" Cushing would inquire when the assistant manager brought the matter to his attention. "Is his food complimented?" When told that both were, Cushing would reply: "I think he's getting a good bargain," and thereafter leave it up to the assistant to tell the man politely that what he had was the best he would get.

Not long after he became manager, Mr. Cushing had the city of Boston place a small bench for his exclusive use in a traffic island in front of the Boston Statler. In fine weather it was his custom to repair to this sanctuary after a hard day of adorning his lobby and sitting behind his bare desk. There he would take his ease, clad tastefully in tweeds for the out-of-doors, smoking his panatela and admiring the height, breadth and beauty of his building. A great many of his friends around Boston knew of this custom, and they would make it a point to walk by the traffic island, and exchange the time of day with Cushing. The great man would receive them royally, like a king on a throne or, perhaps, like Mr. Bernard M. Baruch on a park bench.

The present Statler manager who most closely conforms to the traditional innkeeper type is James H. McCabe, former general manager of the New York house and now vice-president in charge of West Coast operations. The lobby of the New York house is so large that strangers frequently confuse it with the main concourse of the Pennsylvania Station, the world's largest railroad terminal, which is just across Seventh Avenue. Such an immense place is bound to lose all semblance of personality and become simply an institution for sleeping and eating, if it is not infused with some dynamic type of host. It was McCabe who gave the place its warmth and intimacy.

McCabe is a banty-looking Irishman, with squinty eyes, large ears and a voice like a bullfrog. He conforms in many respects to the traditional innkeeper type, who was no great shakes on payroll control and cost accounting, but who met and greeted his guests. McCabe has been heard from time to time to state that he is leaving $30,000 in his will to defend in court the first hotel manager who shoots a hotel auditor—provided, of course, that the shot is fatal.

His circle of friends throughout the United States is said to be larger than that of any other living hotel man. In any case it is an impressive number. Each Christmas McCabe may send out around 8,000 greeting cards, and receive up to 12,000, which provides something of a storage problem around the holiday season. Once when he was ill in a hospital, Walter Winchell announced the fact over the radio, and the hospital had to put an extra operator on its switchboard to handle the calls about McCabe.

McCabe started out with E. M. Statler as an assistant manager at the Cleveland house shortly after it opened in 1912. A few years later he was sent on to St. Louis, when the Statler was being built there, to prepare the social groundwork and make the proper contacts against the opening of that hotel.

After "opening" the Pennsylvania in New York—he was an assistant manager at the time, but any hotel man, from dishwasher on up who happens to be employed in a new hotel when it opens, always reminisces: "I opened that house"—he left Statler, and was successively assistant manager at the Maryland in Pasadena, Biltmores in Providence and Los Angeles, Columbus in Miami and Book-Cadillac in Detroit. In 1927 he was made manager of the St. Francis in San Francisco, and ten years later returned to the Pennsylvania Hotel (now Statler) as general manager.

Any man who has greeted people in all those hotels is bound to have an immense number of friends, and McCabe, who is gregarious and colorful, has made more of them than most men would have. His friends are constantly calling on him for all sorts of personal services.

One time a young man in his late teens ran away from his home in a small city in the Midwest, and came to New York to make his way à la Horatio Alger. He didn't leave his parents word where to locate him, for fear they would hunt him down and bring him home. So his father, an old friend of McCabe's, wrote the Statler manager, asking him to do what he could to locate the wandering youth. McCabe gave two of his house officers photographs of the missing boy, and told them to hang around the post office general delivery windows. Sure enough, the boy showed up there in a couple of days, and the officers followed him to a rooming house where he was living. McCabe went over to see the boy, brought him into the Statler, and persuaded him to go home to his folks.

There was a time when the wife and daughter of a friend of McCabe's were staying in the New York house before taking a ship for a European tour. There was some mix-up in their minds about the time of the ship's departure, and when they called a porter to take their luggage down to the Cunard docks, he happened to know that the *Mauretania* was at that moment backing out into the North River. The porter called McCabe, who got in touch with harbor authorities and managed to charter a tug. Then he informed the steamship company, which radioed the ship to take it easy on its way down the bay. The tug overhauled the liner in the Narrows, and the two women and their luggage were put aboard.

Several years ago a cold wave struck New York at a time when one of McCabe's old friends, an elderly man from California, was stopping in the New York Statler. This man's wife, who had stayed at home, read of the Eastern cold wave, and sent McCabe a telegram. She said she had packed some long woolen underwear in her husband's bag, but she was sure he wouldn't put it on unless somebody made him. She wanted McCabe to see that he did.

McCabe believes that probably the greatest display of loyalty to him was the case of a friend stopping at his hotel who decided to take his own life because of ill health. This man left his bags in the Statler, but checked into another hotel a short distance away, and promptly leaped twenty floors to his death. He left a note to the manager of that hotel apologizing for the trouble he was causing it. "But," he added, "I couldn't do it at the Statler. I didn't want to bother Jimmy."

5

I'm Sorry, Madam, But . . .

It is possible that the assistant managers of large hotels are the most harassed class of individuals in the history of human frustration. The assistant manager is the man who winds up with 999 out of every 1,000 irate customers when they scream demands for the manager.

A successful assistant hotel manager should have the patience of a priest, the wisdom of an old judge, the physical stamina of a long-distance runner, the imagination of a promoter, the judgment of a loan shark and the manners of Emily Post. He should behave like a practical politician and look something like a successful undertaker. In Statler hotels, the assistant manager is "Mr. Statler" to nine-tenths of the customers. He dresses his part, in winter, in a short plain black, formal-type coat adorned with a carnation, a pearl gray cravat, a wing collar and gray striped trousers. During the summer he looks a gayer bird—an illusion, since assistant managers are seldom gay—in light, grayish blue trousers, double-breasted blue coat, blue and white polka dot four-in-hand necktie and black and white sport shoes.

Each Statler hotel has from four to ten assistant managers, depending on its size. In the larger houses they work in pairs, partially to protect each other. Their station is a desk placed in the most prominent part of the hotel's lobby. Their desk is surrounded on four sides by a wooden wall, about waist high, which gives the impression of an old-fashioned pillory.

The walls tend to shield the assistant manager from physical contact with guests, but their abbreviated height leaves him open to verbal attack from all directions. There are a number of telephones on his desk, so that others may get at him on the wire. On a busy day, an assistant manager is likely to be juggling three telephones, while at the same time he is writing messages and instructions with both hands, and standing off onslaughts on all sides by persons demanding rooms that are not available, seeking lost articles, asking to get checks cashed and demanding to have some employee fired. If he is good, the assistant manager will do none of these things, but leave everybody reasonably happy.

There is a lady who makes her home in the Cleveland Statler, where she enjoys sitting in the lobby late in the day and observing things. One time she was sitting near the desk of the assistant manager, who was trying to talk on his telephones every minute or so, and, at the same time, listen to people leaning over his barrier. This lady took some notes in shorthand of the conversations, starting as the assistant manager was saying to a red-faced man:

"No sir, I'm sorry; we're all sold out."

"Jesus Christ, I been stopping here twenty years."

"I'm sorry, sir, but we have rooms only on reservation tonight."

"God damn it, I think that's a hell of a way to treat me. Do you mean you're not going to give me a room?"

"I'll be glad to try another hotel for you, sir."

"I don't want another hotel. By God, I want to stay here."

By this time, another man had gotten his voice loud enough to command attention.

"Say, I'm a guest in your Terrace Room, and I want to get you to cash this check."

"Are you registered in the hotel, sir?"

"I'm in the Terrace Room."

"I'm sorry, sir. Do you have a credit card?"

"Naw, but I'm in the Terrace Room."

"I'm sorry, sir, but you're not registered?"

"Well, I'm in business down here on Fifteenth Street."

"I'm sorry, sir."

"You mean you won't cash this? Why God damn it, look at the name of the firm printed on this check. Don't tell me they're a bunch of crooks."

"I've lost my glasses in the Café Rouge." A woman's voice now piped above the others. "Will you send a boy to look for them?"

"Have you tried Lost and Found?"

"I've already been there, and they don't have them. Those glasses cost ten dollars and a half. Do you think the waiter could have taken them?"

"Look, Chief," a man wearing a deliveryman's cap had crept up close under the assistant manager's flank, "can I leave these tickets with you. Mr. So-and-So is going to call for them."

The assistant manager scribbled on a pad, while he picked up his telephone that had been ringing for some time.

"Yes, Madame. I'm sorry, Madame, but we have no suites tonight. We are all sold out."

"I'm sorry, Madame that the plane was late, but we have nothing tonight. . . . You are wrong there, Madame. We certainly do appreciate your patronage. . . ."

"Look, Bud." This was coming from the red-faced man, who still wanted a room. "I bet if I slipped ten bucks under that desk of yours, you would. . . ."

People sometimes threaten assistant managers with physical violence, and invite them to combat out in the street. The assistant manager will pass this off as gracefully as he can, although occasionally one of them may absorb a blow. Some time ago in the New York house, a woman, angered because she couldn't get a room, hit Assistant Manager John Shaw on the nose, breaking his glasses.

Usually the people who get the angriest about not getting a room, when they arrive late on a busy day without a reservation, are holders of the company's credit cards. Sometimes, when they don't get a room, they will whip out their credit card, in front of the assistant manager's desk, tear it to bits, throw it on the floor and stomp on it. After this man has left, the assistant manager will try to salvage enough pieces to see how the credit card had been made out. If he succeeds in this, the company mails the man another. Occasionally, after a card-tearing demonstration in New York, the assistant manager will put the card together, and learn that it is one issued by another hotel company.

People also confuse the New York Statler with places other than rival hotels. Women frequently ask the assistant managers about the floors on which underwear or table linen may be purchased. They have confused the hotel with Gimbel's department store hard by. Or else some woman, knowing it is the Statler, will inquire if the hotel's elevator will take her to Gimbel's. The assistant managers often feel like saying it will if she will get off on the twelfth floor and leap twenty feet out the window across the alley, but they usually are able to restrain this levity.

Now and then, some aged lady with lots of baggage, who is arriving early at what she believes is the Pennsylvania Railroad station, will park herself prominently in front of the clock in the Statler lobby to wait for her train. The assistant managers keep an eye open for people who look as though they had made this mistake, and see that they and their luggage get across Seventh Avenue to the railroad station before their train leaves.

Assistant managers are the principal targets in the hotel for inane remarks and foolish questions. Judson Cobb, a former assistant manager at the Washington Statler, claims that a woman once came to him outraged because, she said, the hotel wouldn't cash her check for seventy-eight cents. She'd had to write this check to pay for a drink, having forgotten to put money in her purse. When Cobb had asked where she had taken her check for cashing, she replied: "To the checkroom, of course."

The assistant managers in Detroit say that once when a woman had telephoned from her room to ask what was the check-out hour and they had told her three o'clock, she replied: "I can't stay that long. My bus leaves at one." The assistant managers in St. Louis tell about a woman who had called their desk to say she was going to fly to New York, and asked what weight of baggage she was allowed. When they told her forty pounds, the lady responded, "I weigh more than that."

The assistant manager sometimes has to grapple with the problem of a guest who hides his money from thieves and himself, usually in bedclothing, the wastebasket, the toilet, the chandelier, between the pages of the telephone book or in the Gideon Bible. Assistant

managers—and thieves—know to look first in these places, and the
assistant manager can often find the guest's money without much
trouble when the guest, who hid it, cannot.

What complicates this situation is that the guest is likely to check
out of the hotel and remember his money when he reaches a point
several hundred miles away. Then he will place a desperate call to
the hotel's assistant manager, and ask him to rush upstairs and see
if his money is still there, while he hangs on the long-distance wire.
This once happened in Boston when a man left $5,000 inside the
pages of the telephone directory. Some other guests had already
taken over the room when he remembered about it. Armed with a
new telephone directory and fearing the worst, this assistant manager went to the room. He told the occupants that their telephone
directory was out of date, and he wished to replace it. When he
got outside, he opened the directory, and to his vast relief found the
money that the former occupant of the room had described.

Assistant managers constantly face situations that make no sense
whatever. In the New York Statler, it is customary to set up a towering Christmas tree in the lobby each yuletide. One year, a strange-
looking woman used to come into the lobby every day while the
tree was there, and make a deep salaam before it. Then she would
walk over, face the assistant manager's desk, and make another
low bow. Then she would go away. Nobody ever learned why.

The New York Statler once had a burly Irishman among its
corps of assistant managers. One day a man for whom this assistant
manager had done some favors in the past walked up to the desk
and asked him if he would like some perfume. Thinking the man
had in mind sending a bottle to his wife, the assistant manager said
he would be delighted. Whereupon, the man brought an atomizer
from his pocket, and sprayed the assistant manager thoroughly with
some pungent scent.

It was in St. Louis that a group of ladies approached the
assistant manager to report they had been invited to a cocktail party
General Mills was supposed to be giving in Parlor G. and they could
not find Parlor G. The assistant manager said that was natural,
because there was no Parlor G. in the Statler, and the party was
probably in some other hotel. He then telephoned every other leading hotel in St. Louis, and not one of them had a Parlor G. A short

while later—while the ladies were still standing around clucking—
the hotel learned, through some mysterious means, that the cocktail
party they were seeking was progressing very nicely at the moment
in the Statler in Cleveland, a night's journey to the northeast by fast
Pullman.

Once in a great while a guest will telephone the assistant manager to please send up somebody to read to him from the Bible.
Again, the assistant manager may have to go on a guest floor to discourage somebody from cooking in his room. This happens most
with foreign guests, from India and such places, who often carry
braziers about with them to prepare their native dishes which are
usually spicy and smell up the hotel.

Occasionally, assistant managers have to deal with guests, generally middle-aged ladies, who are afraid of germs. They try to
persuade the elevator operators to take them up and down alone
so they can avoid other guests, who are germ-laden.

There are other guests, usually middle-aged ladies, who are convinced that unauthorized persons are constantly getting into their
room and rummaging through their belongings. To thwart these
mysterious parties, guests with this obsession may set rat traps in
the desk or dresser drawers, which they forget about until they catch
their own fingers. Sometimes they threaten to sue the hotel for this,
and must be pacified by you-know-who.

Then there are still other guests, usually middle-aged ladies, who
are afraid of all men. They become unusually agitated if they hear
reports that prowlers or footpads are operating in that part of town.
One time when some night burglaries were being reported in the
vicinity of the St. Louis Statler, a couple of old maids who lived
there insisted on the assistant manager's accompanying them each
evening when they went up to their room, where they made *him*
look under the bed.

When an assistant manager has been in that work as long as
thirty years, as Frank Bennett of the Cleveland Statler has, sooner
or later he is likely to see the usual situations reversed. For example,
people are often put out of hotels because they have no money, but
once Bennett had occasion to go by a room of a guest he knew from
a nearby small town, and found his room full of money. It was lying
in chunks about the floor, on the table, the desk and the bed. Ben-

nett urged the man to take his money to a bank, or let him try to get it all in the hotel safe. The man, who had been drinking, refused, although Bennett appealed to him as a friend. It was embarrassing to him, Bennett said, to know that all that money was in a guest's room, because if it were stolen, he might be suspected, but the guest remained adamant.

Bennett then went downstairs and told the manager, Howard F. Dugan. Dugan, who had trouble believing what Bennett had reported, accompanied his assistant to the man's room. When they entered, no money was in sight, and the guest told the manager he had no idea what his assistant was talking about. The manager shot a suspicious look at the assistant, as though he might have had a drink or so. Then Bennett noticed that the bed looked lumpy. He threw back the mattress, and there again were piles of money.

The manager counted up to $70,000 before he got tired, but that was enough for him to instruct the guest to turn the money over to the hotel for safekeeping. The guest refused, and Dugan ordered him out. Presently they saw him making his way out through the lobby sadly, his suitcase bulging with cash and a few bills sticking out here and there between the fastenings. It may have been the first time in the history of hotelkeeping that a guest was tossed out because he had *too much* money.

There was another time when a housekeeper on a guest-room floor telephoned Bennett and said to get up there quickly. When he arrived, Bennett found an immensely large woman standing in the corridor, clad only in a blanket. She said she was afraid to go back into her room. "My husband will kill me," she quavered.

Bennett, who figured the husband must be a brute indeed to so terrify such a large woman, put her into another room temporarily, while he went to investigate. He found, in the room from which she had come, a meek, little man with two black eyes and bruises and abrasions about his face. He was crying, and begged the assistant manager not to let his wife back. "When she gets a few drinks, she becomes mean and always beats me up," he said.

The assistant manager brought the woman back to the room anyway, but before leaving the couple, he warned her: "You ought to be ashamed of yourself. If you hit that man of yours again, I'm calling the police."

The assistant managers are also active in happier domestic situations, when newly married couples arrive to spend their first night of wedded delight in a hotel. On almost any Saturday night, from two to six dozen newlyweds will be spending the night in any one of the Statlers.

Whenever newly married couples arrive for a night in a Statler —whether the hotel does or does not expect them or whether it has or has not been informed that they are newlyweds—the assistant manager is expected to do what he can to make them feel welcome and at ease. This includes ushering them out of the line waiting at the room clerk's window, registering them promptly in a room with a double bed, seeing that the bride's orchid is taken for storage in the refrigerator, and sending up to the room a bouquet of suitable flowers.

The assistant managers' duties in handling brides and grooms sometimes go even further than this. Occasionally a commercial traveler, weary and calloused from years on the road, will call downstairs in the night and complain that strange cries and peculiar sounds issuing from a certain room are disturbing his rest. Often, when the assistant manager knows that this room is occupied by a newly married couple, he will go up and reason with the traveling man. He will appeal to him to be tolerant of the situation, employing the "you-were-young-once" type of argument. The traveling man is usually noble about the matter, agreeing to sacrifice his night's rest for the sake of true love.

No matter how hard newlyweds try to conceal the fact, hotel employees can spot them immediately they enter the lobby. Generally they look embarrassed and self-conscious. The bride is usually wearing an oversize corsage, most often an orchid, and there are apt to be bits of confetti and rice clinging to their clothing. But there is one invariable and unfailing rule to distinguish newlyweds: Both brides and grooms *always* wear new shoes. These are inclined to squeak when the groom walks up to sign the guest register. As likely as not, he forgets to register for his new wife. Or else, in his confusion, he will write down one of several peculiar name combinations, such as: "John Jones and Millie Jones," or "John Jones and Mrs. John Jones," or "Mr. John Jones and Mrs. John Jones," or "Mr. and Mrs. John Jones and wife."

One new husband at the Boston Statler got through signing the register all right until he reached the line where he was to put their address. Then he turned to his new wife, and asked, "Where are we going to be living—at your mother's house?" She nodded yes, and he filled in the address.

They claim at the St. Louis Statler that a rural-looking man from the Ozarks arrived one day, arrayed in wedding finery. He announced boldly that he was just married, and wanted two double rooms. When the room clerk asked why two, he answered: "There are four of us: me and my wife and my wife's people."

Sometimes, to the practiced eye of hotel people, the deportment of newly married couples does not forecast a particularly promising wedlock. An assistant manager at the Boston Statler was so impressed one morning when he met on the elevator a couple of newlyweds he had bedded down the night before. The bride, when this assistant manager saw them next morning, was listening to a portable radio she was carrying, and the groom was reading a comic book.

Then there was the time in the Cleveland Statler when Miss Kay Roach, the hotel nurse, was asked to perform a most peculiar function on the wedding night of a middle-aged couple. The bride, who had been a spinster until her marriage that day to a widower, asked the nurse if she would sit in their suite all that night. Miss Roach, who was flabbergasted by this request, didn't go, but she has wondered ever since what would have been expected of her, if she had.

One of the most memorable events of a goofy nature in the annals of the Hotels Statler Company took place in the Cleveland house, where one of the principal public washrooms for men is situated on the mezzanine floor. Opening out of this washroom, but clearly marked, is a fire door that leads out upon the marquee over one of the hotel's entrances. The marquee is about thirty feet above Euclid Avenue, the main street in downtown Cleveland.

This fire door is for use only in emergencies. To keep prowlers and others from entering the hotel for nefarious purposes, the fire door may be opened only by persons wishing to get out of the building. Once a person goes through it onto the marquee, he can't get back until somebody inside the building opens the door.

Late one Saturday afternoon in the fall of the year, a Cleveland business man of some prominence arrived at the Statler, where he and his wife were to attend a large private dinner party. He was to meet his wife in the lobby in front of the assistant manager's desk at six o'clock, but he arrived a few minutes early, so he went up to the washroom on the mezzanine to freshen up a bit. It was never explained why, but when he went to leave the washroom, he opened the wrong door, and stepped out. Instead of being in the corridor, he found himself standing on the marquee over the Euclid Avenue entrance. When he tried the door, he found he could not get back.

The sensible thing to do, he figured, was to shout down to someone passing on the street, explain his predicament, and ask the passer-by to go into the hotel and tell some employee to come up to the washroom, and let him in. Unfortunately for this plan, that section of downtown Cleveland was in a gala mood. A big football game had been played in Cleveland that afternoon. The crowd had returned from the stadium, and was making headquarters in and around the Statler. Impromptu celebrations were in progress on all sides, and a carnival mood prevailed.

Therefore, when the man began trying to call to persons walking by the hotel on Euclid Avenue, they assumed he was a celebrant having a good time, and paid no attention to what he was trying to say. They waved gaily in his direction. Some of the pedestrians winked knowingly at one another, and tapped their skulls.

These reactions tended to infuriate the man on the marquee. He began to shout louder, and to illustrate his predicament with suitable gestures. This merely served to convince passers-by that he was celebrating more violently than those who had passed earlier had imagined. They waved to him more effusively, smiled more broadly, winked more knowingly, and continued more resolutely upon their separate ways. And so, the minutes ticked by to six o'clock and after.

Meanwhile, the man's wife had arrived in the Statler lobby to meet him. The later it got, the more annoyed she became. When 6:30 arrived, and the guests were sitting down at the dinner party they were to attend, a man known to both the lady and her husband happened to pass where she was sitting in the lobby. He told her he had seen her husband in the hotel thirty minutes or so earlier. The lady's anger immediately changed to concern. She imagined some terrible mishap had engulfed her husband, which, as a matter of fact, it had. She appealed to the assistant manager on duty so forcibly that he instituted a search for the missing husband. Several bellboys began paging him. House officers were sent looking for him in remote corridors, in vacant dining rooms, in closets and, in fact, everywhere except on the marquee over the Euclid Avenue entrance.

Out there, the situation was rapidly becoming more and more critical. The man had by now become covered with soot, which lay thick upon the marquee roof, and he appeared to passers-by to be, not only a celebrant, but an indiscreet and violent one and, to some even, a low-type character. This impression gained momentum when the man on the marquee, exasperated because nobody would notice him, became profane. Great flights of bitter invective were flung from his lips at the passing public, and vile epithets resounded up and down that portion of Cleveland's main stem.

His wife was near the point of prostration, and the assistant manager summoned the hotel nurse to look after her. The bellboys and house officers had about completed looking every place they could think of, when a break came in the case. This arrived in the form of a regal-looking and highly respectable local lady who sailed indignantly in through the hotel's entrance, and headed for the assistant manager's desk.

This lady fixed the assistant manager with an irate eye, and announced that she was a respectable citizen and a church worker, and that she resented being called "an old whore" by some drunken hoodlum disporting on the roof of the marquee over the Statler's entrance on Euclid Avenue.

The assistant manager was seized with a sudden inspiration. He dashed up to the mezzanine and out upon the marquee, followed by the bellboys and the house officers. There was their man all right, soot-covered and frothing with rage. They brought him down tenderly, procured for him some new clothing and a bath. And eventually, along about the time dessert was being served, he and his wife joined the dinner party.

When it was all over and peace had been re-established, Ray-

mond McSoley, the manager, observed that it was a fortunate thing
indeed that a true lady, who resented being called a foul epithet,
had chanced to pass. "If we had not had a lady with high sensibilities in the neighborhood," McSoley said, "we might not have
found him until time to put up a new marquee five or ten years
from now."

6

Stop-off in Buffalo

E. M. Statler never did learn how to play. For a good many years he hadn't the time for relaxation, and then it was too late. When he became rich and owned a yacht, he tried to play sometimes, but it never worked out to be much fun. In the end, even his yacht let him down. It sailed out of Charleston, South Carolina, bound for Miami, one day, and was never heard of again. With it went one of Statler's friends and his crew. After that happened, Statler swore off yachting for the rest of his life.

Late in life Statler took up golf, but his irritable temperament, brought on by years of worrying with hotel management problems, had formed him into a perfect golfing dud, who developed the hook and the slice into a high art, and became one of golfdom's leading experts at profanity and invective. Furthermore, something was always happening to shake his self-confidence with relation to that gentlemanly sport. One time, when he was living in his New York hotel, he rode down the elevator, clad for the links in knickerbockers that barely covered his knobby knees, golf socks that hung in wrinkles upon his spindly shanks and a tam-o'-shanter perched unexpectedly upon his Middle Western American head.

The elevator operator, a fun-loving youth who did not recognize the big boss and obviously mistook him for some small-town hick trying to look like a sportsman, suggested politely that Statler try his golfing sometime upon the hotel roof. "This is a very large hotel, sir," the operator explained. "We have a full eighteen-hole golf course up there." Statler retaliated a day or two later by having the hotel institute a special course of courtesy training for elevator operators. But the event no doubt rankled in his soul, for nobody remembers ever having seen him fare forth in knickers again.

With a background such as he had, it was probably natural that Statler should take his pleasures boisterously. Sometimes, his conversation and deportment reverted to the days of the glassworks and the billiard hall. When the Los Angeles Biltmore opened during the middle 1920's, a friend of Statler's, Baron Long, who is lessee of that hotel, invited Statler out to take part in the opening ceremonies. These included an elaborate banquet and speeches by various hotel bigwigs, which were broadcast over the radio. Things went along smoothly until Statler arose to speak. He proceeded to convey his thoughts in such picturesque language that the program was immediately yanked off the air lanes. The tender ears of the radio audience were thus spared further embarrassment, but those present at the dinner seemed to find his remarks stimulating.

Once in a while when he was in a mood of relaxation, Statler behaved something like a country boy showing off in town. Mr. Long recalls he was out on the town one night with Statler in Kansas City, and, at a late hour, the two chanced to find themselves in the railroad station—an edifice of which that city is very proud. Because of the hour, very few people were around. The late night noises of a big railroad station—the feet of travelers ringing on the marble floors, the clank of scrub buckets—had a pleasantly resonant timbre as they echoed softly about the big expanses. As he stood at one end of the station observing the vistas of vacancy and with these reverberations of emptiness falling pleasantly upon his ear, Statler was seized with an inspiration.

"I'll bet you a hundred dollars," he said, turning to Long, "that I can holler louder than you can."

Now, Long is a big man by any standards, but compared with Statler, he was immense. He stands six feet four inches tall. He is firmly built, and has a powerful set of lungs. Long, therefore, accepted Statler's bet with alacrity. He drew in a mighty breath of wind, and gave forth with a roar that reverberated up and down the marble corridors, and was heard by surprised switchmen out in the train shed.

As its final echoes died away in the outer yards, Statler made preparations for his try. He was, as already pointed out, a little man, compared with Long, but he was wiry, tough and determined. Statler dug his toes into the marble flagstones. He sucked in wind until his face was the color of a setting sun in Indian summer. His chest assumed the shape of an immense cannon ball. And then he let loose with an ear-splitting squall, the like of which had probably not been heard since the days of the Rebel Yell, as executed by the ragged cavalrymen of General Nathan Bedford Forrest's Critter Company.

Within the stately station, its effects were sensational. According to reports that may be slightly exaggerated, several electric bulbs were jarred loose from one of the chandeliers. It is said that two citizens, who had missed the last train to Wichita and were sleeping in the waiting room, fell off a bench onto the floor, while a charwoman collapsed into a slop bucket. And it is told that a flight of migrant swallows, which had taken refuge for the night beneath the eaves of the station, flew away in consternation. They did not light again until they reached St. Joe, which is forty-seven miles up the river.

An outraged policeman ran headlong in the direction of the pair, his arms flailing, his face contorted with emotion. He could not speak for some moments, but Long and Statler suspected what was on his mind, and gently explained about their one-hundred-dollar bet. Then they asked the officer if he would be kind enough to render an opinion as to which had won.

"I'll have no part of such foolishness, and I ought to run you in," the policeman responded when finally he could speak. "Two grown men making a row like this at this time of the night. I'll not help you decide anything." He turned to leave, and then spoke an after-thought: "But, I'll tell you one thing. If that sawed-off, scrawny little son-of-a-bitch hollers like that again, I'll shoot you both."

Whereupon, Long paid Statler one hundred dollars.

When Statler came along, Midwestern America was just emerging from that state of culture where the greatest man in many a community was the one who could holler the loudest, get the drunkest, tell the biggest lies and whip the biggest bully. By the time Statler had reached his formative years, standards had reached a somewhat higher stratum; achievements through trade and commerce were more highly regarded than physical valor, and the most flattering thing that could be said about anything was that it was "the biggest in the world." Until his death, that phrase had great allure to the ears of Statler. That is why three of his hotels were "the biggest in the world" at the time they were built, and why the last hotel he constructed still remains the "biggest hotel in New England." It is also the reason Statler happened to start out as a big-time operator in Buffalo.

After he had become financially respectable from his various enterprises in Wheeling, Statler used to go with a couple of friends each summer fishing in the St. Clair River at Star Island, in Canada. Returning from such a junket in 1894, Statler stopped off in Buffalo, where he observed the new Ellicott Square Building under construction. He was interested to learn it would be "the biggest office building in the world." He also learned that the building's management was looking around for somebody to operate a large restaurant there, and that the basement and a part of the main floor could be had for this purpose for $8,500 a year rental. Before he left for home, Statler had a verbal agreement with the renting agent to lease this space, provided he could get up enough money to open a large restaurant.

He got credit for $17,000 worth of decorations and restaurant equipment from the Brunswick-Balke-Collender Company. Kitchen and tableware concerns, including the John Van Range Company, took his personal note for $11,000 more, and Statler put in the only $10,000 he owned. That summer he married Miss Mary Manderbach, whom he had met in Akron eight years before. They moved to Buffalo, where on July 4, 1895, Statler's Restaurant opened amidst a blaze of fireworks and an outpouring of oratory, as Buffalo celebrated jointly the nation's birthday and the opening of the city's great new building.

Buffalo, which is not exactly a festive place, had never been noted as a center of fine dining and the haunt of famous restaurateurs. One reason the restaurant space in the Ellicott Square

Building was unrented when Statler happened by was that nobody wanted to venture a restaurant that large in Buffalo. In fact, after it had opened, John W. Scatchard, president of the Ellicott Square Building, informed Statler that no big restaurant had ever made money in Buffalo.

"Mine will," Statler replied. He based this confident forecast on his restaurant experience in operating an eighteen-by-sixteen-foot lunchroom in Wheeling.

One of his first concerns was to save his waitresses time and steps, so he invented a new type of service table, with compartments for napkins, glasses, butter chips, condiments, cutlery, clean and soiled linen, and, according to Statler, the first ice-water spigots ever built into such a table. He had his guest tables built in octagon shape. It was his idea to seat as many guests as possible, yet give each diner some illusion of privacy. From the first, however, crowding was not one of the restaurant problems faced by Statler.

His restaurant, after the first day, was noted chiefly for empty tables. He learned that the city was not only apathetic, but quite hostile, to the enterprise of anybody who was not a native. Policemen and townspeople steered strangers looking for a place to eat to other restaurants. And while his patronage failed to increase, his expenses did. He managed to pay his bills regularly, but one local wholesale grocer, who figured the place was about to collapse, served him with a process to collect his $180 bill. Statler had that in the cash drawer, but this started a trend among his creditors, all of whom sued to collect.

Naturally, Statler hadn't the funds to pay all these demands, so, after a quick conference with his attorney, William H. Love, he hauled down his sign, changing the name from Statler's Restaurant to George E. House's Restaurant. George E. House was one of his Wheeling friends who had underwritten his lease. Statler then rushed to Wheeling, where he put the name of the home he had built for his mother under her name—and not a moment too soon, either—to stop the John Van Range people from attaching the property.

Meanwhile, a Wheeling creditor had undertaken to attach his billiard parlor, but Statler persuaded the sheriff not to foreclose. Then he talked his Wheeling creditors into sticking by him and giving him more time to pay. He did the same thing with those in Buffalo, after making them a short speech, the substance of which was as follows: "If you will give me a few months, I'll pay you all in full; otherwise, none of you will get a damned cent."

Statler now instituted a great economy drive. He fired his expensive chef from New York, and hired a cheaper one. He got rid of his purchasing steward and his bookkeeper, and did their work himself. He arose at 4:30 A.M., and did his own food purchasing. He put his accounting system on a day-to-day basis. He figured his own meal costs, printed his own menus, kept his own books, made out the checks himself, but in spite of all this, business kept slipping.

Statler's misfortunes finally reached such an ebb that he decided he must stake everything on one final plunge, namely the coming encampment of the Grand Army of the Republic, which was about to bring to Buffalo thousands of Union Army veterans and their families from all over the northern United States. Statler resolved that he would capture their patronage if a lot of food at low prices would do it—a policy which, in view of his recent experiences, he had begun to doubt.

Therefore, he advertised widely in the local press and upon signboards all over the city perhaps the most amazing menu ever offered for twenty-five cents. For a quarter, a person eating in his restaurant could have any part of, or all of, the following: bisque of oyster, olives, radishes, fried smelts with tartar sauce and potatoes Windsor, lamb sauté Bordelaise with green peas, roast young duck with applesauce and mashed potatoes, Roman punch, fruit or vegetable salad with Russian dressing, cream layer cake, Metropolitan ice cream, coffee, tea or milk. What is more, anybody could have as many helpings of anything as he desired.

That tore it. The veterans, arriving in Buffalo with lusty appetites and no overabundance of funds, rallied to Statler's menu. They charged his restaurant with more spirit and vigor, perhaps, than they had demonstrated since storming the heights of Vicksburg. Piles of quarters overflowed the cash drawer. The cashier began to shove them out of the way with her feet. Finally even that became impossible, and she ended the first day of the Grand Army encampment standing knee deep in silver.

It is difficult to understand how Statler made any profit from the venture, considering the prodigious menu he served, but he cleared several thousand dollars, which was sufficient to insure him against bankruptcy for some months to come.

His success with the Grand Army invasion convinced Statler that he had not advertised enough in the past, and he immediately began to make up for this deficiency with a series of hard-hitting, go-getter exploitation campaigns in Buffalo newspapers. "Your wife's labors could be lightened and your business improved by the exercise of a little common horse sense on your part," he chided Buffalo businessmen. "The going-home-to-lunch habit is a relic of village customs. Time, money and labor are saved by eating at Statler's."

His name began to appear frequently in the news columns of the Buffalo press as "Statler, the popular caterer of Ellicott Square" or "Statler, the famed restaurateur." With the Spanish-American War on the horizon, he capitalized on Buffalo's patriotic spirit by removing the potted palms from his restaurant, and hanging bunting. He then hired a brass band that blared out such patriotic airs as "Columbia the Gem of the Ocean," "Yankee Doodle," and "The Star-Spangled Banner," which was a new and exciting kind of dinner music.

Stimulated by improving business, Statler proved he was full of all sorts of tricks. He continued to allow customers to gorge themselves with as many servings as they chose for twenty-five cents, but he began adding more expensive dishes, such as quail on toast at forty cents, to augment the regular table d'hôte. People flocked in from all parts of Western New York State to eat some of Statler's widely advertised Yum Yum ice cream. The ice cream was molded into the shape of a Japanese woman, who carried a tiny paper umbrella over her shoulder; concealed inside some of the servings were five-dollar gold pieces, which finders could keep. This brought in such a heavy trade in ice cream that a special staff was employed to do nothing but open Japanese umbrellas and stick the handle into the frozen lady's hand.

Statler sold books of six twenty-five-cent meal tickets for the price of five, and printed upon each book was a series of numbers. A drawing was held each week, and the holder of the lucky number

won "a magnificent $300 piano." For several years, Statler distrib-
uted more pianos around Buffalo than Steinway did. Statler even
relapsed into the muse now and then in his advertising, with such
limpid verse as:

> Rarest dinners we contrive
> To serve at low expense,
> One table d'hote at twenty-five
> And one at fifty cents.

Statler's Restaurant had many special awards for persons who
ate there, such as:

For one week only STATLER will give each cash purchaser of a twenty-
five-cent meal, absolutely free, as long as they last, a KATZENJAMMER
PUZZLE, the greatest puzzle of the Nineteenth Century—impossible of
mathematical demonstration, and can be solved with equal ease by the
youngest school girl or the most learned scholar.

By 1901 Statler had paid all of his debts and had $60,000 in the
bank. He now began to bend an eager ear toward the sound of
distant band music. One of the "biggest carnivals in the world" was
about to advance upon Buffalo, and E. M. Statler could never hope
to resist a thing like that.

7

Wine, Women and Song

During the dark hours from midnight to dawn—or, more specifically, from 11:00 P.M. until 7:00 A.M.—a large hotel is in charge of its night manager, whose duties are as lonely and dreary as the hours he keeps. The night manager is an assistant manager who has been exiled to Siberia.

Throughout the day and early evening, the lobby is generally exciting, often gay. The night manager's lobby is inhabited by drudgy women with scrub brushes and slop buckets. His ears are beset by roarings of the vacuum cleaners working on the lobby carpets. When that quits, an eternal whispering of adding machines persists the rest of the night from the cashiers' cages. There the night auditors, grim in their shirt sleeves and eyeshades, probe among yesterday's account sheets for mistakes, made by happier, frivolous people, who work during the day.

There are several duties the night manager must perform in the course of a night, most of them dismal. During his first hour or so after coming on duty, when the house is full, he is involved with sending to other hotels weary travelers who have arrived late, without reservations. It is discouraging to any hotel man to send business out of his house, in the first place, but the night manager often has to turn away families with small, tired children. The smallest little girl is probably dangling asleep across the shoulder

and stomach of her father, who looks worn out himself and unhappy that they left home.

Often the only hotels with vacancies are the second-raters, with
gloomy rooms, dowdy furniture and sloppy service. But the man
with the big family, who is not aware of the sort of hotel to which
he is being sent or else is too tired to care, accepts the night manager's note to that hotel with a look of doglike gratitude.

He feels better about sending to second-rate houses persons who
had reservations, but arrive at 1:00 A.M. instead of 9:00 P.M.,
when they had said they would. They usually give the night manager a great argument when he tells them their rooms have been
sold—a policy of the hotel when there is a demand for rooms,
and persons, expected early in the evening, do not show up by
midnight.

As the supper room prepares to close, the night manager may
have to approve checks for a few people he never heard of, who
have overspent and haven't enough cash to pay their bills. Then a
credit card holder and good customer of the house may barge in,
feeling no pain, seeking finances to prolong his celebration in one
of the city's late spots. If he is unable to sign his name legibly on
his check, the night manager may accept a raggedly written I.O.U.
for about a third the amount the guest was seeking originally. The
night manager usually limits the amount of cash he lets this guest
have, for which the guest will likely be thankful in the morning.

Late on Saturday nights or on Sunday evenings, when the liquor
stores are closed, the night manager will often get some visitors,
not guests of the hotel, who want to buy a bottle of liquor after
hours. They seem to have the erroneous impression that the hotel
is willing to jeopardize its liquor license, which may be worth a
half million dollars a year, by selling them an illegal bottle of
whisky for a couple of dollars above the regular price.

The night manager must also keep an eye open for bums, who
stray into the lobby now and then. These may be panhandlers,
trying to mooch a quarter from some guest before the house officers
chuck them out. Or they may be characters such as the "Market
Street Gandys" in St. Louis, a "mink-slide" type that every large
city has. These are men of middle age with no visible means of

support who subsist largely upon cheap wine. As the fall of the year comes on and the damp cold creeps up from the river bottoms into that city, these men begin to look for a warmer place to sleep than the alleys and doorways off Market or Sixth Streets.

If such a character has had sufficient "goof balls," he may stride boldly up to the room desk, announce that he has no money, but he desires a room, a girl and a bottle of liquor. More likely he will slip into the lobby and try to capture for the night an easy chair behind a column. Or else he may try to slip downstairs into the men's washroom, where he will crawl under the door of a pay toilet and make himself comfortable on the tile floor.

Some nights, particularly during a convention or a football weekend, the night manager has a noise problem. The worst noises that beset a sleeping hotel are loud singing and laughing in rooms, and women talking and running up and down the corridors. The singing is frightful, of course, but women in the halls are probably worse. Their voices are shrill and can penetrate up and down for several floors. If there are several roomfuls of people in one party, the women enjoy making trips from room to room, glasses in hand, chatting with one another en route and indulging in loud whinnies of laughter. The management tries to reason with them to be quiet, but it is a well-known axiom in the hotel business that the most unreasonable of all people are women who have had much to drink.

Occasionally, there are unique situations relating to noise, such as Joe Picciotti, night manager at the New York Statler, encountered when some Lebanese people were holding a convention in that house.

About two o'clock one morning, irate guests began telephoning the night manager, stating that some sort of war dance was in progress upstairs. Picciotti found a room filled with Lebanese, standing and sitting around the walls in a circle. Two men were beating tom-toms and two others were playing flutes that looked to the night manager like the kind snake charmers use. To these weird and dreadful sounds, a young Lebanese woman was doing some sort of Eastern dance in the center of the circle. Nobody was drunk. They were all quite serious about the matter, but it sounded something like the hubbub of the market place of Baghdad.

Picciotti announced that, tribal customs notwithstanding, this noise had got to stop. It might be all right on the wind-swept steppes of Lebanon, he continued, but it was out of place on the tenth floor of the Statler hotel. The crowd was reasonable about this, and, to Picciotti's consternation, adjourned the session to the hotel lobby, where the men resumed their activities with the tom-toms and flutes, and the girl went back into her dance.

Great crowds of Lebanese from all parts of the hotel came down to observe and applaud this spectacle. Picciotti was at a loss here as to what his attitude should be. He finally decided to allow the dance to proceed, which it did until 5:30 A.M. After all, they were not keeping guests awake upstairs, he reasoned. Furthermore— although Statler's books of instructions to its employees and executives are most comprehensive and embrace almost any known situation likely to occur in a hotel—there was nothing in any of the books covering ceremonial dances of the mysterious East.

The night manager's most demanding task, however, is preserving the morals of the hotel by superintending the ejection of sundry women of ill repute who attempt to get into the house. Usually the guests, their libido fired by strong waters, drag them in from some low bar. Sometimes they pick up girls in more auspicious places. In any case, the Statlers want no part of these women. Aside from the morals of the house, the management is concerned about the welfare of its guests. Few women are going to accompany a man they do not know to a hotel room unless they have some extremely ulterior purpose in mind.

A member of the United States Senate once left a gay party at the Boston Statler at four o'clock in the morning with a good load of whisky in him and a strange young woman in tow. He awakened in his room a few hours later to find his door unlocked and the young woman gone with his money and watch. The Senator threatened to bring all sorts of pressure in Washington to make the Statler pay him $600, which the company flatly refused to do.

The Statlers do their best to maintain an atmosphere that encourages men to bring their wives there instead of their girl friends. While some of these latter—along with some independents, or professionals—get through the portals in spite of all of Statler's restrictions, the company's reputation for being straight-laced is high.

Fathers of young ladies in girls' schools, such as Stephens College at Columbia, Missouri, or Wellesley College at Wellesley, Massachusetts, have told their daughters for years that, if they are in a large city, such as St. Louis or Boston and are in need of help or advice, to go to the manager of the Statler Hotel.

The hotel staff begins to man the ramparts to defend the house from infiltrations of undesirable women in the late afternoon during the cocktail hour, when the bars are full. For, according to Eddie Laughlin, headwaiter at the St. Louis Statler and in charge of the Lounge Bar there, a first-class bar can become the same as a bordello in no time, unless the staff that runs it is careful and firm.

If a young woman, unknown to them, comes into the Lounge Bar at the St. Louis Statler and lingers too long over a drink, the captains of waiters become suspicious. When she is ready to leave, she is apt to give some man the glad eye as she walks slowly out. The next afternoon, if she comes back, she doesn't get a table.

"If we relaxed that policy," the headwaiter says, "in two or three days, a dozen of these babes would be sitting around, waiting for some pickup. Some of them would be professionals. Some would be married girls, looking for some extra money.

"We've also got to watch the men. When a guy puts down his drink on the bar, and turns around and surveys the room, he is generally looking to see what promising-looking girls are around. Our bartenders suggest to him that he turn back to the bar; his drink is there.

"If the man moves away from the bar and out through the crowd at the tables, when he obviously doesn't know anyone, he probably has in mind joining one of the groups of women. This is called table-hopping. Our captain is instructed to stop him before he reaches a table. He can do this politely by saying something like, 'Did you want something, sir?' This lets the guy know we know what he has in mind, and allows the headwaiter and his captains to run the room, rather than the room running them."

When a man fails to make a pickup in the hotel bar, he may go to a less fastidious place before the night is over. Then, along about 2:30 A.M., when his standards have declined sufficiently, he may heave into the lobby with a female, usually a professional. She may be young and pretty, in a hard-faced way. She may be a veteran with baggy eyes and floppy hips. In either case, if she is not known to the night manager or the chief house officer, they quickly recognize the type.

In the Cleveland house, the night manager, Charlie Heidler, who has been on the job for years, is the house authority on which women are legitimate and married to their escort, and which are not. Heidler, who is short, scrappy and determined, regards this work as a necessary, but unpleasant, task.

"They tried the old double-talk deal on me again last night," he may observe sadly over his bowl of cornflakes in the Café Rouge, when his duties are over. "Some guy comes in about three o'clock, and starts talking to me in a very enthusiastic way about the weather. So I keep my eye peeled toward the side entrance, and sure enough here comes his pal slipping in toward the elevator with this woman. It was 'Old Bessie' again. Sometimes this job is sickening . . . ."

On the other hand, Charles P. Billings, chief house officer at the St. Louis Statler, is a man who glories in his work. "I've got the name with most of the girls," he will shout joyfully, "as the meanest son-of-a-bitch between Chicago and New Orleans."

For a good many years Billings was chief investigator for the Circuit Attorney's office in St. Louis. He has close contacts with the Police Department, which informs him every few days just who is operating where. This has discouraged most of the regulars from coming to the Statler at all.

If a girl is unknown to Billings or the police—maybe some local working girl with a traveling man for a boy friend—Billings has to rely on his knowledge of human nature. One good indication, he has found, is how couples enter the lobby. If a man comes through the revolving door late at night, according to Billings, and a woman is following him, the chances are good they are man and wife. But if a man ushers the woman through the door, and escorts her across the floor, they are very likely not legitimate.

Sometimes the girls who know him will watch from the outside until they see Billings leave the floor. Then the girl and her escort will make a try for the elevators. The bellboys usually know them, however, and inform Billings. There are also house officers who patrol the corridors all night, mainly to watch out for fire. They know which rooms are single and which are double. If they hear male and female voices issuing from a single room as they pass, they inform the chief house officer.

He will then listen at the door. The trick in doing this effectively is to place the ear against the crack where the door is hinged. That is where there is least obstruction between the ear and events transpiring in the room. Also, the sound waves are trapped in the recess the door makes in the room's wall, and voices are quite audible at the hinged crack, particularly if the window is open.

If the conversation leads the house officer to believe that improper procedures are under way, he will inform the night manager. The Statler Company, the leading experts at standardization in the industry, has perfected a standard message for the night manager to convey under these circumstances, to wit: "I understand that you have a visitor in your room. It is against the rules and regulations of the hotel to have visitors. Please ask your visitor to leave."

This is brief, crisp and to the point. Furthermore, it is polite. There are many less dignified terms than "visitor" that the hotel might use. The message has a carefully calculated psychological inflection, in that the room occupant is not asked *if* he has a visitor. The implication of the message is that the hotel knows very well that he *has* a visitor. This makes the room occupant less likely to argue.

Occasionally when night managers have strayed away from instructions and varied their remarks from the standard message, the occupant of the room has been able to get the upper hand. One time when Frank Bennett, of the Cleveland Statler, was serving as night manager, he telephoned a room about a visitor, but his mind was on something else.

"Are you entertaining a woman in your room," Bennett asked absent-mindedly.

"Yes, I am," the man replied. "What do you think I am anyway —a queer?"

Another time when Bennett's mind was wandering, he inquired of a guest if he had a lady in his room. "Wait a minute," this guest replied, "and I'll ask her."

If a room is vacant near the one where the visitor is being entertained, the night manager usually goes in there to make his call, so he will be in position to see that his instructions are carried out promptly. Nine times out of ten they are. In two or three minutes, a door will open down the hall, and a rumpled-looking woman will walk toward the elevators with the dejected attitude common to most people who have seen an important business deal slip from their grasp.

Sometimes, when the night manager calls, the room occupant denies he has a visitor, or else doesn't answer the telephone. In that case, the night manager and chief house officer go back and check the room records. They listen some more at the door to be doubly sure. Then they knock. If the door isn't opened, they go in with a pass key.

The girl may not be evident when they walk in. She is frequently hiding, usually back of the shower curtain in the bath, although occasionally she may take refuge under the bed. More often, she and the man are sitting across the table from one another, chatting with great decorum.

"We are just good friends; our families have known each other for years," they may say with a marked degree of hauteur. Or sometimes they will announce: "We were just having a little business conference at the end of the day." This explanation is unlikely, since it is three o'clock in the morning.

If the room occupant puts his visitor out of the room when he is first called by the night manager, the hotel usually lets the matter go at that. But if he denies he has a visitor, or will not answer the telephone, or resists the efforts of the hotel to get her out, he is likely to be ejected along with his companion.

Back during the 1930's, when the hotel business was in the doldrums, the Hotel Pennsylvania was going out of its way to be solicitous to guests. It was the duty of one of the assistant managers, a Frenchman by the name of Branecelac, to stand near the cashiers' cages and say polite things to guests as they were checking out. He would look over a guest's shoulder, while he was paying his bill, and note his name on the form. Then, as the guest turned to leave, Branecelac would make a bow, and remark in his most solicitous tone: "We were delighted to have you as our guest, Mr. Blank.

We hope that you enjoyed your stay with us, and we look forward
to having you again very soon . . . ."

Early one night, about ten-thirty o'clock and before this assistant manager went off duty, there had been an unusually violent
visiting case upstairs. The assistant manager in charge—not Branecelac—had telephoned the room, but the occupant had refused to
answer. Later, he refused to open his door. A forced entry was
made with the special emergency key.

His "visitor" was sent on her way, and the hotel officers ordered
the man to pack his bag and get out. They stood by and watched
to see that he did. Then they accompanied him down on the
elevator, and stood with folded arms and fierce looks while the man
went to the cashier to pay his bill.

The assistant manager, Branecelac, who knew nothing whatever
about all this, was near the cashier's cage, bowing and smiling and
saying nice things to the guests as they departed, as was his custom.
When the ejected man reached the cashier's window, Branecelac
glanced over his shoulder and got his name. Then as he turned to
go, the assistant manager made his bow, and went into his speech,
to the complete confusion of the ousted man.

"I wish," he was heard to mutter as he left the lobby, "that this
damn place could make up its mind . . . ."

Sometimes a married man will check into a hotel with another
man's wife, whom he registers as his own. On rare occasions, the
wife or husband of one or the other will show up at the hotel and
demand to know what room they are occupying. Until that happens
the hotel probably has no idea anything irregular is going on. However, the management will usually try to pacify the injured party,
and shield the pair upstairs. The reason for that is to prevent law-
suits and possible bloodshed. But, occasionally in spite of all the
hotel can do, such a situation may get out of hand.

One time a druggist from Buffalo checked into the Cleveland
Statler, where he had trailed his wife with another man. He managed to get a suite on the same floor for himself and three private
detectives he had brought along to get evidence. They first attempted to get into the room the lovers were occupying by posing
as a bellboy with a telegram to deliver. But their approach was so
peculiar that the man inside grew suspicious, and telephoned the

night managers' desk. He wanted to know what sort of fool bellboys
the hotel had, anyway.

"There was a knock on my door, see," he said on the wire to
Frank Bennett, "and I asked who it was. This voice said he was a
bellboy with a telegram for me. I told him just to slide it under
the door, and he said, 'I can't. It's on a plate.'"

Bennett, who felt that the hotel had no bellboys that stupid,
asked at the mail desk, and was told that no telegram had been
sent to that room. He decided he'd better go investigate. He
knocked at the door of the man who had telephoned, said he was
the assistant manager, and the man opened the door.

At this point, Bennett was trampled to the floor by the enraged
husband and his private detectives. They had been lurking around
a corner waiting for the door to open so they could pounce for
evidence. In their fervor to get into the room, they had completely
run over the assistant manager.

There was plenty of evidence there for the detectives, but this did
not seem to worry the woman, who was defiant rather than cowed.
She confronted her husband squarely, and informed him that she
was through with him, no matter how many detectives he put on her
trail. There was a short pause here in the conversation, as the
husband was at a loss for something to say.

The man who spoke next was Bennett, who by this time had
managed to get off the floor, collect his wits and take in the situation. Hoping to make the best of a bad matter, he suggested that
the thing for the husband to do—since he had obviously lost his
wife's esteem—was to be noble about it, and congratulate the
other man.

To Bennett's utter amazement, that is what he did.

Besides being alert for men bringing women into the hotel, night
managers have to look out for girls operating on their own. Occasionally when one manages to get into the hotel and complete her
assignment, fate steps in to foil her before she gets away. In Cleveland, late one night, such a young woman was leaving the hotel
through a door used by employees that opened upon a dark alley.
The door was on a night latch so that it could be opened only from
inside the building. As she went out, the door slammed shut,
catching her skirt. The girl remained imprisoned there—not caring

to abandon her dress—until some of the early hotel staff came to work.

Now and then, girls who do not have a male escort will undertake to get into a hotel by working in pairs. One, who is known to the house detective, will go into the lobby, and make a dash for the bank of elevators, with the house officer close at her heels. The other, taking advantage of this diversion, gets into another elevator, and rides to one of the guest-room floors. This is usually after 11:00 P.M., when the floor clerks have gone off duty.

"Then," according to one observer at the Boston Statler, "her idea is to stand around in the corridor near the elevator lobby. Pretty soon along will come some jerk, and she will say, 'Don't I know you.' And he will say, 'Your face does look familiar.' The next thing he knows, he is waking up with a dope hangover and no dough."

This is one reason why the Statler managements watch out for women as closely as they do. Knock-out drops, better known as "Mickey Finns," are indispensable parts of the equipment of prostitutes in large cities. The most popular Mickey Finn concoction is chloral hydrate, a white crystalline powder. "Roll artists," as experts in this field are known, attempt to get some man to take them to his room, where they will slip the powder in his drink when he isn't looking, just like in the old melodramas.

Some guests will manage to get women into any hotel—no matter how flossy or luxurious its reputation, or how high its prices are or how exclusive its patronage is supposed to be—but the Statlers think they have the best record among hotels for running their houses clean.

The night manager's duties seldom include ministering to victims of the Mickey Finn, who usually do not recover sufficiently to start screaming, from pain and anger, until long after the night man has gone home. The latter stages of his stint, in fact, are peaceful and dull. The last stragglers are generally in bed by 4:00 A.M., and the lobby is quiet until around 6:30 A.M. when guests begin leaping out of elevators trying to catch their trains in five minutes.

Later in the day the man who was doped and rolled the night before tells his story to one of the regular assistant managers. Then he must make arrangements with the credit manager, in case all his funds are gone. The whole business of men who are caught in the deadfalls of the great city is sordid and stupid, and it is not often that one comes along that ends on a bright note, such as an exchange of letters from a soldier stationed in one of the midwestern Army camps and the manager of the Hotel Statler in St. Louis, which follow:

Dear Sir: I'd like to try to explain my action in leaving your hotel last evening without settling my account. I know that my departure was entirely illegal, and that I left myself open to legal action. On Tuesday evening I went over to East St. Louis, Ill., and was unfortunate in running into one of the oldest pitfalls for soldiers. I met a woman—if she could be called that—and after spending time and money with her, I woke up Wednesday morning and found I had been doped and rolled of my remaining funds.

I tried unsuccessfully to obtain financial aid from the Salvation Army, Veterans' Welfare and Red Cross. The only thing they had to offer was sympathy. After being unable to secure aid, I found it necessary to return to my post before I had a charge of A.W.O.L. Since returning here, I have started contacting my folks, and will receive financial aid from them, I'm sure.

I want to ask you to be patient with me, knowing that anything you choose to do would be perfectly legal, and grant me two weeks to straighten out this delinquent account. I left my baggage in the room as security, and when I send a money order to you covering the bill, I shall also send ample funds to have that baggage mailed to me. Hoping you will be able to grant me two weeks to straighten out this account to your satisfaction, I remain. . . .

Dear Corporal: I am just in receipt of your letter of June 7th, which I appreciate very much indeed. Naturally, I am very sorry to hear of your unfortunate experience, but I suppose that sort of thing comes to most of us some time or other in life. I think the best thing in this matter is to simply charge it off to experience.

As far as your hotel bill is concerned, we will consider the matter closed. We were delighted to have you as our guest, and hope that after you have completed your service for Uncle Sam, we may have the opportunity of again serving you on your future visits to St. Louis.

We are only too happy to return your baggage to you at our expense. I hope when you do have occasion to visit St. Louis again, that I may have the opportunity of meeting you personally. Sincerely, Donald M. Mumford, Manager, Hotel Statler, St. Louis, Mo.

Dear Sir: I would like to take this opportunity to express the deep feeling of gratitude I owe to you in connection with my recent stay at your hotel. I find it difficult to get words to convey my sincere thanks for the magnanimous expression of charitable tolerance accorded to me in this matter.

It's a good feeling to know that in these times of unrest, world greed and the like, soldiers are not forgotten by men in your high standing. Experiences of the nature of mine in East St. Louis are common, and always appear in a sinister light. But the manner in which my case was unraveled makes me proud to be wearing the uniform of the one nation that believes in fair play for all. . . .

8

The Big Hello

In 1877, James Breslin, owner of the old Gilsey House in New York, became the first American hotel man to outfit his employees in livery, thereby creating the bellman as he exists today—an American personality type that has become as well-known as the rube farmer or the city slicker.

The bellman—that is his official title, although the terms "bellboy" and "bellhop" are probably in wider usage—is more definitely the trademark of a hotel than any other of the approximately 150 classifications of employees required to operate large hotels. The average guest is more aware of the bellman than of any other functionary, because he renders the more obvious types of services. The bellman is the hotels' chief dispenser of what Jimmy Durante calls "The Big Hello."

Hotel bellmen are a strange combination of patience and arrogance, of amiability and malevolence, of deep understanding and utter stupidity. No functionary presents a more touching picture of long-suffering faithfulness than a bellman, when given a wet, squirming baby to hold in a busy lobby, or when he is trudging patiently from one women's wear shop to another trying to match some material for a lady guest, who is waiting anxiously in the

rest room with a torn dress. No insufferable ingrate can demonstrate more scorn than a bellman when he receives no tip, or what
he considers an inadequate tip, for fetching a package of matches
a distance of twenty feet. Nobody on earth can be more exasperating than a stupid bellman when requested to perform any service
at all.

Some bellmen are young, fresh-faced and ambitious. Some are
middle-aged, shrewd, all-knowing, like wicked old dogs. But, as
a class, they are amazingly ingenious at freeing a stuck zipper,
or consoling a depressed drunk, or procuring in the middle of the
night the heads of three dozen Rhode Island Red chickens and a
flag of the Dominican Republic, as a bellman of the Boston Statler
was able to do for some college fraternity initiates. All bellmen
answer with alacrity to the call of, "Boy," regardless of their age,
and most of them would go through hell for a large enough tip.

When Mr. Breslin first put uniforms on his bellmen, they objected
strenuously to being thus regimented, but the custom spread
within a few months to all the larger American hotels. Until then,
the only livery for hotel employees had been a round, hard cap,
with a stiff visor and a brass plate bearing the hotel's name. These
were worn exclusively by porters, who handled the trunks and
heavy baggage.

In spite of the early objections of bellmen, it was not long before the uniform was regarded as a great attraction. It may be
partly the uniform, along with the fact that they can make more
money hopping bells, that causes some men to remain "bellboys"
most of their lives, declining promotions to more dignified positions
in hotel work, such as room clerks. It is probably the uniform, plus
an atmosphere of romance that most people associate with hotel
life, that causes many men, young and old, to yearn to be a bellhop.

At the time he outfitted his bellmen, Mr. Breslin also had uniforms made for his elevator operators and doormen, who, next to
bellmen, are the most apparent employees to guests. There are,
however, probably more employees in a large hotel whom the guest
never sees than those who are visible.

The company maintains a department under Robert F. Brydle,
a vice-president, to keep apace with various union rules in Statler
cities so that one labor classification will not encroach upon the

functions of another. In Washington, for instance, a housemaid can remove a room-service tray from a guest room only as far as the door. The kitchen staff takes it from there. In other Statler cities, maids may take a tray to the service lobby on each floor. Brydle's department also has charge of the Recreational Council in each hotel, which sponsors dances, shows, card parties, choral groups and an annual bowling tournament between employees of the firm's various houses. Statler, incidentally, was the first hotel-operating company to provide vacations with pay for employees and free health and accident insurance.

These matters, however, are of little interest to guests, except indirectly, as satisfied employees tend to give a higher type of service, or so the Statler Company likes to believe. The guest is more interested in getting in a hurry the package of cigarettes he orders from downstairs than in the working conditions of the person who brings them.

Delivery of the guest's cigarettes or shaving cream is a part of a bellman ritual of operation that is as religiously followed as a church ceremony, and which has been in existence ever since the modern conception of hotels came into being.

On an ordinary day at the New York Statler there will be from twenty to twenty-eight bellmen on each of the two main shifts, from 7:30 A.M. to 3:30 P.M. and from 3:30 to midnight. The largest shifts are on Fridays, the biggest check-out day. The first front boy on the early shift is always the shortest boy in height. The second boy is always the second shortest and so on. When the 3:30 shift comes on, the tallest bellman is first front boy, and so on. Nowadays the front boy does not run errands to rooms, as front used to do. Front is always the boy assigned to show a guest to his room and take up his baggage. Or else, if all the hotel's ten porters are busy, the front boy is sent to bring down luggage, and see to checking out the guest. These duties are almost always good for a tip. Average tips for rooming a guest will vary from twenty-five to fifty cents, while check-out tips range from fifty cents to a dollar.

The front boy at the New York house always stands beside a lobby post just to the left front of the bell captain's desk, near the middle of the lobby. The second boy's station is beside a similar post at the bell captain's right. The third boy stands near the cashier's window. The others boys in the progression have various posts about the lobby, and advance from one to the next, like baseball players on the base paths.

The boy who has completed his front call goes to the back-boy position, which is under the clock at the western end of the mezzanine balcony. While there, he is supposed to watch out for baggage being deposited at the Seventh Avenue entrance, and he brings the baggage in to await the guests being assigned rooms. He is seldom tipped for this. The new arrival's tip usually goes to the front boy, when he carries their baggage upstairs and rooms them.

From the under-the-clock post, the back boy progresses to a stand three or four feet to the north of the assistant manager's desk, where he is available for errands that functionary requires. His next post is at the bank of elevators, where he helps guests carrying their baggage down. Next he goes to the Thirty-third Street entrance, next to the foot of the stair leading to the east mezzanine balcony, and so on around until he is third, then second, then front boy again.

At any of these posts before second boy, the bellman must run any errand any guest requests. The only assistance he is not allowed to render is to remove luggage from the rack back of the assistant manager's desk. That is the exclusive right of the front boy. If, while he is completing an errand a guest has requested, this bellman's turn as front boy arrives and passes, he loses his place in the progression, and must start all over again as back boy. If, however, this happens while the bellman is carrying out an assignment from the captain, he automatically becomes next front boy when he returns to the floor.

There is a battery of numbers back of the room desk. When one of these numbers lights, it means a bellman is required at a certain place in the lobby. The boys are expected to keep an eye on this board, and answer its signals immediately.

In an eight-hour shift, besides his front assignments, a bellman will answer maybe twenty calls to rooms. These are usually orders for cigarettes, newspapers, razor blades or shaving cream, but occasionally a call comes from a guest who is lonely. He wants a bellboy to listen to his troubles. Sometimes these guests will dole out half dollars every five minutes or so as long as the bellman will hang around and listen to him.

Bellboys and captains are often asked by guests to procure whisky after hours, or women. The whisky requests outnumber those for women ten to one. When the bell captain tells a guest that he will not co-operate on the woman situation, the guest often becomes sarcastic: "Do you mean you are bell captain in a big hotel like this, and can't get me a girl?" The hangover guests seeking whisky usually start out bravely by ordering a quart. When the bell captain says that is impossible, the guest will reduce his demand to a pint, and finally ends by begging for a single drink, which the bell captain won't produce.

During big conventions, mainly those of veterans, the bell captain receives requests from delegates to assist them in various strange projects. At the American Legion convention in New York in 1947, a delegate tried to tip the Statler bell captain, Charlie Ashbaugh, fifty dollars to let him bring an automobile into the lobby. Some other delegates, who didn't tip anybody, showed up in the middle of New York with a herd of cattle, which they drove into the Statler lobby. The bellmen had to abandon their other tasks for the unusual assignment of shooing cows out of the lobby by waving brooms at them.

John Springer, bell captain of the Boston Statler, once received orders via short-wave radio from a yacht at sea. The yacht, owned by a steady Statler customer, was heading for Boston when the owner wirelessed the bell captain to meet his ship when it moored in the harbor that night, and bring along a dozen steaks and a dozen lobsters. Springer saw that they were there.

The New York Statler, with a good number of foreign guests who stop there regularly, has two bellmen who speak thirteen languages between them. They serve as interpreters for guests both in the hotel and elswhere. Henry Gisbert, who speaks Spanish, Portuguese, French, Italian and Greek, was once assigned by the hotel to accompany a South American businessman on a two-week tour of New England industrial plants. Gisbert served as interpreter for the man, who was buying machinery.

Once when a wealthy Spaniard, who had stopped often at the Statler, came to New York for an operation, he persuaded the hotel to allow Gisbert to look after him at the hospital. And there was the time when Gisbert stood by, at the father's request, while a baby was being delivered. This happened when a wealthy Mexican family, en route to Spain, was delayed at the Statler when the wife gave birth prematurely. The father insisted that Gisbert be allowed in the delivery room to give him reports on progress. The child, a boy, was delivered successfully, and twelve years later, when the family was again in New York, they gave a party with Gisbert and the boy he helped to birth as guests of honor.

The Statler Company has printed a booklet that instructs bellmen in all matters they are likely to encounter when rooming a guest. The bellman is told how many lights to turn on when showing the guest into the room, if the day is cloudy, or how many if it is sunny. He is instructed to watch the guest's facial expression and try to determine, without asking, whether the guest is pleased with his room. If the bellman judges the guest is not, he reports this to the assistant manager, who inquires if the guest would like to be changed. Statler bellmen, when leaving a newly roomed guest, are instructed to avoid saying: "Can I do anything else for you?" This is a standard closing line with bellmen in many hotels, but the Statler people feel that it sounds too much like a reminder to the guest that the bellman is now ready to accept his tip.

But, like almost every functionary in the hotel business, bellmen are occasionally confronted with situations not covered in the book of rules. One time at the Buffalo Statler, which has many brides and grooms as guests because of its proximity to Niagara Falls, a new husband arrived covered with confetti and confusion. The confetti was from the ceremony an hour or so before. The confusion was because he now could not find his bride. He informed the registration clerk and bell captain that his bride had disappeared an hour before not three blocks from the Statler, where they had reserved a suite.

The bell captain sent all the bellmen he could spare to search for the missing bride, and one of them did find her locked in the rest room of a nearby filling station. She had gone in there, and the door had jammed somehow so she couldn't get out. She had failed to attract the attention of the station's attendants by screaming and pounding. But when one of the Statler searching party chanced to pass nearby and heard faint sounds of distress, he investigated. Bellmen are more accustomed to persons who get themselves in ridiculous situations than filling-station men are.

Another time at the Buffalo Statler, a bellman named Red Benson was called on a Sunday morning to the room of a guest who was in an equally ridiculous situation. This guest had packed in a trunk all of his belongings, except the suit he was expecting to wear on the train. When he closed it, one trouser leg of the suit was caught between the jaws of the trunk top.

The guest learned this when he attempted to pick up his pants to put them on. When he tried to open the trunk to rescue them, he found that the key he had would not work. There he stood without his pants and train time getting nearer. Bellman Benson managed to knock the trunk lock off with a heavy hammer, and extricated the man's trousers. He tied the top shut with a rope, and the guest made his train. It was not until several hours later that Benson learned that the guest he had been helping was Ray Milland, the movie actor.

Bellman Benson happens to be the Buffalo Statler's principal liaison man between the hotel and Governor Thomas E. Dewey, of New York, when the Governor is stopping in that house. Benson is usually relieved of his regular duties, and assigned to the Governor's suite to run errands and help keep the place clear of job seekers and persons who wish to tell the Governor how to run the state. When the 1948 Presidential elections were held, the Governor invited the bellhop to come down to Republican headquarters in the Roosevelt Hotel at New York to help celebrate his victory. Benson made the trip, which turned out to be one of the more dismal experiences of his career.

Usually, when Governor Dewey is stopping at the Buffalo Statler, he invites Bellman Benson to have a meal with him and Mrs. Dewey in their suite. The first time this happened, the Governor insisted on the bellman removing his coat, as it was a hot morning. Benson demurred, but the Governor, thinking he was just being modest, removed the bellman's coat himself. He hasn't done that again because Benson, like most bellmen in hot weather, doesn't wear a full shirt under his coat—just a dicky for an impressive shirt front and support for his black bow tie.

A Statler bellman who shows annoyance at the size of his tip is subject to dismissal. But occasionally a bellman will hit upon a plan to get a great many tips he does not deserve in a manner that makes the guests, who are being taken, glad to tip him. Something of the sort happened one time at the New York Statler in connection with a big banquet, attended by about fourteen hundred persons. Half of these guests were ladies, and the banquet sponsors had arranged for each lady to receive an electric lamp as a favor. These were to be distributed after the dinner by a bellman at a counter in the foyer outside the ballroom.

Before the guests began to file out, this bellman carefully broke two or three of the lamps, and offered one of the broken ones to each lady guest. The lady would quickly notice that it was broken. She would call it to the attention of her escort, who would show it to the bellman. He would express appropriate concern, and say that he would try to find the lady a whole lamp. He would then take an unbroken lamp from the big supply, and hand it to the lady. Her escort would give the bellman fifty cents or a dollar and thank him profusely. The bellman cadged a couple of hundred dollars that way before the night was over.

For every sharper among hotel bellmen, there is usually a young innocent who is just learning his way about the big city and the hotel business. One time in the New York house, a new bellman was sent upstairs to remove a guest's luggage. The bell captain was astonished a few minutes later to see this boy wheeling a baggage truck through the lobby with the air-conditioning unit from the room where he had been sent for the luggage. The boy had thought it was a trunk, and was about to load it into the automobile of the departing guest.

Another time at the Boston Statler, a young bellman fresh from a New Hampshire farm was rooming three young women, who observed a fireplace in their suite's living room, and asked the bellman to light a fire. He did not know that the fireplace was a dummy, without a chimney, and intended only for a gas log. The boy had the impression that the log was real, and attempted to set it ablaze with some newspapers and wooden coat hangers he piled about it as kindling. The fire didn't burn well, but great clouds of smoke poured out into the suite and along the corridors. When the fire department arrived, the firemen found the boy, his eyes streaming with smoke tears, still fanning his fire vigorously.

Once when the Copley-Plaza Hotel in Boston was short on bell-men, the management pressed into bellboy service one of its door-men, Archie Hayes, who promptly messed up his first rooming assignment. The singer, Giovanni Martinelli, accompanied by his valet, was checking into the hotel, and Archie was sent to room them. He managed to mix the two room slips so that he put the singer in a $4.50 single room and the valet in a large suite that contained a grand piano.

The next day Martinelli complained to the management that his room was so small it deafened him and he could not get proper range when he tried to practice singing in it. The valet looked up the doorman-bellhop and tipped him five dollars. He said his apart-ment was the nicest accommodation he had ever had in all his career as a gentleman's gentleman.

Archie left the Copley shortly after that, and took up with the Statler, where he was allowed to operate as a doorman exclusively, and where he has become one of the better-known personalities of downtown Boston. It is Archie's contention that the doorman's "big hello" is more important than the greeting the guest receives from functionaries inside the hotel because the guest gets from the door-man his first impression of the hotel's brand of hospitality.

Furthermore, Archie maintains that doormen work much harder than bellmen. Once, to prove his point, he strapped a pedometer around his leg to record the mileage he walked during one eight-hour shift, and persuaded a bellman, Frankie Console, to do like-wise. At the end of the day the doorman and the bellhop compared their mileage. Archie was pleased to learn that he had walked seven-teen miles, while the bellman had done a mere eight.

Hotel doormen are required to open the doors of every car that arrives under their marquee—Archie Hayes once counted 279 doors he opened in eight hours. He sees to parking guests' cars, removing their luggage and sending their cars to the garage. Sometimes, when a bellman isn't available, the doorman will bring the baggage into the lobby himself. Archie, a skinny type, can manage as much as 250 pounds of luggage by arranging the bags under his arms so that the weight of one bag presses against the weight of another, thereby creating a balance that makes the load seem lighter.

A doorman who understands human nature is in a position to get more tips than almost any other employee around a large hotel. The most opportune time for this is on a rainy or snowy day, when taxis are scarce and large crowds of guests are waiting under the marquee for transportation. Under these circumstances, people usually tip the doorman according to how they see others tip. If a man who gets a cab tips the doorman fifty cents, the next guest in line will probably tip the same amount. If another guest doesn't tip the doorman anything, the next in line probably will not tip him either. When a smart doorman finds his tipping chain is broken, he takes immediate steps to start the tips flowing again.

The doorman will glance over his shoulder and if he sees a man he knows, whose name may be Jenkins, the doorman will shout, when the next taxi draws up, "This cab for Mr. Jenkins!" Jenkins, surprised and pleased, will probably tip the doorman fifty cents or a dollar, and the tipping chain is rolling again. If the doorman doesn't know any of the waiting guests, he will pick out one who looks to be a good tipping type, and get the next cab for him.

Occasionally, a traveling salesman will tell Archie Hayes that on the following Friday, at approximately six o'clock, he is going to drive up to Archie's entrance, and with him is going to be the president of his company. The salesman wants to make the boss feel good, so he asks Archie to give the president the "big hello," and address him by name. The salesman must tell the doorman the name to say, because it has been maybe ten years since this company president has stopped at the hotel.

This, however, makes the president feel the more pleased and important when he rolls up to the hotel, and the doorman addresses him enthusiastically by name—after all those years. Both he and the salesman will probably offer the doorman generous tips, but ethical doormen never accept double tips. They are merely skillful in rendering split-second judgment as to which tip is the larger.

Like most hotel employees who deal with guests, doormen must be diplomats. Occasionally a man enlists the assistance of a doorman to straighten out difficulties with his wife or his lady friend. A regular guest at the Boston Statler once told Archie Hayes that he had gotten in trouble with his steady girl when she returned from a trip and found another girl's tennis shoes in his car. He asked Archie to help him convince his regular girl that the shoes were an accident. The man said he would drive up with her to the Statler entrance at 5:45 o'clock that afternoon. He asked Archie to say the following:

"Hello, Mr. Brown, I'm glad to see you. When I loaded you the last time, I made a mistake and put in your car a pair of tennis shoes that belong to somebody else. If I don't get them back, I'll have to pay for them, and I wonder if you have found them."

The man told Archie he would tip him well for this service, but that, in order to make it convincing, he would have to berate the doorman violently, calling him a number of impolite names. Archie said he understood, and it was all right. The procedure went as scheduled that afternoon. Archie said his piece, and the man responded with such an impressive barrage of profanity that the girl was favorably impressed, and the pair made up.

But the man never did tip the doorman. This was back during the middle 1940's, and Archie still broods about it. "He never left me a nickel," the doorman sometimes reflects, "and I let him call me a son-of-a-bitch. It looks like that should have been worth a dollar anyway."

Elevator and telephone operators, who have almost as much direct contact with guests as bellmen and doormen, are seldom tipped for their services.

In order to get the guests to and from their floors and to keep them supplied with food, linen and service, the New York Statler has twenty-seven elevators in all, sixteen passenger cars and eleven freight. Unless there is a large convention in the house, when two nonstop cars operate between the lobby and the meeting rooms and display space on the top floor, not more than ten of the twelve passenger elevators are used at one time and only that many during the peak hours from 8:00 to 10:00 A.M. The cars stop automatically on floors for which the operator pushes the control buttons, and the comings and goings of each of the cars is controlled by the elevator starter.

Convention delegates cause elevator operators more grief than most guests because the delegates are usually so busy talking that they will not announce their floor until the elevator has passed it. Or else so many delegates will pile into a car, in spite of the operator's protests, that their excess weight burns out the car's brakes, and puts it out of service for several days.

On the other hand, some religious sects disapprove of elevators. When they hold a convention, the hotel quarters them on the lower floors to save them as much stair climbing as possible. Then there are some people who are just naturally afraid of elevators, although some of them can be coaxed aboard the slower freight cars.

Elevator operators are required to keep an eye open for guests who are trying to smuggle their pet dogs or cats to their rooms in laundry bags or hat boxes. Sometimes people will try to get large animals on the elevators, as one American Legion convention delegate did at the New York Statler. He showed up at the elevators with a policeman's horse he had rustled while the policeman was having a cup of coffee. It was this man's idea to take the horse to the top floor of the hotel, then telephone the Police Department that one of its horses had been found attending the convention sessions. He was sure this would amuse the Police Department.

During the summer, when families are on vacation trips, the children sometimes entertain themselves by riding up and down elevators. They may do this with approval of their parents, who regard elevator riding as an excellent way to keep children occupied. Again, children will take to the elevators without parental approval, getting off and on different cars on different floors to confuse pursuit. These matters are trying to elevator operators, but they are seldom tipped for their trouble.

The hotel telephone operators figure that they give more hellos, little and big, and come in for probably more abuse from guests than anybody else on the staff, but they are seldom tipped. Marie Mowery, chief operator at the Detroit Statler, reported that at the end of their convention in the summer of 1951, the Daughters of Isabel, a Catholic organization of women, sent the telephone staff a twenty-five-dollar tip. This was the first tip of that volume the telephone staff had received since 1943.

A good many guests, often women, will give the telephone operators a hard time by attempting to order everything they want directly from the operator rather than calling the proper department. Some women psychiatrists, in convention in Detroit, for instance, tried to order their food from the telephone girls instead of calling room service.

"Operator," one would say, "I would like a chicken sandwich, sliced, with plain bread, a little butter, mayonnaise on one side— *no interruptions, please*—and I want it right away. That is all." And the lady psychiatrist would hang up.

Telephone operators frequently get calls from women guests who say they can't get a hook on their dress fastened, and please send someone to help them. Occasionally a one-armed guest will ask the operators to send somebody to wash his back. Women guests call the telephone department for advice on what type of dress to wear down to dinner. Others call in the morning to ask how the weather is, rather than looking out the window to see for themselves. Many people living in the suburbs call Statler hotels to learn how the weather is downtown, and people from all over the cities will telephone to inquire the time of day.

When a long-distance call arrives at a Statler hotel for a guest room, the operator is required to check with the caller as to the name of the guest desired, even though the caller knows his room number. Otherwise, some interesting complications are apt to take place. One of the strangest of these occurred at the Detroit Statler when a call arrived from Chicago for a certain room number. The call was from the wife of a traveling salesman who suspected him of running around at night with women. She was calling to reassure herself that he was in his room and in bed, as he should have been at that hour.

However, this man had checked out of the Detroit house late that afternoon, unknown to his wife in Chicago, and had moved on to the Cleveland Statler. The room in Detroit, which his wife thought he was still occupying, had been taken that evening by another traveling salesman from Omaha, who had his wife along. This woman, too, suspected her husband of playing around while on the road, and she was accompanying him to see that he behaved himself.

When the wife in Chicago called what she thought was her husband's room number in Detroit, the Detroit Statler operator neglected to check on who was in the room, and put the call through. The wife of the salesman who was occupying the room answered, causing the wife in Chicago to leap immediately to the conclusion that this was the voice of some mistress who was sharing her husband's room. At the same time, the wife who was thus suspected concluded just as quickly that the woman calling her husband in the middle of the night from Chicago was some character with whom her husband had been having a clandestine affair.

There followed a confused and violent conversation between these two wives. Fortunately, since one was in Chicago and the other was in Detroit, no physical damage was done, but it took the Detroit Statler's telephone department half the night to straighten out the misunderstanding.

The telephone department of the Washington Statler pulled a more embarrassing bloomer when President Truman was attending a private Masonic dinner in a suite in that hotel in December, 1950. He picked up the telephone, and said to the operator: "This is the President. I am expecting a long-distance call. If it comes through, please ring this room."

"Please repeat your name," the operator said.

"Harry Truman," the President replied, and suddenly found himself holding a dead wire. He had to call the manager and get him to persuade the operator that it really was the President.

All of which goes to show that, in the hotel business, when somebody mentions to an employee that he is the King of Siam, and would like to bring his white elephants into the lobby, his request should not be taken lightly until it is checked. For the King of Siam is who he might turn out to be.

9

The Inside Inn

Any photographic collection representing Buffalo's Pan-American Exposition is bound to contain a picture of "Statler's Hotel," or, in the case of the Louisiana Purchase Exposition in St. Louis, "Statler's Inside Inn." For E. M. Statler was as much a part of these two expositions as were "The Streets of Cairo," the gigantic balloon ascensions, and the Dance of the Seven Veils. Statler got into the act like this:

When Buffalo was ready to stage its big show, Statler had been in the restaurant business there almost seven years. Most of that time he had been cavorting in a frantic series of publicity gymnastics to attract enough people to his eating house for him to pay his debts and become the first big-time restaurateur to survive Buffalo's lethargic habits about dining out. He was out of debt by 1900 and had $60,000 in the bank. When the city began to talk about its big celebration, to be held a year later, Statler concluded that his $60,000 was adequate as the financial nucleus for building "the world's largest hotel" to help house the visitors.

On $60,000 Statler could not hope to build the world's largest *and* finest hotel, but the temporary house needed for the fair visitors didn't have to be another Waldorf. What was needed was an immense, cheap, showy building that could handle efficiently huge crowds of guests. It gave Statler an early opportunity to realize his ambition of owning "the world's largest hotel" with a mere outlay of his $60,000, plus two or three hundred thousand he was able to borrow. Even with his reputation for paying off his debts under unfavorable conditions, he could probably not have borrowed the amount he did in an atmosphere less charged with boom or bust than Buffalo's was with the big fair in prospect.

During the several months his hotel was under construction, Statler spent eighteen hours a day on the site. He studied the blueprints until he knew the plans better than the contractors did. This was the beginning of a reputation he enjoyed in later years as the hotel man who knew more about hotel design and construction than any architect. But, with all his attention to construction, Statler was not so much interested in the structure itself as he was in an experiment to see if he could produce "perfect service" on a big scale. He had begun to conceive service, not so much as a matter of bowing servility, but as a concrete, salable piece of merchandise.

Statler's Hotel, which was just outside the exposition gates was only three stories high, but it covered nine acres and had 2,100 rooms, designed for housing 5,000 persons. The corridors totaled five miles in length. The structure contained over two million feet of lumber, most of it plastered to help give the illusion of permanency to the building, which would be torn down when the exposition closed. The dining room seated 1,200 persons, and the hotel's front-office setup, including fifty bellboys on duty at all times except late at night, was designed to room up to 500 guests an hour. Rates were $2 to $2.50 per day per person, including all meals, but guests could stay in the hotel without taking meals there for $1 to $1.50 a day.

Statler evaded the problem of "skippers," who leave without settling their bill, by selling each guest upon arrival a ticket entitling him to one week's stay. Every time he entered the dining room, he passed through a turnstile, and the ticket was punched for that meal. If the guest did not stay out the week, to which he was entitled on the ticket, his money for the time he didn't stay was refunded. This ticket system, inaugurated by Statler, has come into wide use since at resort hotels, on excursion steamers and in other boarding places where the American plan is observed.

On its face, no hotel man had any right to undertake such an immense operation without a background of years of experience. Statler, who had never operated a hotel in his life, undertook it in the hope that he could make up for his lack of practical experience with the ideas he had been mulling over for years on simplification and standardization of services. A good many hotel owners smiled knowingly when they heard about the audacious undertaking of the inexperienced Statler. But, once his operation was functioning, the industry itself admitted he was doing a remarkable job. After visiting the exposition and staying in Statler's Hotel, a writer for *The Hotel Gazette* reported:

The system at Statler's is fine—bellboy, chambermaid, dining room and office—all perfected. Manager Statler is a wonder. With all the hustle and bustle, the hotel has an air which is pleasing. They are never too busy but what a bellboy may be had at once. The cashier is never too busy to change a five-spot for you. The clerks—room, key or mail— find time to answer courteously a thousand questions an hour. In the dining room you are promptly waited on and served with good food.

The Pan-American Exposition, on the contrary, was an immense flop. Citizens of Buffalo love to boast about their cool summers, but the summer of 1901 was so cool and wet that even some Eskimos, who had been transported there as an attraction, took pneumonia and died. The shivering crowds quickly grew disgusted, and went away to look at Niagara Falls before departing for home. They were not warmed to enthusiasm by such wonders as the "Gigantic Electrical Display" or the "Hawaiian Holiday, with Opu the Man Fish and Burning Mount Kilauea." They were not heated up even by "La Cocoa, the Premiere Danseuse from the Streets of Mexico City."

A good many things other than the weather went wrong. A boa constrictor escaped from Bostock's Menagerie and crawled around the streets terrifying people. Pickpockets descended upon the festivities and lifted so many jewels and valuables that guests who had braved the weather on the exposition. An unfortunate white dog wandered too near the encampment of the "Indian Congress of Two Hundred and Twenty-five Redskins." Some hunters of the tribe captured this miserable beast, and the Indians sacrificed him as an offering to the Spirit of Vegetation. This was the Indians' way of praying for better weather, and they obviously had the good of the exposition in mind, as well as their own comfort. But the fate of the innocent dog outraged the SPCA and dog lovers everywhere.

The weather improved in August, and everyone began to hope the exposition might take on new life and end in a blaze of glory, stimulated by an anticipated visit from President McKinley. When the President did arrive, early in September, he was greeted with wild enthusiasm by the public and particularly the fair promoters, who set off a twenty-one-cannon salute so near the President's private train that all the windows in the forward cars fell out. The President spoke that night on the Esplanade before 50,000 people, and later shook hands with a number of them, including Opu the Man Fish. Then, on the following day when a file of persons were marching up to shake hands with the President in the Hall of Music, he was shot by an anarchist.

The President lingered for a week before he died, but the Pan-American Exposition died before he did. There were some half-hearted efforts to keep it going, but, to all effects, that dreary pageant expired when the President fell on the steps of the Hall of Music.

Most of those financially interested in the exposition lost what they had invested, except Statler. He didn't make any money, but he did manage to break even, although his huge hotel, built to handle 5,000, seldom had more than 1,500 guests at a time. His standardization and simplification methods—together with the lessons he had learned about cutting costs when his restaurant had been almost on the financial rocks several years before—had saved him from ruin in his big hotel splurge. And so, after nine wild months as the builder and operator of "the world's largest hotel," Statler went back to being just "Statler, the Famed Restaurateur of Ellicott Square."

A couple of years after the Pan-American Exposition closed, Statler received a telegram from the promoters of the Louisiana Purchase Exposition, being arranged for St. Louis the following summer. They wanted to know if he would be interested in building and operating the "biggest hotel in the world" for their show. That "biggest in the world" phrase was one Statler couldn't resist. So he wired St. Louis from Florida, where he was tarpon fishing at the time, that he would be right up. He may have figured, at least, that the summer in St. Louis would not be cold.

The St. Louis Fair was to be the most ambitious of all the expositions, far more glittering and splendid than the one in Buffalo. Thus Statler felt obligated to create a larger and more fantastic hotel than the one at the Pan-American Exposition.

His new creation, which took six months to build and cost $450,-000, was located within the exposition grounds. Thus, at the suggestion of John Wiley, editor of *The Hotel Monthly*, Statler named it The Inside Inn. It had 2,257 rooms, hundreds of private baths, a staff of 2,000, acres of public rooms, some corridors that were almost a half mile long, a lobby over a hundred yards long, two dining rooms that seated 2,700 people and "the world's largest kitchen" that measured 120 by 260 feet. It was built principally of yellow pine, burlap and stucco. Again the latter material was used on the outside to give the temporary structure the appearance of great permanence. This was achieved remarkably well in the two immense towers that reared as a façade and looked as solid as the pyramids.

The hotel was furnished with jute rugs and cheap furniture. The interior walls were made of fire-proofed wallboard and covered with fire-proofed green burlap. On the outer walls, wooden ladders were nailed between each vertical row of windows so that, in case of fire, guests might escape that way, if they were terrified enough. Tunnels were dug under the hotel so that guests might exit through them if they came down into one of the enclosed courts during a fire.

Perhaps Statler's most interesting innovation was his bellboy service. Bellboys could not very well operate from the lobby, with some rooms a half mile away, so Statler put a chair for a bellboy at all the corridor intersections, where he could keep a lookout for signals from the guest rooms. These were transmitted by a wooden semaphore arm, fitted into a socket beside the transom to each room. A string was attached to each device, which the guest might waggle to get attention. If the arm dropped to an acute angle, it meant the guest desired ice water. If it went on down to a right angle, the bellboy was to come to the room for instructions. It was a speedy and adequate system, provided the bellboys didn't fall asleep.

Statler signed a contract with Fuller & Company, of Chicago, calling for $60,000 worth of advertising, an immense outlay for those days. "If people don't come to the fair, we'll need lots of advertising," Statler pointed out. "If they do come, we can easily afford it"— a line of reasoning upon which advertising concerns have based their sales talk ever since.

Shortly before the exposition opened, Statler wrote a sort of platform for his hotel, which later was to develop into some of his guiding principles for his permanent hotel organization.

The policy of this house is to please [he wrote]. No guest will leave the house displeased, if concessions will please—the amount of concessions to be charged to advertising. . . . No employee is to be retained who cannot please guests. . . . Guests are invited to complain and suggest improvements and betterments. . . . Complaint office will be maintained where a competent stenographer will take down on properly numbered blanks in triplicate all complaints and suggestions. . . . No verbal complaints or suggestions received. . . . The rate for one or two or more in a room will be on the door, printed and maintained there at all times. Any room clerk who charges more will be dismissed.

The great exposition opened on April 11, 1904. It had been widely advertised, and a great many thousands of persons had added themselves to the city's population for the summer. All of them who could get there were on hand that morning to try to be the first through the gates. The Inside Inn was in readiness, and Statler had arrayed himself properly to take part in the opening ceremonies, but he never got there.

Just as he was ready to leave for the gates, his chef, Louis Rosenbloom, sent word that something was wrong with the twenty-gallon coffee urn in the kitchen. Statler went down to have a look, accompanied by the chef and the coffee boy. They were bending down to see why puffs of steam were coming from the bottom of the boiler when the entire urn blew up, and showered the three with gallons of scalding water.

They lay on the floor begging for someone to throw cold water over their bodies until an ambulance arrived, and took them to a hospital, where the coffee boy, Charles Goodrich, died. The chef, the least burned of the three, was in the hospital for six weeks. And

Statler—while the cannons boomed and the flags whipped and the
mayor spoke at the opening of the big celebration—lay close to
death in St. Anthony's Hospital.

Within a few weeks, the doctors were able to start grafting skin
upon Statler's scalded legs, but Statler was more worried about what
was happening to his hotel than he was about his own recovery. He
had put everything he owned and all he could borrow into it, and a
few bad weeks could ruin him. Some of his waiters tried very hard
to do just that.

There were two dining rooms in The Inside Inn, an American-
plan room where guests ate who paid for their rooms and meals
together, and an à la carte room, where they paid at the completion
of each meal. Under this system, waiters "buy" the meals they serve
in the kitchen, pass a food checker on the way to the dining room,
who ascertains the value of the order, and the waiters are paid in
turn by the guests. With the big boss laid up in the hospital, some
waiters would fill pop bottles with whisky, and the checker marked
down the order at the price of pop. The waiters then resold the
whisky to the guests at whisky prices, and pocketed the difference.
Or they might buy two orders of toast in the kitchen, which they
split into three or four orders to serve that many guests.

Two women employees whom Statler had brought with him from
his restaurant, his secretary, a Mrs. Prince, and his head waitress, a
Mrs. Kocher, saw what was going on, and fired every waiter in the
hotel. Their places were taken by waitresses in both dining rooms.
The graft stopped, and the girls, who were mostly college students
and schoolteachers in St. Louis to see the fair, were outfitted in
white blouses and full-hipped skirts. They were accorded widespread praise by writers attending the fair for their modest and
decorous behavior.

Various other troubles haunted The Inside Inn, including a
threatened strike of bellhops, but this was quelled by Statler's head
bellman, a former Army man by the name of Richardson. Then a
disgruntled fire official threatened to close the entire hotel, but he
was outshouted by Statler's secretary.

By the time Statler was able to get back to his hotel in a wheel
chair late that summer, the Louisiana Purchase Exposition was in
full swing, and The Inside Inn had developed into a leading attrac-

tion on its own. It was swarming with all sorts of Americans who had come to the fair, including "Montana's Galaxy of Beauty"— thirty girls from that state who had each won a free trip to the fair by being elected the most popular girl in her county.

There were conventions of undertakers, carpenters, confectioners and the National Editorial Conference. The West Point cadets attended in a body, and it became a regular sight afforded by the Inn to watch them being fed. They would march into the big American-plan dining room a half hour before the regular mealtime, fall out into the various lines leading to their seats, and were seated at a command. They finished their meal in the military precision time of twenty minutes, all 1,200 of them.

Theodore Roosevelt, Jr., his cousin, Philip, and brother, Kermit, attended the fair, and one day the President's son performed as "manager" of The Inside Inn where the boys were quartered. The high point of their visit, so far as the newspapers were concerned, was little Kermit getting a stomach ache from three helpings of watermelon.

In the heavy heat of the St. Louis nights, The Inside Inn pulsed with the sounds of thousands of people attempting to sleep and having a hard time doing it. The bedrooms were bathed in the reflected glow of lights along "The Pike" and "The Cascades," and the acoustics inside the house were excellent. All sorts of sounds resounded over the transoms and through the thin walls. Cooings of bridal couples mingled with the yells of disconsolate infants, and people trying to sleep in one room were disturbed by conversations from next door concerning the wonders of the exposition, such as paper underwear and the Sistine Madonna done in embroidery.

"The Inside Inn is a constant joy," *Collier's Weekly* reported. "It is not entered on the list of exhibits, but of all the shows at the Fair, it is the most entertaining and extraordinary."

Compared with the Pan-American Exposition, the St. Louis Fair was an immense success. Admissions totaled about twenty million, and the sponsors realized a profit of about a million dollars, which wasn't as much as they had hoped for, but it was pretty good as investments in "World Fairs" go.

Statler's Inside Inn was frequently jammed with 5,000 guests, and in rush periods, as high as 1,400 were roomed in an hour. When the fair had closed, and The Inside Inn was wrecked and sold as junk for $30,000, Statler emerged with $300,000 profit. He retired to Florida to regain his strength from his burns, and to plan for starting his chain of permanent hotels.

10

The Criminal in the Corridor

Each year, the Hotels Statler Company loses about forty-three cents of every $1,000 income to hotel skippers, a shifty type of character who enjoys a hotel's hospitality for a brief season, then leaves without paying the bill. There are two kinds of skippers: professionals and people who just run out of money.

The second type is easy to detect, because people staying in hotels without funds are inclined to eat almost all their meals in the hotel so long as they can get them by signing their name to the restaurant checks. They will also charge everything else possible, including their cigarettes and tips to the room-service waiters. A room-service waiter and the old-time maids, in fact, are excellent spies for the hotel manager on the condition of a guest's finances. They can sense, beyond his new luggage and fine clothes, at what point his money runs out, and his friends, who have money, quit answering his telephone calls. To a waiter of long standing, this polished poverty has a distinct and repulsive odor that his nose quickly detects, the way old doctors can smell certain diseases.

The credit department has its own signs and portents that warn it when a guest is in financial straits, and may be contemplating a run-out. One of these may be unusual hours the guest is keeping, sleeping during the day and eating at strange times of the night.

This indicates he is probably not spending his time doing anything financially constructive.

The housemaids report to the credit manager, upon whom falls the responsibility of seeing that guests do not skip, when she finds that guests have been storing the hotel's towels away in their luggage. This is of interest to the credit department—not so much for the individual act—but because it indicates that if a man will pilfer the hotel's property, he might try to escape paying his bill.

Bellboys are expected to report to the credit department when some male guest propositions them to find a woman. The Statler management regards this as irregular and unethical and not indicative of the highest type of character. Furthermore, there is always the chance that a man with such things on his mind will pick up some unsavory female, and bring her to his room. There she may slip some knock-out powders in his beer, roll him of his funds, and leave him in a financial plight where he cannot pay his hotel bill, even if he would like to.

When sizing up a guest suspected of having skipping tendencies, it is the management's practice to note the type of telephone calls he has made. If there are some long-distance calls apparently made for business reasons, the chances are that the guest is legitimate. A person intending to cheat the hotel seldom makes long-distance calls because the hotel has a record of who is on the other end of the wire. Thus if a man skips, the hotel can probably trace him. Another skipper check is to examine the way the guest made his reservation: whether he wrote for a room, called for a reservation on the telephone, or just walked in and engaged one. If he wrote, the chances are he is all right, because letters can be traced.

Any guest who is stopping for the first time at a Statler Hotel, or most other hotels, for that matter—and provided the hotel has not been assured ahead of time that he is of sterling character—is going to be investigated by the credit department after his bill reaches a certain figure, usually $100. At that point, the credit manager will probably render a bill. If this is not paid in one day, the credit manager will study the itemized bill for "suspicious" charges, such as too much whisky being ordered to that room or the fact that the guest may be taking all his meals in the house and signing for them. The credit manager will then go up and have a look at the guest's baggage and effects while their owner is out of the room. If the baggage is good and the man's clothing gives the appearance that he is there on a legitimate stay, the credit department will allow the bill to run for a couple of more days before taking steps to collect. Otherwise, the credit manager may lock the door so that the guest will have to see him, and come to an understanding about things, before he can get back into his room.

If a guest checks in at a hotel with nondescript old baggage such as nobody would mind leaving, or if his luggage feels unusually light to the bellboy carrying it to the room, these facts are reported to the credit department. The maid who cleans the room will let the management know if the man has brought along nothing of any worth.

While the appearance and contents of his luggage have always been regarded as probably the best gauge a hotel can have of a guest's stability, this is in no wise infallible. Once, an attractive young woman registered at the St. Louis Statler, where, in a week, she ran up a large bill. The management wasn't particularly worried because her abundant luggage was of fine quality. Her dresses and accessories were first rate, and she had two fur coats. Then one day the police came, and they disclosed that the lady was a celebrated shoplifter, and all her fine things had been stolen. The hotel was stuck with the bill, and representatives came from a local department store and removed all her fine clothing and bags.

On the other hand, a housemaid at the Boston Statler reported one morning, after putting a guest's room in order, that his luggage contained exactly five items: three bricks and two Manhattan telephone directories. The guest, who had checked in the night before from New York, had left the hotel early that morning, but the credit manager lay in wait, and confronted the guest when he returned late in the day. He did not look like a hotel skipper to the credit manager, however, and sure enough he was not. He had caught the Boston train in New York the night before, after leaving an office party, where some pranksters had removed his clothing from his bag, and substituted the bricks and telephone books. The man hadn't known these were in his bag until he arrived at the Boston house and opened it.

Most people who run out of money in a hotel, and thus become involuntary skippers, do so because they are victims, in the hotel parlance, of "the good old hooch." Bellboys, waiters or housemaids report to the management when guests are drinking to excess in their rooms, and the credit manager is apt to make an unexpected call. He usually chooses to make this call early in the morning, when his victim is at a physical and mental low. Obviously the guest does not enjoy this visit, and neither does the credit manager, unless he happens to be a misanthrope.

Such a scene is too painful to dwell upon here. It is a situation that the professional hotel skipper almost never encounters. His type does not drink to excess, or run around with women, or have any "suspicious" charges upon his bill. He may sign for four or five meals in a week and have a reasonable amount of laundry done. But he doesn't order up whisky to his room, or make long-distance calls or disturb anybody. His conduct is that of the model guest, and he usually brings along respectable luggage and a nice layout of clothing. Only the amateurs bring old bags full of bricks and papers.

The usual length of his stay is six days, which gets him out of the hotel just before the weekly bill is rendered. He may contrive to remove his luggage secretly the night before he himself leaves. Or he may leave behind the bags he has, which have usually been stolen anyway. He can remove his clothing by carrying it away in innocent-looking bundles to his next abode. But the suave, polished skipper will simply pack his bag, call for a porter and leave the hotel without going by the cashier's window. The trick here, which makes this a fine art, is that it takes a man of extreme poise to walk out of a hotel lobby under these conditions without looking so guilty that he excites suspicion.

One of the coolest skippers the Statlers ever had was a gentleman who once resided in the Cleveland house for three months without paying for anything. His method was as follows: He registered under a fake name, of course, when he first came to the hotel, and asked for a room on an upper floor. After six days, with no unusual charges on his bill or peculiar conduct to arouse the interest of the management, he would call a bellboy, as though he were checking out in the regular way, and have his bag carried down to the lobby. There he would have it checked in the hotel checkroom.

After an hour or so, and at a time when the porter who had

brought it down had gone off duty, the man would redeem his bag at the checkroom, go to the registration desk, where he would register under another fake name. This time he would ask for a room on a lower floor. This procedure went on every six days for three months. The man never came near the room clerk's desk except to register, so that his face would not become familiar to the clerks. He also chose a time to re-register when the room clerk who had assigned his room six days before was not on duty.

His purpose in asking for a room on an upper floor one week and one on a lower floor the next was to avoid being recognized by housemaids and housekeepers on floors he had recently inhabited. He was finally caught, however, because a housekeeper had been transferred from the floor on which he had spent the previous week to the floor on which he was currently in residence. Meeting him in the hall, this housekeeper spoke to the guest, calling him by the name he had used when he was living on her previous floor. The skipper then made a serious mistake. He denied he was the same person. This aroused the suspicions of the housekeeper. She reported the incident to the management, and the man's residence was moved from the Statler to the county jail.

Once, a man and his wife, whose home was in Brooklyn, lived two or three days a week in the New York Statler over a period of two months without paying for the hotel room, food or services. They used a series of fake names, combined with a set of disguises, including wigs and false whiskers. It was their practice, when quitting the hotel, to abandon the bags they had. This was no loss to them, since they had contrived to steal the luggage from department stores, or from railroad or bus stations.

It finally reached the point where these two were bringing in, and having laundered at the Statler, their sheets, napkins and table-cloths from home at the hotel's expense. They were caught finally because the laundry reported that a peculiar thing was going on. Somebody kept sending back the same flatwork every other week, but it always came from a different room and from people with a different name. It didn't take the management long after that to get wise to what had been going on.

Sometimes skippers go about beating hotels in a grand manner. During the war, two Mexicans arrived at the Detroit Statler, bearing convincing-looking credentials that they were members of a Mexican Government purchasing commission. When the Statler management learned that one of the city's large manufacturers of machinery was negotiating with the pair about a large order of equipment, the hotel extended them bountiful credit. Some of the city's Mexican population gave a grand ball for the pair one night in a southwest Detroit lodge hall.

.On the sixth night of their stay at the hotel, the two entertained a group of their new Detroit friends at dinner in the Statler's Terrace Room. The party continued until a late hour in their suite. But when the maids arrived to clean it next morning, they found that nobody had slept there. When the credit manager arrived immediately after receiving this chilling report, all he could find of the hotel's distinguished guests were some stale cigarette butts, some empty bottles and stained glasses lying about and three empty champagne cases. He still quavers every time he remembers this sad sight, and recalls that one of the men had signed hotel checks in the amount of $1,200. The other had been more conservative; his checks totaled only $400.

The credit manager attempted to check on exactly who the men were and where they had come from through some of the local Mexicans who had given the party in their honor. It turned out they didn't know any more about the pair than the hotel did, although some of the women did report that the two men were excellent dancers.

Once in a while, a credit department's investigation of a suspected hotel skipper has turned up instead another type of pest, namely a prowler, or hotel thief. This once happened some years ago. Thieves had broken into a suite in Boston's Ritz-Carlton Hotel, a block or so away from the Boston Statler, and had taken $15,000 worth of jewels from a family named Whittimore.

A few days later, Tom Troy, then credit manager of the Boston Statler and later manager of the William Penn in Pittsburgh when it was under Statler management, went upstairs in the Boston Statler to look over the luggage of a guest he suspected might be a potential skipper. The man had registered five days before. He was unknown to the Statler management, and several things he had done indicated he might have skipping inclinations.

His luggage and effects seemed substantial enough, but Troy was interested in some peculiar-looking celluloid strips he found in one of the man's valises. He didn't know what they were, but took one of them back with him to his office as a possible clue to the man's business, assuming the strips were samples of some product he was selling.

In the credit office, Troy found waiting a Captain Crowley, head of the Hotel Squad of the Boston Police Department, who had dropped by on a routine visit. He was much interested in the celluloid strip when Troy tossed it on his desk. When he learned where Troy had gotten it, Captain Crowley asked to be locked in that room, where he waited until the guest returned, and arrested him. A search of the room disclosed the missing Whittimore diamonds. The police captain had recognized the celluloid strip as an implement that burglars use to slip between the door and its jamb to force back a spring lock.

The Statler hotels do not use spring locks, and are never troubled with burglars using celluloid strips, but few hotel thieves use them anyway. Most hotel prowlers work between the hours of 4:00 and 6:30 A.M., walking the halls and trying doorknobs in search of an unlocked door. They have found that most people sleep soundest during this period. Furthermore, guests who do not return to their rooms until the early-morning hours are usually more careless about locking their doors than those who retire early. In spite of all sorts of warnings from the management, on any given night in the 2,200-room New York Statler, an average of seventy-five guests will go to bed without locking their doors.

On a night when a large and convivial convention group is stopping in the house, the night watchmen have found as high as 275 unlocked doors. Thieves have a system of hanging around on the fringe of gay parties, and making friends with somebody whose better judgment has become befuddled by rum. The thief may accompany this guest to his room, and make off with his valuables when he falls asleep. Hotel house officers are forever on the alert to spot characters who may be following guests who have been out on the town celebrating, and are on their way to bed. In these cases, the guest doesn't know the thief is on his trail, since it is the latter's plan to observe the room his quarry enters. He will hang around the halls a few minutes, then try the door on the good chance that the man has fallen into bed and never thought of locking his door.

Most thieves, however, walk the halls and try doors as they come to them, starting not long before dawn. They usually continue operations until some early-risers have begun to stir, in the hope that a guest may step out of his room, perhaps to get his newspaper, then fail to relock his door when he goes back. Probably seven out of ten guests will not relock their door in this situation. If the guest does not relock the door, the thief will wait until he hears the shower running, then enter the room and remove what he can find. The guest, involved in the shower, can't hear him, and couldn't do much about it even if he did.

A thief who once operated in the Detroit Statler had a method of persuading guests to take their morning baths at his convenience. He usually worked on Sunday mornings, taking advantage of Statler's policy of slipping morning newspapers under the guests' doors. On Sundays, the papers are usually so thick they have to be left in front of the doors. The thief would look for a door from which the paper was missing, indicating the guest had been out for it. Chances were he had failed to relock his door.

This thief would descend to the lobby, and call that room on the house telephone. He would announce that he was the hotel's plumber, and that the water in that section of the building would be turned off in twenty minutes. He would advise the guest that he had better take his shower at once, if he intended to bathe that day. The thief would then go back upstairs, and hang around until he heard the shower start, then enter and proceed with the business at hand.

A hotel prowler was once caught in the Cleveland Statler because he owned an alarm clock. One week, several guest rooms were robbed. House detectives were reasonably sure this was being done about 4:00 A.M., by somebody registered in the house. They thought it likely that this thief slept during the early night, arising about 3:30 A.M. They checked with the telephone department to see if anybody had been leaving wake-up calls for that hour. Nobody had, so a search was made of all the guest rooms in the hotel. In four-teen of them were found traveling alarm clocks owned by the occupants. An officer was stationed near each of the fourteen rooms to watch during the early morning hours, and sure enough, along about 3:30 a man slipped out of one of these rooms, and started softly down the corridor, trying doorknobs. When he found one that was unlocked and entered, the detective followed him in and made the arrest.

An experienced hotel thief, who specializes on creeping into guest rooms while the occupants are asleep, will seldom take valuables that the guest would miss immediately upon waking. If a guest is sleeping normally, a prowler's visit usually does awaken him, although generally by the time the sleeper's subconscious mind tells him something is wrong, the prowler has gotten what he came for, and gone. The room occupant, who has a vague feeling of uneasiness, will usually look to see if his valuables are where he left them, and if they appear to be, he goes back to sleep. Otherwise, he will spread a burglar cry, and the prowler, who may have just left the room, may be caught in the corridors. At best, such an alarm ruins his chances of entering any more rooms that early morning.

One guest in the Cleveland Statler awakened about four o'clock one morning with an uneasy feeling. He switched on the bed lamp, and looked at the valuables he had placed on the night table before going to bed. His wallet was there. So was his $300 watch, a diamond ring and twenty-one dollars in loose bills. The man went back to sleep. But the next morning he found that $450 that had been in his wallet wasn't there any more.

This robbery, one of several in the hotel that week, had an interesting postscript. The hotel's chief house officer, Fred Collins, believed that all the rooms had been entered by the same prowler, and that he was registered in the house. He had all the occupied rooms in the hotel searched during the day for some clue as to who the thief was. In the closet of one room they found two suits, from which all labels had been removed. The officers were sure this was their man, and waited for him to come back, but he never came. Apparently he had gotten wind that he was suspected, and left without his suits and other effects, which contained no letters, papers, labels or laundry marks that gave the detectives any idea of who he was or where he came from.

Collins interviewed the maid who had been cleaning that room.

She remembered that the day before she had taken an empty, cracked medicine bottle from his wastebasket. She recalled this because she had scratched her finger on a piece of its jagged glass when she reached into the basket to remove some discarded newspapers. Collins then had the janitors search all the barrels containing waste materials. They finally found the bottle. It had contained a prescription filled by a drugstore in Chattanooga, Tennessee, and its label still bore the prescription number. The hotel communicated with the Chattanooga Police Department, which learned from the drugstore, through the prescription number, that the medicine had been supplied to a resident of that city, who was wanted at the moment for a safe robbery.

When a hotel prowler enters a guest room, and removes the occupant's money, but leaves his wallet behind and his watch and jewelry, there is a reason for this beyond the one already mentioned. An experienced thief shies away from jewelry because it is easy to identify. He hates to have stolen wallets around because —and this might appear to be a minor problem to the layman— wallets are extremely hard to dispose of. A good example of how a stolen wallet can get a thief in trouble happened once at the Statler in Cleveland.

One morning, a gardener working in a small garden of the Union Club—haunt of Cleveland's aristocrats of trade and commerce and located just across the street from the Hotel Statler—found a man's wallet that had been wrapped carefully in a page from a recent issue of the *New York Times,* and tied with a heavy cord. When he learned that no club members had reported the loss of such a wallet, he took it over to the Statler. It was quickly identified as the property of a guest who had reported a strange experience in his room the night before.

The guest had put his wallet, containing $235, on the night table beside his bed when he retired. During the night he had a confused dream about a big man who was wearing a broad-brimmed, western-rancher-type hat being in his room. When, in his dream, the guest had asked the man what he was doing there, the intruder had replied: "You had better close your door when you go to bed at night." Then he went out, closing the door behind him. When the guest awakened next morning, his wallet and money were gone.

The wallet was brought to Frank Bennett, the senior assistant manager, who was most interested in the paper around it and the cord with which it had been tied. He concluded that the paper had been used both to conceal the wallet and to give it more weight. The only reason more weight would be desired, he reasoned, was because somebody wanted to throw it as far as possible.

This accounted for the cord, which was probably to hold the paper in place around the wallet and also provide leverage for the thrower. The only reason the assistant manager could figure why a person would wish to throw a wallet, in the first place, would be a desire to get it as far from his person as possible in the shortest possible time. And, considering where it was found, the person must have been in a room in the Statler, fairly high up on the Union Club side.

The cord also looked familiar to Bennett, much like the cord used on window shades of Statler guest rooms. A comparison of it with a window shade cord showed they were identical. Bennett then started the hotel's house dicks looking into all rooms fronting on the Union Club for a window shade with a cord missing. They found such a window on the ninth floor.

Then the house officers talked with the maid who had cleaned that room. She had disposed of a pile of Sunday papers from that room only an hour or so before, and was able to produce them. There was an issue of the *New York Times* for the past Sunday, with a double page missing from the magazine section. This page corresponded to the paper wrapped around the wallet.

Thus fortified, the hotel had the room's occupant arrested when he came in at lunchtime. He admitted the theft after a session with police. He turned out to be a one-time oil operator from Texas or Oklahoma, who had gone bad. But as a hangon from his oil-drilling days, this man still wore a wide-brimmed, western-rancher-type Stetson.

Sometimes when criminals are registered in hotels, but are operating elsewhere, they are caught because hotel employees keep their eyes open. In Boston once, the newspapers carried scare stories about a certain "Red-Headed Terror," who was holding up

filling stations and liquor stores in a series of bold robberies. He
seemed to be a red-haired man, quite young, who carried two guns,
and for a couple of weeks nervous people were seeing him around
every corner.

One night, some junior executives of the Boston Statler were
bowling for relaxation, and the conversation turned to "The Terror,"
and what manner of man he might be. This caused one of the room
clerks to mention something that had been on his mind for a week.
He said he had been wondering about two young fellows who were
occupying one of the hotel's suites. But they had pronounced it
"suit," as though talking about a suit of clothing, when they registered. The clerk noticed that they had plenty of money at the time.

Now the thing that puzzled him, he said, was why two young
men had enough money to afford a thirty-five-dollar-a-day suite
when obviously, from their pronunciation of the word, they had
not been accustomed to staying in suites before. The credit manager, Albert Morris, who was present, concluded immediately that
the pair were probably the "Red-Headed Terror" and a pal. (As has
been indicated, credit managers are a suspicious lot, inclined to
expect the worst.)

He felt about this matter so strongly that the bowling game soon
was abandoned, and the Statler employees repaired to Police
Headquarters, where they related their suspicions. The police were
convinced sufficiently to raid the suite, and there found the "Red-
Headed Terror," his pal and two girls.

There was another time in the Buffalo house when a robber with
a pistol held up some traveling men who were playing poker in
one of the suites. The next day, the lady in charge of the cigar
counter noticed a man who bought a newspaper and turned rapidly
through it to the page where an account of the robbery was carried.
He read it with such fervor that she became convinced he was
probably the robber. She was able to convince police that they
ought to look. They broke into this man's room—he was registered
in the hotel—found him asleep, with the guns he had used in a
dresser drawer with some of the jewelry he had removed from the
salesmen.

Usually when hotel prowlers are caught, either in the act of
stealing from a room or under suspicious circumstances, they feign

illness or intoxication in an often-convincing manner. Once in the New York Statler, where two men were sharing a room during a convention, one of them awakened in the middle of the night and started to the bathroom without turning on the light. He was amazed when he stepped squarely upon the back of a man lying on the floor. He yelled and grabbed the man. His roommate in the other bed awakened, turned on the lights and called the house officers.

The man on the floor contended stoutly that it was all an accident. He said he had been out on the town drinking, and had merely come into the wrong room. Seeing both beds were occupied, he said, he judged the men in them were people he had met and probably invited to share his room. He said he had taken the floor in the best tradition of hospitality. Since this line of reasoning is not unusual among men who have had too much to drink, the house detectives were inclined to believe him. They were convinced he was all right when they found he was registered in a room down the hall, as he said, and that the luggage there was of a type he described. So they let him go.

Two days later, house detectives from the New Yorker Hotel, a couple of blocks west of the Statler, showed up at the Statler looking for this man. They had traced him from their hotel, where he had stolen the baggage that had been in his room at the Statler. He had been using the Statler as a base of operations for preying on guest rooms in hotels all about the Pennsylvania Station area.

At the Cleveland house some years back, $350 had been stolen from an assistant district attorney in New York, and a guest in the house. He had put the money in a dresser drawer, after removing the suit he was wearing to send out for pressing. When he put on another suit to go down to dinner, he forgot to transfer the money from the dresser to his pocket, and when he came back to the room after dinner, his money wasn't there any more.

The district attorney suspected a bellboy who had been in the room to take the suit to the presser, and had probably seen him toss the money in the drawer. The chief house officer, who was a friend of the bellboy, didn't agree. He asked the D.A. if he had seen anybody lurking in the corridor when he came out on his way to dinner. The victim did remember seeing a man going into a room down the way, number 1027.

By the time the investigation had reached this stage, it was the day after the robbery, and the man who had occupied 1027 had checked out. The hotel investigated the name and address under which he had registered, and learned they were both fakes. He had signed the registration card in a bold, distinctive handwriting, and the hotel felt strongly that the man who had done this writing was the thief. Some clerks were put to work going through Statler's old registration cards for some years back, looking for other examples of the same handwriting.

They found several old registration cards bearing it. Furthermore, they learned through a cross-file check of hotel records that on every occasion, over the years, when a man who had signed the registration card in that handwriting had been in the house, some room robberies had been reported.

The names and addresses were different on all his registration cards, but the hotel had the handwriting photographed and enlarged. Copies were posted back of the counters where members of the front-office force would see them every day. The room clerks and cashiers were instructed to be on the lookout for somebody who signed his name in that handwriting. The signature became so familiar that finally, nine months later, when this man registered again in the Cleveland Statler, the room clerk recognized the handwriting immediately, and informed the chief house officer.

He brought in two city detectives and established them in a room across the hall from the one assigned to the man with the distinctive signature. They planned to watch over the transom all night, if necessary, until the man emerged and started trying doorknobs. They would follow him, and pounce when he entered some room.

The detectives watched all night, but, to their surprise and disappointment, the man never stirred from his room. Along about eight o'clock next morning, the detectives were overcome by thoughts of food. They went down to have breakfast, abandoning their watch until that night.

However, a few minutes after they had gone to breakfast, one of the hotel's night watchmen was making his last round before going off duty when he ran into something unexpected. He was one of the patrolmen who roam the hotel halls all night, mainly to watch out for fires. He had not been one of those charged with bagging the thief. Therefore, he was surprised when he encountered in the hall a guest carrying his own bag toward the elevator, who seemed to get highly excited when he saw the watchman.

In his agitation the guest dropped a ring of keys he was carrying. They skidded across the floor, through the open doorway leading into the lobby of the service stair. The keys disappeared into a dark corner. But the man, after looking in the direction they had gone, abandoned them, and made for the elevator at a half gallop. The watchman poked about in the service lobby, and found the keys. He recognized them as master keys that could open guest rooms. So he ran to the house telephone in the guest elevator lobby, called the assistant manager on the main floor, and told him that a thief was coming down on the elevator, and might, in fact, have already arrived in the lobby.

They got the man just as he was piling into a taxicab at the side entrance. It turned out that he was the one who had robbed the New York District Attorney, and that he was wanted for a long series of hotel burglaries all about the country, dating back for years. The man explained later to police why he had not emerged from his room the night they were watching.

He said that always, when he first entered a hotel room, he would lock the door. Then he would pull a table close to the door, get on it, and peer through the transom to see if anyone who looked like a policeman had followed him. He had done this when entering the Statler room the evening before, and had, of course, seen the detectives take up their watch of his door. He had watched them, more than they had him, all night, and was waiting for them to get tired and go away, so that he could make a dash out of the Statler.

The staff of the Cleveland Statler looks back with pardonable pride upon this example of criminal detection, but the hotel prefers to forget, whenever possible, the time some men stole the lobby rug. They arrived in the middle of the day, claiming to be from a large rug-cleaning house that had orders to take the rug, which was roughly about sixty-by-forty feet. They were so convincing as cleaners that whoever was in charge of the lobby had some bellboys stand around the rug to keep guests from walking across it until it could be properly rolled, and delivered to the truck outside. The truck drove off, and the Cleveland Statler has never seen it since.

Perhaps an even more ridiculous case occurred in the New York Statler when some men showed up, claiming they had been sent to get a tapestry and clean it. This was during the lifetime of E. M. Statler, who had purchased the tapestry in Europe for $30,000, and had hung it as the central ornament of the Café Rouge in the New York house, one of the largest hotel dining rooms in the world.

The self-styled cleaners, who claimed to represent a well-known firm which specialized in the care of *objets d'art,* arrived about three o'clock in the afternoon, when the waiters were setting up tables for dinner before taking their afternoon time off. The headwaiter, not stopping to inquire who had ordered the tapestry cleaned, was most concerned about how it was to be removed. He was afraid, if it were carried out the main entrance, it might spill dust on his fresh linen and napery. So he prevailed on the men to back their truck to one of the large windows, facing on Thirty-second Street, and take it out that way.

Later that day, the headwaiter let it be known in the manager's office how efficiently he had handled the removal of the tapestry. His satisfaction took a rough jolt when the manager inquired: "What tapestry?" By the time the executives had put the pieces of this silly puzzle together and learned that nobody had ordered the tapestry cleaned, it was too late. It was gone, and may, to this day, adorn the art collection of some eminent gangster.

And then there was the time when the same sort of trick was worked at the same hotel with Vincent Lopez' piano. Vincent played a season at the then Pennsylvania, back when it was brand new, holding forth in the Grille, a popular luncheon and evening dancing spot one level below the main lobby. The hotel provided the musician with a large and very fine grand piano.

One day some men in overalls showed up looking for that. They said they had been sent by the maker, who wished to take it to the factory for tuning. Whoever was in charge of the dining room was quite co-operative. He sent to the engineering department for some helpers, who brought along hoists, skids and ramps to help ease the piano out of the Grille, and up one flight and into the truck.

The men drove away with it forever, waving gestures of gratitude to the hotel's engineers. And when Lopez came down that evening to play, he had to make out with an accordion.

Perhaps there is a lesson in all this for persons aspiring to a career in hotel thievery. It appears that most thieves who go around pilfering pocketbooks and jewelry from guest rooms get caught in the end, but those who steal lobby rugs and tapestries disappear forever. Thus, if a person wants to be successful as a hotel thief, it would seem that he should think and act big. Steal a piano!

A Room and a Bath for
a Dollar and a Half

During the middle 1940's, when Frank Sinatra was regarded in certain circles as the greatest man in the world, an interesting series of events would transpire each time the eminent singer checked into the Waldorf-Astoria Hotel. On such occasions, the Waldorf staff would gird itself for action in much the same manner that garrisons of castles of the Dark Ages used to make ready when word came that the barbarian hordes were heading in their direction.

The hotel's telephone switchboard staff was thoroughly briefed to anticipate several hundred calls a day in which childish voices would announce that they were Mrs. Sinatra, and ask to speak to their husband. Meanwhile, the Waldorf's strong-arm squadrons, consisting of twenty-eight uniformed patrolmen and a dozen or more plain-clothes men, flexed their muscles preparatory to defending the hotel at all costs from the invasion that was sure to come. Platoons of bellboys, porters and pages were held in readiness as reserves.

The invaders, who were to be distinguished by their floppy moccasins, soiled bobby socks, and slightly insane gleam in their eyes, never made a frontal assault on the Waldorf, but employed infiltration tactics. Their scouts would first reconnoiter until they determined on which floor their quarry was quartered. Then the main body would flit in by side entrances, one by one. They would steal up fire stairs, creep along hallways when nobody was looking and lie in wait in dark corners. When their victim emerged, they would descend upon him, shouting their war cry, "Speak to me, Frankie," and all was confusion until the hotel's flying squadrons arrived, herded them into freight elevators, and chucked them out.

The Waldorf's employees—the old-timers, that is, who remember the graceful days of hotelkeeping when all famous hotels were sacred places for the exclusive entertainment of the *haut monde*—regarded such interlopers as the court of Louis XVI looked upon the beggars of Paris. I recall on such a night a conversation with an ancient former *chef de rang*, or dining-room waiter, who was then working on room service. He had just come back to the room-service kitchen after serving a meal on the same floor where Sinatra happened to be residing, and had chanced upon a group of hostile bobby-soxers being herded away. The barbarians were putting up a lively scrimmage at the time and their loud insults, hurled at the house officers, resounded up and down the corridors.

"Such cattle! Such swine! Such rabble!" the old waiter exploded. "Such trash as this would never have dared to think of coming into the Waldorf in the old days. They would have hesitated even to have walked on the street past our building. And if they did pass, they would have done so with their heads uncovered and their eyes respectfully in the other direction."

The most interesting thing about the old waiter's outburst was that forty years before he would probably have been almost as horrified if he had observed within the Waldorf the type of people who by the 1940's had become its best customers, namely, business-men and well-to-do commercial travelers. For the Waldorf, one of the few luxury hotels ever built in this country, was conceived upon the same idea on which most luxury hotels in Europe were built—as a place for millionaires and royalty to disport. That is the idea a good many people seem still to have of what good hotels are sup-posed to be—although they have little idea what such service en-tails. Some hotels still attempt to give the impression that this function is what they perform, among them the present Waldorf-Astoria.

This is a delusion. The Waldorf-Astoria, which represents the acme of luxury in the mind of the average American, is essentially a commercial hotel, with luxury-hotel overtones. If it did not operate this way, it would not be in business now. With the exception of a few resort places, this holds true for almost any other hotel in the United States. The pattern of the luxury hotel, as it was in its greatest ascendancy, was laid down by Cesar Ritz, of Paris. Nowadays the Waldorf-Astoria and almost all other large-city hotels are operated not so much according to the tenets of Cesar Ritz, whose name has become synonymous with luxury hotels, as along the lines of E. M. Statler. This means standardization, simplification and keeping a close eye upon the account books.

Otherwise, they couldn't afford to stay in business now, with royalty a thing of the past and millionaires fast heading toward extinction. Most of the few hotels which might claim to be exceptions to this—such as some of the exclusive houses on the East Side of New York—are really not luxury hotels, but residential apartment dwellings for permanent and some transient trade. They never undertake the elaborate dining and large functions that the Ritz and the old Waldorf used to sponsor; they can't afford the help, the equipment or the space.

There isn't much question that Ritz and Statler, although they operated in completely different strata, have been the two leading figures that the hotel business has known. For that reason, a brief examination of who Cesar Ritz was, what he represented and what he did might be appropriate here.

In some ways the careers of the two men were alike. Both came from humble parentage, and both achieved immense success in the hotel field. Both were expert in dispensing hotel service, as well as in hotel design and in creating hotel customs and practices. Their similarities stopped about there. The people to whom they catered were poles apart.

Ritz directed his attention to the royalty, the high society of Europe and to the booming millionaire trade, which was overrunning Europe from the Western Hemisphere. As for Statler, his appeal was to the common, middle-class American, who, until then, had been pretty much neglected by good hotels.

Cesar Ritz was born in 1850 at Niederwald, a village in the Swiss Alps, the son of a farmer. He herded his father's cattle until he became an assistant wine waiter at Brieg, but he always dated his entry into the hotel business from 1867 when he went to Paris during the International Exposition. He learned the principles of preparation and service of fine foods as a waiter at Voisin's from the proprietor, a man named Bellinger, who was widely acclaimed by international gourmands. Bellinger taught Ritz the arts of properly basting a duck, decanting a burgundy and carving a roast expertly into thin slices, pressing the meat with the knife in such a manner that the juices ran temptingly, and in such a position that the customer could not help but notice how succulent it was.

Ritz advanced from waiter to maître d'hôtel at the Hotel Splendide in Paris, then began following society to places like Vienna, Nice, Riga and Locarno. It was the era of the famous European jaunts of such prominent wealthy Americans as J. P. Morgan, who was buying museums out of their art treasures; Jay Gould, who was seeking rare tulip bulbs, and Commodore Vanderbilt, who was bragging all over Europe about how he started the Staten Island Ferry.

Besides these wealthy patrons, Ritz served most of Europe's royalty at dinners given by Emperor Franz Josef at Les Trois Frères Provençaux, in Vienna. Ritz quickly picked up the likes and dislikes of the royalty he served. He knew that the Prince of Wales, unlike most Englishmen, preferred his roast beef well done. In fact, he liked lighter meats, such as roast chicken, better than beef. He was a poor conversationalist, but enjoyed listening. He liked a good cigar after dinner, and, when he smoked cigarettes, preferred a brand put up by Laurens, of London.

Ritz got ahead, not only by strict attention to his royal guests, but by remembering their preferences. He used this knowledge for many years to impress lesser patrons by recommending to them the type of cigarettes the Prince of Wales smoked or a bird done after the fancy of Franz Josef. Ritz knew so many of Europe's royalty and high society that when he took over management of a hotel, he could send out some letters of invitation to the right people, and the hotel would be reasonably sure of a successful season.

It wasn't only bowing and scraping to royalty that brought Ritz his success. He was an expert hotel man, particularly in food, and maintained that, no matter how luxurious and beautiful its appointments, a good hotel stood or fell by its cuisine. He was the first to recognize fully the culinary genius of Auguste Escoffier, whom Ritz first employed as chef at the Grand National Hotel at Lucerne, which Ritz was managing. Escoffier later worked as Ritz's chef at the Paris Ritz, the Carlton House and the Savoy in London.

During the 1880's, Ritz started a policy that became known later as "The Ritz Plan" by getting rid of the heavy, hard-to-clean draperies at windows of the expensive hotels. He replaced them with light muslin curtains and light drapes, and his furniture was made light and cheerful, as opposed to the heavy, somber pieces then in vogue. He built large windows that would let in plenty of sunlight that was accentuated by spotless white walls.

As early as 1893 he put bathrooms in every apartment in the Grand Hotel in Rome, and he established the type of hotel livery that is generally followed up to the present. Some of his costumes, such as knee breeches of silver and green, aren't used any more, but some of his other rules of hotel dress are religiously observed, such as the white tie and white aprons for waiters, black tie for headwaiters and the morning coat for the upper staff members and the manager.

Ritz even started dinner music. That happened in 1895 when he had taken over management of the fashionable Savoy Hotel in London. He noticed an oppressive silence hovering over the dining room there during meals, which alarmed him. On the continent, the Italians, Germans and French always were full of conversation that made a pleasant and attractive hum throughout the dining room during the meal. But the British, when they were in England, at least, ate in silence, and the room seemed to him to be gloomy and sad.

That season Johann Strauss and his orchestra had been imported to play in London, and between concerts the great composer-conductor and his musicians didn't have much to do. Ritz hired Strauss and his men to play each evening at his hotel to infuse a bit of

Vienna's lilt into the dreary occasion of dinner at the Savoy. The Strauss aggregation went over so well there that the better hotels have been providing dinner music ever since.

A number of hotels bearing Ritz's name were built in American cities. They were built and furnished according to Ritz's ideas, and operated, through the Ritz Development Company, according to his techniques. William Harris, of London, formed the Ritz Development Company to exploit Cesar Ritz's ideas on a world-wide basis. It was purely a managing and operating company, and financed no construction. Capital had to be raised locally. The Ritz Company supplied only the name, the manager, the good will, the patrons and mutual advertising, and shared in the profits.

Perhaps the main reason that Ritz was able to operate such luxurious hotels was that he never owned a large part of them, and never had to take a great financial risk. Most of his hotels came to him through the grace of patrons, who were rich and admired him. These patrons would build ornate hotels, along the lines of fine palaces, and invite Ritz to operate them.

On the other hand, Statler came up the hard way in a raw-boned, two-fisted atmosphere. He had to fight for everything he ever got by taking all kinds of financial chances and bulling through by his ability and toughness. But more important, Statler, who probably never saw a duke in his life, was not interested so much in catering to high society as he was in the coming common man. This was natural because he personally was a common man, and the only people he knew or had ever met were men in that undistinguished stratum.

The field in which Statler operated was not as glamorous and as rarefied as the atmosphere in which Ritz performed, but in the long run, it has turned out to be more economically and socially healthy. The most famous hotels built in the United States in recent times have been almost exclusively for the average man. The society of grand dukes and their ilk collapsed during the First World War, and the sort of hotels that they inhabited have been collapsing ever since, among them, recently, the Ritz-Carlton Hotel in New York.

The sort of hotel service, food and accommodations that the American public expects today was conceived, more than anywhere else, at Statler's old Buffalo hotel, which was completed in 1907, the same year that the Ritz-Carlton Hotel was begun in New York.

Here for the sixth, and last, time in his career Statler put everything he owned into a new project. Into the Buffalo hotel went all the profits from his restaurant, from operation of The Inside Inn, plus half a million dollars borrowed from local bankers. He had picked up most of the ideas he intended to incorporate into his hotel from Pullman and smoking-car conversations with drummers, who could speak interminably upon the subject of what was wrong with existing hotels and what should be done to improve them.

The most remarkable feature of his Buffalo house was the bath-with-every-room idea. In those days this was as unheard-of as equipping each guest room with a telephone, which he also did at Buffalo. Until then, guests in the better-class hotels washed their faces in a basin built against the bedroom wall, beneath a strip of oilcloth to protect the wallpaper, and went down the hall to the bathroom. They summoned service by pressing an electric call bell. In the cheaper houses they hollered for service, if any, and did all their toilet down the hall. Or else they didn't bathe.

There are, broadly speaking, two schools of thought on the proper manner of dispensing hotel hospitality: The Gushing, or "Is-Everything-All-Right-Sir," School, as opposed to the Restrained, or "Don't-Disturb-the-Guest-Unnecessarily; He'll-Let-You-Know-Damn-Quick-If-Everything-Isn't-All-Right," School. The former theory, among commercial hotels, probably reached its greatest flower under the late Ralph Hitz, operator of the New Yorker, the Netherland Plaza and other hotels during the late 1920's and early 1930's. Hitz's men sometimes telephoned or called personally upon guests on the hour every hour to inquire if they were pleased with their room, the service, the view, the weather, the policy of the hotel and the state of the nation.

Statler was a firm advocate of the opposing, or Restrained, School of hospitality. He believed that most hotel guests prefer to be left alone. In fact, Statler used to point out that whenever he was a guest in one of the highly solicitous houses of another operator, it was usually when he had seated himself comfortably in the bathroom that some assistant manager downstairs chose to ring his telephone to inquire if he was getting enough attention from the staff.

With the idea of making each of his rooms a sort of self-sufficient citadel for the guest, Statler, besides installing telephones, equipped each with a writing desk stocked with pens, ink, laundry lists and telegraph blanks. The rooms had such additional equipment as the already mentioned pincushions, stuck full of darning materials, mirrors and clothes closets. He built a mail-chute opening, and put a big clock on the wall in each elevator lobby.

These conveniences, which are taken for granted now, were innovations with Statler. They could have been included without too much trouble or expense before he came along by any operator of first-class hotels who had thought of them. The business of putting a bath in every room, however, was another proposition entirely. The expense of such a thing made it out of the question in popular-priced hotels with anybody except a crazy man like Statler. In fact, baths in many rooms were too advanced and expensive for the flossiest of hotels in this country or Europe. The original Waldorf-Astoria in New York didn't have such convenience, nor did such ornate houses as the Grand National Hotel at Lucerne or such small and exclusive houses as the Splendide in Paris.

Statler's thought was that hotels were seldom sold out of rooms in those days, and, since there were always a number of hotels in any sizable city with rooms to offer, the traveling public would go first to the one offering most of what, as he said, "the average man wants." Since he had found the average man would delight to have a private bath if such a thing were feasible in a hotel, he concluded that if all his rooms had private baths, they would be filled before any of the rooms in other hotels were. And since the greatest profit in any hotel operation is in its sale of rooms, he concluded that his bath-with-every-room idea would pay for itself in a very few years.

Furthermore, every respectable hotel had to provide several large public baths on each floor, and Statler figured he could eliminate these and substitute a private bath with every room at a cost only thirty per cent greater than the cost of building the ordinary number of public baths. He was able to do this because of a plumbing system he originated with the baths of each two adjoining guest rooms back-to-back so that the fixtures in each bathroom opened into a common shaft.

He also situated his bathrooms in a vertical arrangement by floors so that each pair of baths on one floor was immediately above the corresponding pair on the floor below. This makes for immense savings, both in construction costs and in space. Furthermore, the mirrors Statler built over the wash basin in each bathroom were removable so that the interior of the plumbing shaft is made easily accessible for repairs and maintenance.

Besides housing the bathroom plumbing pipes, Statler's shafts also carried the heating pipes for the rooms. These come out of the shaft in the bathroom and are built around the walls of the room, inside the baseboard, to a radiator situated under the window. Statler's plumbing ideas have become common practice in the construction of most multiple-dwelling structures and even in office buildings, and his system has come to be recognized in all Schools of Architecture as "The Statler Plumbing Shaft."

The group of Buffalo bankers who had loaned Statler the half-million dollars to help build his hotel were so impressed by his practical innovations that, with practically no urging whatever, they advanced him another $150,000 to tide him over the first few months of operation. He never needed this money. The hotel was a financial success from the start. Travelers reacted to the bath-with-every-room idea and other innovations as Statler had hoped they would. He cleared a modest $30,000 his first year of operation, and profits increased thereafter. When the new Buffalo Statler was built, this house became "The Hotel Buffalo."

Statler managed this hotel himself. His office was near the room clerk's desk, near the dining-room entrances and near the service stairway, so he could receive guests' complaints while they were hot. As the years passed, Statler seemed to get an increasing delight from listening to guests' complaints—and then correcting their source—in the way that some people enjoy listening to symphonies. When one of his guests sought him out to compliment his hotels and their service, Statler was unspeakably bored. At such times he would pull his left ear as a signal to whatever assistant manager happened to be in sight to come and rescue him on some pretext or other. He wanted to be taken preferably to the presence of some irate guest who would charm him with a tirade about the soup in the coffee shop being cold.

One time Tetrazzini wired from New York that she was arriving in Buffalo that night, and would like a three-room suite. Statler had nothing larger than two connecting rooms, but he accepted the reservation anyway. Within ten hours he had a doorway cut through a wall, had a door hung and the new wood covered with quick-drying paint. When Tetrazzini arrived, a three-room suite was waiting for her.

Cesar Ritz once did the same sort of thing, but on a grander scale, when he was managing the Grand Hotel at Monte Carlo, and the Prince of Wales wired that he would arrive twenty-four hours later. The Prince had never stopped before at the Grand, which had no royal suite. Ritz had one constructed within the twenty-four hours, driving a large group of carpenters, painters, decorators and plumbers at the task, which was finished just in time for him to slip into a tailcoat to greet the arriving royalty.

The basic difference in these two episodes was that while the Grand Hotel's suite remained a royal suite from there on out to be inhabited only by kings and princes, at Statler's house, immediately Tetrazzini had checked out, his three-room suite became three doubles again.

Every room in every suite the Statler Company has ever built, from the first house in Buffalo on, has been arranged so that it can serve as an individual room, if necessary. Not long ago, some officials of Statler who were visiting the much-publicized Shamrock Hotel in Houston, Texas, were horrified to find that their suite, of a sitting room and two bedrooms, had only one entrance to the hall, that through the living room. Any Statler hotel would have had a door in each room opening into the hall.

Although it is hallowed by some hotel men as the place where modern hotelkeeping began, the Hotel Buffalo is not exactly an impressive or beautiful building. It is rather squat-looking, by modern standards. Its exterior is covered with a material that gives it somewhat the appearance and texture of a tortoise shell. The lobby is a low room with a worn tile floor. It is encircled on two sides by a low mezzanine with a brass railing. The space above the elevators is adorned with an old-fashioned, meaningless painting of maidens in Grecian costume gazing into a swan pool.

The main dining room, known as the Arbor Room, is a dome-shaped place, intended to resemble a grape arbor with plaster grapes and vines. This room would never win any artistic awards, but the arrangement of the kitchen—which is on the ground floor, and opens directly into the hotel's three dining rooms—is something that almost anybody who thinks he is an authority on hotel design should study.

Upstairs, the guest rooms have the familiar Statler look. There is a compact writing desk built into the top drawer of the bureau. In the closets the coat-hanger rod is built just below and protruding just outside a head-high shelf, and a pants-presser, made of a bent steel rod, is fixed to the inside of the door. There are some furnishings that are not like what Statler put in his other hotels, principally the beds. These are four-posters, some carved to represent various ominous-looking creatures, such as American eagles staring fiercely down from the headboard in the direction of the sleeper's face.

Although the Statler Company sold the old hotel some years back, its present owner keeps it about the way it always was, including the Old Man's original signs, which are hung up in the back of the house, intended to keep employees on their toes. Perhaps the sign that most typifies Mr. Statler is one that still hangs in the kitchen, which reads:

ALL LEAKS MAKE BIG BILLS.
There are 2,146 faucets in this hotel.
A dripping faucet consumes fifteen gallons of water a day.
One one-thirty-second inch opening consumes 160 gallons of water a day, costs $1.14 a quarter.
One one-sixteenth inch opening consumes 1,280 gallons of water a day, costs $4.32 a quarter.
One one-eighth inch opening consumes 2,560 gallons of water a day, costs $18.45 a quarter.
One one-fourth inch opening consumes 10,250 gallons of water a day, costs $73.80 a quarter.
WATER IS A COSTLY ITEM OF EXPENSE, AND THE ABOVE INDICATES CLEARLY HOW MUCH CAN BE WASTED THROUGH CARELESSNESS.

Now, the Ritz-Carlton Hotel in New York probably never had such signs in its kitchens and back-of-the-house. In the days when it was conceived, the hotel industry in general was not too much concerned with saving on time, space or materials. And a luxury house, such as the Ritz-Carlton, by its very nature could not be too much concerned about conserving fine foods or fine liquors, let alone drops of water.

"In the Ritz dining room in the good days," Charles Silvani, maître d'hôtel, was recalling one day in the late summer of 1951 while wreckers were destroying that famous hotel, "we would always recognize our good patrons at the door. Maybe one of them had a party of four.

"I would say to him, 'Sir, today the lamb is very good.' He would say, perhaps, 'All right, bring me lamb.' So, for the party of four, we would tell the chef to prepare a whole saddle of lamb, especially for Mr. Blank. The lamb would come in with all the trimmings. If it was cake for dessert, we would not send in portions; we would send in the whole cake. People like this gentleman would not pay the bill. He would say to me, 'Take care of the bill, Charles, and see that the waiters get their tips.'

"In the Ritz, we tried to please every guest with luxuries. If in the morning he pressed the button for the waiter, the waiter was there instantly, and the food was prepared immediately, and served in his room. The waiter would leave no bill, but see that the charge was made against the guest on his regular room bill.

"In those days, many people who took suites wanted them to be like home, like a luxurious, splendid home, and we tried to serve that way. But now, and for some years past, there are not enough people who live in that manner. So the plant, the building of the Ritz, was out of date. Yes, on the outside it looked like a good building when it was demolished. But there was too much waste space. For example, the ballroom, which was fifty-two by ninety-six feet, was not always in use, and above it there was nothing . . . no rooms to produce revenue."

The Ritz-Carlton in New York, although it was successful financially, is typical of the fine hotels of the departed era of "the grand manner," because it was essentially a rich man's toy. It was one of a number of fine hotels about the globe that were under Ritz management for years.

The Ritz-Carlton, of course, was built for a grand scale of living. An average guest room was twice the size of an average guest room in the Washington Statler. Some guest-room ceilings were twenty-four feet high, as compared with nine-feet ceilings in the Washington Statler.

At the time it ceased to function, the Ritz setup called for two employees for every room. Earlier in its career, the Ritz used to have three employees for every room. This compares with slightly under one employee per room in the Statler system. There was personal maid service on every floor of the Ritz and valet service headquartered on every third floor. Guest rooms had three buttons, one for the maid, one for the waiter and one for the valet. When a button was pushed, one of these functionaries responded instantaneously, because they were always waiting in close proximity.

Frank Swadley, general manager of the Ritz until it was closed, says the hotel was making some money up to the last. But its clientele, although fiercely loyal, was diminishing. People who could afford, or who cared for, this luxurious service were dwindling. The management no longer regarded its immense rooms and towering ceilings as great attractions. The Ritz management now thought of these airy spaces as nonproducing assets, the way the late E. M. Statler would have viewed them in the first place.

Structural changes made necessary in the Ritz by new fire laws would have cost an enormous amount. So the William Astor Estate, which had become its owner, decided to wreck the old Ritz, and sell its site for $250,000 for construction of an office building. By the end of 1951, there was nothing left of the Ritz-Carlton at Madison Avenue and Forty-sixth Street except a hole in the ground and in the hearts of its more sentimental patrons.

Now, it would be foolish to try to compare Mr. Statler's first house in Buffalo with the Ritz-Carlton in terms of a grand hotel. There is no comparison. But as an enduring idea in hotelkeeping, the old Buffalo house is of far more importance than the Ritz-Carlton ever was.

The Ritz was torn down because it had outlived its era—and a short era it was, from a historian's viewpoint. But the old Hotel Buffalo, an unbeautiful but practical house, is still about as efficient to operate as it was when it was opened three years before the Ritz-Carlton.

12

Floods, Fires, and Sudden Death

To the manager of a hotel, the most ominous sound in the world is the telephone ringing in his living quarters late at night. Managers of most large hotels, including all of the Statlers, live in the house in one of the larger suites. They keep the entrance of their living quarters looking as much as possible like all the other doors along the corridor. When approaching or leaving his apartment, the manager is apt to move furtively, casting quick glances over his shoulder, as though he is afraid that somebody will find out where he lives. This, in fact, is precisely what he does fear.

During the working day, he is screened effectively by the assistant managers, his secretary and office force from crackpots with immense and meaningless complaints and suggestions. At night his only defense is anonymity. If the location of his living quarters were generally known, he would be answering the door all night. He would have the same trouble if he were accessible by telephone. For that reason, hotel operators ring the manager's apartment only when old friends are calling. After midnight, even these calls are stopped at the switchboard. They put through only calls that are real emergencies. Thus, as one Statler manager has said, when the telephone does ring during early morning hours, "it usually means a flood, or a fire or sudden death."

From the standpoint of physical damage to the building and the cost of making repairs, floods are usually the most serious. A leak, even a small one, coming through the fancy ceiling of a public room, will cost at least $1,500 to repair. There is plenty of water, water pressure and opportunity in a large hotel to bring on a flood. In the New York Statler, about 600,000 gallons of water are used every day, which is enough to supply 10,000 homes, or a city of 45,000 persons. A flood can be caused by situations ranging from a broken pipe or a loose connection to some fool doing of one of the guests.

Sometimes a traveling man will arrive at a hotel at night, too late to get a suit pressed. He may employ an old sartorial trick of men on the road, as follows: He will hang his suits in the bathroom, turn the hot shower on full force, close the door, and allow the steam to work on the wrinkles. This takes half an hour or so, and the traveling man may wander away downstairs and forget all about his steaming clothing. Something may happen to clog the drain, and, before long, floors thereabouts are steaming with hot water. In some of the rooms below, pieces of wet plaster are beginning to come loose from the ceiling.

Sometimes, when a bathtub starts to overflow, guests become panicky, and can't co-ordinate their thoughts and actions sufficiently either to turn off the water or open the drain. That happened at the Cleveland Statler in a room occupied by two women from France. One of them was taking a bath, and, being unfamiliar with American plumbing, was not able to turn off the water immediately. Whereupon, both she and the other woman abandoned all efforts in that direction, and began to scream. Fortunately the woman not in the tub seized the telephone presently, and screamed into that.

The operator could not make head or tail out of the excited French phrases, but she did gather the impression that the woman was in need of assistance of some sort, and put the call on the phone of an assistant manager. He couldn't make out what she was saying either, but he, too, concluded something was not as it should be, and he'd better get to room 956 immediately.

The assistant manager dashed up a minute or so later, and found the woman who had called standing in the door, waving her arms, shouting in French, and pointing in the direction of the bathroom. He scarcely needed these directions to detect the source of trouble, since the floor by this time was covered with an inch or so of water. He rushed into the bathroom upon the second woman, still screaming, still in the tub and still in an undraped condition. The assistant manager, a modest and discreet man in all hotel matters, hurriedly backed out, but the first woman planted both hands in his back, and shoved him at the bathroom door. Then, abandoning her native tongue for clear and effective English, she shouted: "To hell with her; get in there, and turn off that damned flood."

Floods occasionally result after the water has been turned off for plumbing repairs. Somebody will turn a tap, and when the water doesn't come, leave it on. When the water is turned back on, this tap may cause a flood. Such repairs are usually made late at night, when most of the guests are asleep, and floods from this cause are seldom on bedroom floors. In the New York house recently the water was turned off after midnight in an office section of the mezzanine that is not occupied at that hour. The plumbers forgot that the photographer, who makes pictures of celebrants in the Café Rouge, had a studio there. He turned a tap in his dark room, and when no water came, went home, forgetting to turn the tap back as it was. About 8:30 that morning the flood was discovered when the credit manager a floor below began to complain of water dripping on his head.

One of the most peculiar occurrences, in the nature of a flood, in Statler annals, happened in the Washington house back when it was quite new, in connection with Statler's use of leftover pieces of hotel soap in guest bathrooms, which are gathered up by the maids, and sent to the laundry. The pieces are melted together, cut into large bars and used both by the laundry and in the employees' wash rooms.

Late one afternoon a laundry employee was melting used soap, with steam from a pipe built directly from the boilers to the laundry for this purpose. The steam into the laundry was shut off a few minutes earlier than usual that day, before the soap was fully melted. The employee left the kettle full of semiliquid soap standing

under the opening of the steam pipe, intending to finish the job
when he came back the next day. When he arrived at work the
next morning, the kettle was still where he had left it, but all the
soap was missing.

The employee concluded that somebody had taken it. What had
happened, actually, was that, when the steam was shut off the evening before, a vacuum was created in the pipes, which sucked the
soap into the heating system. The pipes and boilers were soon
gurgling with 5,000 gallons of soapsuds. This was not evident during
the night, but the next morning, as the engineers began building up
pressure, the radiators and heating connections began to behave in a
most singular manner. They hissed and spewed and began to give
off lovely clouds of bubbles. The engineers were completely mysti-
fied at first, but some guests thought the bubbles were pretty, and
applauded them as some new innovation having to do with hotel
cleanliness or beautification.

The most memorable and historic flood in the history of the
Statler organization occurred three or four years ago as a result of a
small fire that broke out on the top floor, near the elevators, of the
New York house. It was only a paint fire, which city firemen extinguished easily with chemicals. However, the firemen downstairs
got the impression it was more serious, and turned on the pressure
into a two-foot pressure pipe that runs up the middle of the building. No water was being used from the top to relieve this pressure,
which built up until the pipe split about the level of the mezzanine,
and an appalling stream of water gushed forth. It poured off the
mezzanine balcony into the lobby, where a flood six inches to a foot
deep soon swirled.

At this point, an official connected with one of the South American
republics, who was arriving in New York for the first time, walked
—or rather slopped—into the lobby of the Statler, where he had
reservations. He was surprised to notice the rugs floating about like
green scum on a pond in summer. Chairs, sofas and smoking stands
were drifting past the registration desk toward the exits, from which
great freshets were pouring into the streets. Hastily-summoned
hotel employees, some in hip boots and others with their pants
rolled above their knees, were wielding brooms, mops and buckets
in a valiant effort to dispel the flood.

The South American, who was absolutely amazed by what he

saw, touched a passing employee upon the arm and inquired gently what in the world had happened. This employee, with the natural reluctance of all hotel people to admit there had been a fire, replied casually: "We're just doing our spring cleaning."

The South American digested this. Then he said: "I have wanted to visit the United States for many years. I have always heard about the—how do you say—the, the lustiness, the natural exuberance of your great country. In our country we have been told how, when you in the United States begin a job, you never let anything stand in the way of its speedy completion. . . . But," and he lifted one foot out of the water and surveyed his dripping shoe and trouser leg, "do you not believe, in this case, you have carried this too far? . . ."

Hotel guests are inclined to view floods as more amusing than disastrous, because neither they nor their property are often endangered, but a good many guests are terrified at the thought of a hotel fire. Some of them travel with a length of stout rope, and insist on getting a room on the lowest possible floor so they can tie the rope around a steam pipe and dangle it out a window to the ground—a sort of private escape that would probably kill more people trying to get down than fires would. Yet, these same people have dozed off to sleep at night smoking a cigarette that caught the mattress afire. Others have dropped hot ashes into wastebaskets near window draperies, which is probably the greatest single cause of hotel fires.

The big hotel fires in recent times have been disastrous mainly because of open stairways from one floor to another. These create up-and-down drafts that feed fires. E. M. Statler may have been the first hotel man to recognize the value of enclosed stairways, for he built all his enclosed from the first, when few hotels did. The chance of a disastrous fire in a hotel these days is pretty remote if the house is properly built and operated, although there are more hotel fires than the public realizes that are confined to one room.

Such a fire often consumes all the furniture, rugs and draperies in a room, and once in a while the occupant also, particularly if he is in a heavy sleep, brought on by whisky. Frequently a fire is reported in time to be extinguished before much damage is done to either the room or the occupant, who may sleep throughout the entire procedure, as one woman did not long ago in the New York house. Her mattress and a small part of one hip were on fire when the firemen came rushing in, and she didn't awaken while they were there. They turned her over, squirted out the smoldering mattress, then turned her back again, and went away.

Again, the occupant of a room may become so stricken with panic that he forgets to inform the hotel that there is a fire in his room. This happened once in the Detroit Statler, when a maid saw smoke coming from under a door, and summoned the house fire brigade. The only thing burning was a part of the seat of an easy chair, but it was producing an awful smoke. After they had put out the chair seat, the firemen heard a weak voice emitting from the bathroom. They found the room's occupant in there—a man fully clothed sitting in a tub full of water. He had been taking a nap, when he awakened to find his room full of smoke. Assuming that the whole building was on fire, he had concluded that the bathtub was the best place for him.

The Statler hotels each have a fire department, which can take care of most situations that arise. Its personnel is made up mainly of engineering department employees, who number 140 in the New York house. Most of them are trained in fire fighting, and stand ready to answer an alarm while they are on duty. If a fire is reported late at night, when only a skeleton engineering staff is at work, they are assisted by a group of picked bellmen, porters and house officers.

A good many alarms of fire are turned in at hotels—more of them false, fortunately, than real. Occasionally somebody outside the building will mistake through a window the glow of the red lights over the exit doors along the corridors for the glow of a fire. Guests in the house sometimes report a fire when they smell what they believe to be smoke, but which is really the fumes of some chemicals that sufferers from asthma burn to relieve their sinus congestion.

Probably the most celebrated of all Statler false alarms, which received international attention, occurred about four years ago in the New York house. Around ten o'clock one evening a guest, who was walking along a corridor, smelled what he took to be wood smoke, and informed the floor clerk. She smelled it, too, and, looking down a corridor, saw smoke coming from under a guest room door. She called the fire department, which presently came dashing down the hall, its members putting on their rubber coats, gas

masks and asbestos suits, pulling the hose cart, brandishing extin-
guishers and unrolling lengths of wall hose as they ran.

They crashed through the door and into the smoking room—to the
profound astonishment of two Englishmen, who had been sitting
there all evening in earnest conversation, while they smoked
calabash pipes loaded with a pungent English blend of tobacco
that traces its derivations to the Near East. The two British guests
had been so engrossed with their talk that they had not noticed the
clouds of smoke until it got so thick they couldn't see one another.
Then one of them opened a window, and the draft had swept some
smoke out under the door. It had an aroma unfamiliar to American
noses—an effluvium which, according to the firemen, was something like burning paint and tarpaper.

Accounts of this happening were carried on news-service wires,
and broadcast in England the next day by the British Broadcasting
Company. The wife of one of the men involved heard this on her
wireless set. She sent her husband a stern cable inquiring if he did
not think it was in rather bad taste, on his first visit to America, to
become embroiled in such ridiculous publicity.

The "sudden death" telephone messages that most disturb hotel
managers in the dead of night usually concern suicides. Many people who are contemplating suicide choose hotels, probably because
they feel more anonymous there. Occasionally, an experienced assistant manager or room clerk can spot a person who checks in with
this in mind from the way he behaves while registering. He is likely
to come in at night, with little or no baggage. He may appear somewhat vague and distracted, want a high room with windows over
the court. If the management suspects he has suicidal intent, a
house officer or bellboy is sent with him with instructions to remain
in the room on various pretexts until the police can be summoned.
A number of persons contemplating suicide have been detected by
other hotel guests, who noticed them coming constantly to the window, and looking out time and again over a period of hours.

People usually like to be alone when they take their own lives,
but occasionally one prefers to have an audience. In Detroit, about
the time the war ended, a soldier, who was not registered in the
house, stopped a maid in the top floor corridor, and asked for a

cigarette. When she gave him one, he lit it, took two puffs, and in the midst of thanking her, stepped over the window ledge.

Once in the Cleveland house a man was sitting in his room talking to a business acquaintance when he picked up the telephone and called his home in Toledo. It was answered at home by the man's son, to whom the man announced he was about to take his own life. This confounded the other man in the room, as nothing of this nature had been suggested in their conversation, up to then.

Before he had time to think or act, the other man put down the telephone, walked across the room, and leaped out the open window. It then became the tragic duty of the man left in the room to pick up the phone and tell the man's son in Toledo what had happened.

Some people constantly threaten suicide who never intend to go through with it. A man used to come to the New York Statler years ago when it was the Pennsylvania. He would order a number of cocktails to his room, and drink them. Then he would order an elaborate dinner. When he had eaten, always alone, he would telephone his mother-in-law, who lived in Trenton, New Jersey, and whom he disliked intensely. The room service waiters who served him used to hear him informing her that he would probably do away with himself before that night was over. They never took him seriously. In the end, he did die at the Pennsylvania, but not from suicide. After one large dinner, he was stricken with acute indigestion.

Occasionally, somebody will go about suicide in such an awkward and roundabout way that he could hardly expect to succeed. A young Italian, disappointed in love, checked in once at the Detroit Statler. When he got to his room, they learned later, he arranged on the table and desk a display of religious pictures and photographs of the girl who had disappointed him. Then he drank a bottle of iodine. This burned his throat, and he rushed to the window to get air, where he yelled so loudly that some people in the Hotel Tuller across the street heard him. They called the Statler management, and the hotel nurse, Miss Minnie Dust, brought him around.

Again in Detroit, a man undertook to choke himself to death with smoke from his clothing, which he had piled in the center of the room, and set on fire. The hotel's chief house officer, Charles

Thompkins, managed to drag him out of the room, although he put up a lively scrap and attempted to hide under the bed. It turned out he had been brooding about a friend who had died in a hotel fire.

And there was the case in St. Louis of the man who checked into the Statler late one afternoon, brooding about losses he had just suffered at the race track. He hung himself with his belt to the shower-curtain rod. It broke, and he fell into the bathtub with such a thump that a passing housemaid heard it and called Assistant Manager Fred Smith. He was able to talk the man out of his desperate intentions, and sent him home to Southern Illinois in a taxicab.

Some people who are unsuccessful in suicide attempts may turn on the hotel and sue, as one man did who jumped unsuccessfully from the twelfth floor of the New York Statler. He fell through the laundry skylight on the third floor court at the moment a laundry employee was wheeling a truck loaded with soiled linen beneath the skylight. The man hit in that, suffered some broken bones, but lived to sue the hotel for $250,000. He charged that his fall was an accident, caused by the hotel's window ledges' being built too low to the floor. The hotel won the suit, after proving that its window ledges were higher from the floor than the average in hotels. Several months later, the same man was successful in a suicide leap from the fifteenth floor of another hotel further uptown in New York.

It was through the same laundry skylight that a woman fell in one of the most remarkable unsuccessful suicide attempts on record. This woman suffered from asthma, which prompted her to leap from room 1611. The heavy wire netting in the fire glass of the skylight wrapped around her like a ball, as she came through. It broke her fall, and she, too, landed upon a pile of soiled linen. She wasn't knocked unconscious, and was talking when they carried her to a hospital. After a few weeks there, she not only recovered from her injuries, but she has never suffered from asthma again.

The strangest of all Statler stories connected with an attempted suicide was the case of a retired businessman who lived in the New York house. Because of bad health, he decided one day to jump from the hotel roof, twenty-three floors above the street. He walked out on the roof to the end of one wing, and stood contemplating the depths below, apparently trying to summon enough courage to jump. A woman who was gazing out a window at about the same

height in a building across the way happened to notice him. She
decided he had suicide in mind, and called the police.

Whereupon, great excitement ensued. Droves of police patrol
cars, fire trucks, emergency-squad and rescue-squad cars appeared
on the streets below, and a crowd started forming. After some careful and commendable work, the policemen, firemen, rescue and
emergency squads managed to get the man down before he jumped.

That was fine, but there were to be some interesting repercussions.
Several days later, with the Thanksgiving season approaching—a
time of great activity in hotel dining rooms and kitchens—an insurance company sent one of its safety engineers over to work at the
Statler. He was to spend several days inspecting the kitchens with
the idea of uncovering accident hazards to food department employees.

The engineer finished his assignment on the afternoon before
Thanksgiving Day. He had noticed the pastry chef baking some big
mince pies that looked tempting, so the engineer asked the chef
about the chances of getting a couple of them to take home for
Thanksgiving. The chef said sure; they would be ready in twenty
or thirty minutes.

Since the day was fine and clear, the engineer rode up to the hotel
roof to kill the half hour by viewing the New York sky line. Having
heard nothing about the suicide-minded guest of two weeks before,
the engineer happened to walk to the exact corner of the roof where
that gentleman had stood. While he admired the view, it chanced
that the same woman who had spotted the other man was looking
out the window again. She saw the engineer standing on the roof,
and decided he had suicide in mind, too. Again she called the
police.

Presently, the engineer noted more than usual activity in the
streets and avenues below. Fire trucks were drawing up to the curb,
and firemen were getting off them with nets and ladders, but the
safety engineer could see no fire, or even smoke. Police, emergency-
squad and rescue-squad cars were arriving, but he could see no
accident or no riot.

Great crowds of people were assembling in the streets, and were
staring in obvious excitement up the hotel walls. So were hundreds
of other people who had poked their heads from windows of nearby

buildings. It was all quite puzzling to the engineer. He had what seemed to be an excellent vantage point, but, although he leaned far over the ledge and looked in all directions, he could not make out what was happening.

Then a door leading onto the roof from inside the hotel opened, and a group of policemen came on the roof. The engineer on the ledge was too busy watching the crowds to pay much attention to the policemen. If he had, he might have noticed that the officers were drifting in his direction with elaborate casualness.

Finally, one of the policemen maneuvered himself into a favorable position. Then, with a magnificent leap, he was upon the safety engineer, crashing him to the roof with a great thud. The other policemen swarmed up, and before he knew what had happened, the engineer found himself trussed in a strait jacket.

Then, as the policemen got their breaths, one of them said to the engineer: "Just what did you think you were going to do?"

"Why I," replied that unhappy man, in an explanation that has lived in history, "was just waiting here for a couple of mince pies."

13

Parlor, Bedroom and Bath

The greatest change in the concept of a hotel guest bedroom since E. M. Statler built the first "every room with a bath" back in 1907 has been dictated by the advance of civilization in one of its most intimate respects, to wit: the majority of people no longer like to sleep together.

Since the early 1940's, there has been a great conversion from double to twin bedrooms in hotels old and new. The Statler Company started this trend—in supplying more twin beds, not in changing sleeping habits—around the middle 1930's with the invention of the studio bed, which serves as a sitting-room sofa during the day and as a sleeping couch at night. Until a dozen years ago the bedroom arrangements in all Statler houses averaged sixty per cent rooms with double beds, twenty per cent with twin beds and twenty per cent single.

But when the Washington Statler came along in the early 1940's, its proportion was fifty-one per cent twin bedrooms, twenty-seven per cent single bedrooms and only twenty-two per cent rooms with double beds. The company has since been converting bedrooms in its older houses toward the Washington proportion, and the new Los Angeles Statler has gone even further in isolating people when they are asleep. It has seventy per cent twin bedrooms, ten per cent single and twenty per cent double. The company felt it should retain some double beds to take care of large men, who do not like to sleep in a single bed. Then, of course, there is the bride and groom situation.

After married couples have passed the newly-wed stage, the majority of them not only prefer to sleep separately; they have definite preferences on what positions in the rooms they want their separate beds. The Statler people have studied this problem at length in their Washington house, and have come up with some findings. These conclusions now serve as guides in designing the shapes of bedrooms in the new houses and in rearranging the bed positions in the company's older houses, wherever feasible.

Most of the twin bedrooms in the Washington and Los Angeles Statlers and the majority of those converted from double bedrooms in the older houses have studio-type beds. These are built against the wall, and during the day are clothed in slip covers, like a sofa. The bureaus, chests of drawers and night tables are designed to look more like living room than bedroom furniture. Thus, during the day, the effect is that of a sitting room.

The maid removes the slip covers at night, turns down the bed and gets pillows from a storage compartment in the bottom of the night table. That part of the bed that serves as the back of the sofa during the day is hinged. It is lifted like a trunk lid, and the couch assumes the size and appearance of a regular single bed.

The Statler Company introduced the studio bed during the grim days that the 1930's brought the hotel industry. The studio bed was intended primarily to appeal to people who prefer to sleep alone.

It is likely that people never enjoyed being kicked about in a bed by someone else, but accepted it as one of mankind's burdens, probably for the simple reason that there were not enough beds to go around. But by the time the 1930's arrived, a strong prejudice was being voiced by men, even brothers, against sharing the same bed. A lot of married couples felt the same way. Men who usually had a room alone in the better hotels sometimes had to double up in the same bed with a friend when the house was crowded at conventions and such.

These men protested loudly, but all hotels, including Statler hotels, were hampered in catering to this sudden advance in elegance because most of the hotel rooms were built for double beds. They were not of the proper size or shape to take standard twin beds gracefully. So the Statler Company invented the studio bed, which was more flexible for bedroom arrangement than the standard twin. Studio beds looked well almost anywhere in the room, as long as they were against a wall. They also made possible the living-room-by-day feature.

The first studio beds were tried, as an experiment, in the Cleveland Statler in 1937, then in the Detroit Statler. They were so popular that not only the Statlers, which started them, but the Presidential yacht, *Williamsburg*, are equipped with this type of sleeping accommodation. Most other first-class hotels throughout the country have been using the same thing, since Statler sold its patent for studio beds to the Simmons Company, which had made the studio beds for Statler originally.

During the past several years, Statler engineers have been experimenting with new plastics and other materials for building wall partitions between bedrooms. They are looking for something that will allow walls to be thin, because of towering construction costs, and yet insulate rooms against sounds from next door more effectively than the old thick walls. This has become more necessary than ever since the coming of air conditioning. An air-conditioned room is sealed against street noises, to a large degree, but this causes noises from adjacent rooms to become more pronounced and annoying. It is the same condition that causes a loud noise in the middle of the night to be more startling than the same noise when it happens during the day.

Outside of conditions brought about by the changing times, E. M. Statler's bedrooms were pretty nearly perfect, technically. Excluding the studio bed, which was a product of changing times, most of the changes the company has made in its bedrooms since the founder's death have concerned the appearances of the rooms, rather than their functions.

Statler first began to pay real attention to the looks—instead of just the functional uses—of his bedrooms, or any other portions of his hotels for that matter, when he decided to build in Cleveland his second permanent house. Of his original hotel in Buffalo, he had boasted, "There is not an inch of waste space in it; not even a grand

staircase." He had incorporated into the first Buffalo Statler everything he knew—and more than anyone else knew—about the prac-
ticalities and conveniences of hotel construction. He was not concerned at the time with the aesthetic, a fact to which the old Buffalo
Statler still bears testimony.

But when he decided to build a hotel in Cleveland, a few years
after his Buffalo house was in operation, he felt a challenge to construct a marvel of taste and beauty. He announced he would build
there "the *finest* hotel in the world." He didn't accomplish that
entirely, but the Cleveland Statler may likely have been, for a number of years, the finest hotel in the Midwest.

Although he had resolved to make his Cleveland house beautiful,
Statler's ideas about beauty were obscure to the point of being nonexistent. He had a distaste for the rococo architecture, then highly
popular in the better types of hotels and now generally condemned.
But his attitude was not based upon offended aesthetic sensibilities.
He merely regarded the frills and furbelows of the Louis XV style
as bothersome dust catchers.

A year before he began his Cleveland hotel, Statler had built a fine
home in Buffalo. His idea of decorating that was to invite several
decorators to bid on adorning it on a room-by-room basis. He proposed that his wife, his secretary and himself should sit as a board
to select a separate decorator's plan for each room, depending on
which they liked best.

If this scheme had carried through, he would have had a home
consisting of a jumble of period rooms, each expressing a different
temperament, which well might have driven all its occupants out of
their minds. Fortunately, his wife and secretary persuaded him to
settle on just one decorator, whose plans they regarded as superior
in most of the rooms. The others were paid and dismissed, and the
lucky bidder turned out to be Louis Rorimer, of Brooks-Rorimer
Studio of Cleveland.

Statler was so pleased with his house that he engaged Rorimer
to decorate his Cleveland hotel. Rorimer was to remain in charge
of all Statler decoration until some years after the hotel builder's
death. At first, however, Rorimer's notions about hotel decor seemed
outlandishly expensive to Statler, who has always regarded such
matters as secondary. He protested that plans Rorimer submitted

for decorating only one public room in the Cleveland house would cost more than it did to decorate the entire Buffalo Statler.

"Your Buffalo hotel *does* give that impression," Rorimer replied stiffly, thereby effectively silencing Mr. Statler at least once in his life.

Not long after the Cleveland Statler opened in 1912, the Old Man had begun another of the same size in Detroit, which opened in 1915. Both houses had 700 rooms originally, but within a few years Statler had enlarged each by 300 rooms. The Cleveland and Detroit Statlers thus became the first two 1,000-room hotels outside of New York. Since that time "One Thousand Rooms, One Thousand Baths" has become the standard size that most large hotels advertise, whether they actually have that many rooms or not.

His hotel in St. Louis, which opened in 1917, was undertaken by Statler at the request of some local bankers. They wanted a new hotel for their city, and remembered him favorably from his operation of The Inside Inn there during the Louisiana Purchase Exposition in 1904.

For the grand opening of each of his hotels, Mr. Statler adopted a pattern of dignified gaiety. Around 2,500 local civic and social leaders were generally invited to the party, which included tours of the new house from cellar to guest rooms. A grand banquet was served, usually with three seatings. Prominent local society sopranos rendered solos. Statler provided the most popular orchestra of the area to play for the dancing, and all of the hotel's profits for the evening were donated to charity.

It was during such an opening of his Detroit house that Mr. Statler explained his ideas about a building and its furnishings to some newspaper reporters, when they came upon him sitting in a low-backed chair, an arm thrown comfortably over its back in a resting position. "I had to battle to get this chair made without a lot of back," he said. "The artist said it ought to be high-backed with a knob on it, but I said, 'Make it low and comfortable so a man can hook his arm over the corner. If it is comfortable, it will be artistic.'"

While Statler's furnishings in all his later hotels were far more artistic than in his first house, they remained practical. Rorimer, his decorator, designed a number of patterns and color schemes—

mainly in deep browns, reds, blues and greens—but the colors were interchangeable from one scheme to the others. Thus, if a drapery had to be replaced in a room, any one of several patterns in the storerooms would harmonize with the rest of the colors in the room.

This idea served a double purpose: It permitted the economies of mass buying, yet prevented some housemaid from hanging up stray decorations that clashed with everything else in the room, and offended the aesthetic sensibilities of the more fastidious guests. Statler decorations are still based on the principle of mass buying and blending of different color combinations. But otherwise, the hotels' decorative scheme has undergone some startling changes since the Old Man's death.

Mr. Statler's death occurred about a year before the depression, which stopped all hotel decoration. During the 1920's a hotel operator would build a skyscraper hotel quicker than he would buy a pincushion during the early 1930's. By the time the mid-1930's arrived, hotel interiors had taken on the gloomy appearance of unprosperous funeral parlors. Not only were the rugs, furniture and hangings wearing out, but hotels, in clinging to their aging trappings, were not keeping up with the public's changing tastes in interior decor. The trend was away from the dark hues and parlorlike motifs, held over from the Victorian age, and toward light, bright, cheerful apartments.

Perhaps one reason why the hotel business remained in the doldrums even after other businesses had begun to recover from the panic was that hotels were so dreary. At least, that was the thinking of a new set of executives—including Arthur F. Douglas, now president of the Statler Company—whom the owners brought in around 1937. Their job was to try to pep up the organization's sagging morale and grab off, if possible, a larger chunk of what hotel business there was in those slow times.

The company set up the Statler Studios as a separate corporation, under a hotel decorator named Kenneth McCann. He operates under the direction of H. B. Callis, senior vice-president, to handle decorations, and buy materials at a ten to twenty per cent saving. McCann and Callis set about to make rooms look more like sun parlors than funeral parlors. New carpets of lighter, brighter hues that were not expected to last more than seven years were put down. The old-type carpets of heavy black, gray, burgundy and deep greens and blues were built to last half a lifetime. Lighter paint was put on the walls, and cheerful-looking draperies were hung.

The old dark finish was removed from the furniture. The wood was bleached, and the pieces made to look more streamlined. Headboards were cut down and footboards were removed. Mirror frames were junked, and the mirrors were hung from the wall above the dressers. Old furniture got new and brighter upholstering, and the firm bought new chairs, tables and floor lamps.

One of the most important changes was the new pictures for hanging on the walls. For many years hotel pictures had been probably the most somber of all art, favoring stern gray-and-white etchings of the Grand Canal in Venice, the Cathedral of Notre Dame or St. Paul's in London. Sometimes when a hotel decorator wished to be devilish and colorful, he hung a few pictures of some 1905 belles, with big hats, usually either clutching a rose between their teeth or peeping roguishly over a curly tress. Statler's new pictures were colorful and interesting, running to landscapes, seascapes, marine and fishing scenes. People talked about them, and wrote letters to the company to learn where copies might be had.

About this time the company came along with its new studio beds. Then it built the Washington Statler, with its radical departure from hotel rooms of the past, like sets in a modernistic movie. The company has gone even more sunburst in its Los Angeles rooms.

In designing its Los Angeles house, the Statler people also devoted great thought to making bathrooms more attractive. They decided to extend the porcelain of the wash basin a couple of feet to one side to form a sort of make-up table for women guests, or a shelf for men's shaving things. But that had already been done at the Terrace Plaza Hotel in Cincinnati. Besides the fancy basin, Statler wanted something entirely new, and concluded that of all bathroom fixtures, probably the toilet seat could stand the most improvement and beautification.

Toilet seats in most hotel bathrooms are a simple wooden yoke without a solid top. This fixture can be used for one purpose only. The Statler people figured, since the toilet had to be there, they might make further use of it as, perhaps, a dressing-room chair. The company had bath-supply manufacturers make all manner of fancy toilet seats, even to seats upholstered in white leather. These turned out to be a trifle too expensive. Statler finally decided on a wide, wooden seat of graceful design, which makes a handy and comfortable chair in the bathroom, and which may introduce an entirely new and artistic use of the homely toilet.

For all its bathrooms, Statler specifies that bathtub drains be two inches in diameter, instead of the usual inch and a half. The larger pipe allows a bathtub to empty fast enough so that the receding water seldom leaves a ring, which reduces the work a maid has to do. Mr. Statler had this idea originally and would frequently use a stop watch to check the drain speed of his bathtubs.

Several years ago, the company installed on all its showers Speakman shower heads, which are expensive and give very powerful spray. They are highly popular among the guests, but caused, at first, great woe among the organization's houses. The new heads shot water with such force against the tile that it penetrated to the underlying cement, and most Statler bathrooms had to be retiled. The Speakman heads, however, paid off in popularity. They are so popular, in fact, that the company has had to equip them with vandal-proof set screws to prevent guests from removing the heads, and carrying them away. For the same reason, Statler hotels never use rolls of toilet paper. There is always a container built into the wall, which dispenses toilet paper through a slit two sheets at a time.

One of the most important of all Statler bathroom fixtures is the large hook, situated about the same height as, and just to the right of, the basin. When this hook isn't handy a person will use a face towel once, then toss it into the wastebasket. If a hook is there, and since the towel is usually barely dampened by one use, the guest will probably hang it on the hook, and use it again. The company has found that these hooks cut by almost half the number of face towels used a day in a hotel.

Mr. Statler never put light switches in his bathrooms. His idea was to turn the light on and off with a chain attached to the light socket. The company now installs switches at the door, although they cost twenty dollars each. It has found that people will turn out the bathroom light more often when a switch is handy at the door, and the company saves money on electricity in the long run. Mr. Statler once experimented with a device that turned off all the lights in the room when a person left, and locked the door from the outside. He abandoned this because it cost more to keep the device in repair than the value of the electricity it saved.

Occasionally the company will get what seems to be a bright idea that turns sour. Somebody got the notion that a threshold between a bedroom and bath was unnecessary, so these were eliminated in the Washington Statler. The idea was bad because, when maids scrub the bathroom floors, the water gets to the carpet of the bedroom, and stains it for an inch or so away from the door.

Another mistake in the Washington bathrooms was a decision to put the towel rack at a position different from the place Mr. Statler had always stipulated, which was immediately above the mirror. The reason he had selected this position—although the company had forgotten this when designing the Washington house—was that people often prefer to stand in the tub and dry themselves when they have finished their bath. If the towel rack is over the mirror, they can easily reach the towels while standing in the tub. There is a great advantage to the hotel here; it cuts down immensely on the bath mats that must be sent to the laundry every day.

When the Washington house was being planned, it was decided to install larger and more ornate medicine cabinets than the other houses had. These stuck up too high on the wall to make it practical to have the towel rack over the cabinet. The rack was put on the wall on the other side of the medicine cabinet from the bathtub.

Bathers now could not reach the towels easily while in the tub, and the Washington Statler, as a consequence, has the nasty situation of twice as many bath mats to launder every day, in proportion to its size, as any other house in the chain. The other bad result is that some people try to reach the remote towel rack anyway, while standing in the tub. Sometimes they lose their balance, and grasp the rack to steady themselves. Eventually the towel racks loosen, and pull off. They must be replaced and that portion of the wall replastered.

But then everybody has got to make a mistake once in a while, no matter how thoughtful and scientific they may be. Even Mr.

Statler could not anticipate every eventuality, such as the guest in the Detroit Statler who attempted to take his gymnastic exercises one day on the bar that supports the shower curtain. The rod broke, and he fell into the tub, raising a large knot on his head. He brought suit against the company on grounds that the hotel ought to provide shower-curtain rods strong enough to support the athletically-inclined.

14

The Eighth-Floor Ghost

Every couple of months or so, a lady by the name of Mrs. Olive Saunders checks in for a weekend at the Boston Statler, where she likes to sit around the executive housekeeper's office and talk shop. Mrs. Saunders was never in the hotel business, but for years she was chief housekeeper at the McLean Sanitarium, an institution near Boston for mentally deranged persons from well-to-do families.

Some years back, Walter Carney, front-office manager and hotel wit at the Boston Statler, asked this lady if her idea of relaxing for a weekend by sitting around the housekeeping department of a large hotel, as contrasted with her work in the mental institution, wasn't something like leaping out of the frying pan into the fire. "Yes," she said, "but I don't have to work in this one." Mrs. Saunders has been retired for some years now, but she still comes back occasionally to the Statler. "I get homesick sometimes," she explained to Carney one day, "and it's such a long way out to McLean."

This is intended as no reflection upon the Boston Statler, because in any large hotel the behavior of a certain percentage of guests borders on the lunatic fringe. Even gentlemen whose manners are impeccable elsewhere will casually drop lighted cigarettes upon the thick carpets of hotel parlors, and grind them into the pile with their heels. They do this in a detached manner that nobody seems to notice particularly, except the hotel management, which suffers dreadfully.

Employees at the Boston Statler recall a convention of school-teachers once that came when the hotel was brand new, spick, span and shining with no scars of battle from careless guests and rowdy conventions. When none of the hotel staff was looking, some convention people, using long nails and heavy hammers, affixed thirty-five signs to the walls of one public room. The signs all said simply, in large letters: THINK.

But the strangest of all behavior on the part of guests takes place on guest-room floors and in their own rooms. One Saturday, when a football game was being played in St. Louis, Mrs. Grace Davidson, executive housekeeper of the Statler there, chancing to look out a window, saw a guest emerge from the hotel gameward-bound, carrying some pennants, whistles and one of her department's carpet sweepers.

The housekeeper spent most of the rest of the afternoon establishing exactly who this guest was, and placed a charge for the carpet sweeper on his bill. Then she lay in wait to denounce him upon his return. Along about dark, the guest returned from the game. He had lost his pennants and whistles, but he still carried the hotel's carpet sweeper. It was undamaged. He put it back in the place he'd gotten it, and Mrs. Davidson removed the charge from his bill without mentioning the matter to him. That was fifteen years ago, and Mrs. Davidson hasn't figured out yet why he took it.

The average guest doesn't abuse his room, or even disarrange it to speak of. An efficient maid can put most of her rooms in order in fifteen minutes each—rooms that have been occupied by men, that is. It always takes longer to do a woman guest's room, as woman are messier than men, in hotels anyway. There is one exception to this rule. Catholic nuns are the neatest of all hotel guests. They generally put their own rooms in order, and do a better job than the maids. Nuns and priests, incidentally, are the most reliable of all types of hotel guests about tipping the maid.

The hardest work the maids have is cleaning suites that have been occupied by a partying crowd, usually at a convention. It may take three hours or longer to clean the cracker crumbs, popcorn, ashes and ground-up cigarettes out of the carpets. The walls and even the ceilings may have to be washed to remove stains left by pop and whisky, and smears of ink and lipstick.

Miss Delia Cooper, executive housekeeper at the Cleveland Statler, says it took her staff three months after a certain convention of schoolteachers in 1948 to remove all evidences of orange peel the teachers had left under the carpets, back of radiators, behind picture frames, under door sills, in linen closets, and on the service stairways.

At this convention, three hotel floors were occupied by Chambers of Commerce from most of the Union's states and territories, which set up booths to display the flora, agricultural, mineral, manufacturing, domestic and wild-life products of their sections.

Most of all there were oranges by the hundreds and hundreds of bushels, from Florida and California. The teachers fastened upon this fruit, and ate it in prodigious quantities, strewing the peel in all directions. Miss Cooper has estimated that more orange juice was consumed at this convention than any national convention of the American Legion ever drank of whisky. Even today, somebody in the hotel's housekeeping or maintenance staffs occasionally turns up a blackened, brittle old piece of orange rind from some remote crevice.

Sometimes a guest, infuriated by something or other, will set about deliberately to wreck a room, as one man did in St. Louis one crowded night when the management refused to let him keep his room until nine o'clock without paying extra. He smashed all the glass in the room, and ground it into the carpet. He slit open the mattress, and gutted the pillows, decorating the room with feathers.

Another time, a maid sent a call to the supervisor to come in a hurry because a man was cutting up the carpet in his room. By the time the supervisor arrived with a house officer, this man had removed several oblong pieces from the carpet. He explained, logically enough, that he was about to take his children on a fishing trip, and did not want to get fish scales on the floor rugs of his car. So he had decided to cover them with carpet from the hotel.

Some guests, who are not destructive, are not familiar with hotels. They may give the housekeeping department trouble because they can't find things in their rooms that are supposed to be there, or else they do not recognize these objects, even when they do see them—drinking glasses, for example. The Statler Company goes to great trouble to sterilize all drinking glasses for guest rooms, and wraps them in a fancy coat of cellophane. A good many guests, unfamiliar with this procedure, will call the housekeeper and demand some drinking glasses, mistaking the wrapped ones on the bathroom shelf for ornaments.

In some of the older Statler houses, the bathtub drain is worked mechanically with a lever, which causes guests to call the housekeeper demanding a rubber stopper, so they can use the tub. The rack of clean towels is over the mirror in the bathroom—a location the company believes it has established as the most scientifically efficient of all locations for towels. Yet many people, stopping in a Statler for the first time, can't find them. Human beings generally do not notice much above eye level. There are a few guests, apparently accustomed to old-fashioned plumbing, who call the housekeeper to report that the chain is missing from the toilet. One man resided for three days in the St. Louis Statler before realizing his bathroom had a toilet. It was concealed behind the door, when it was open. He had been going down to the barber shop men's room until a housekeeper tipped him off.

Night maid service is another Statler practice, which alarms many first-time guests. In the evening, usually when the guests are out at dinner, maids go into the rooms to remove the spreads, and turn down the beds for the night. Guests who are not accustomed to this frequently get the impression that robbers, or members of a spy ring, have given their rooms a going-over. Sometimes it takes the housekeeping department half the night to convince them that everything is all right.

Life in a big city hotel is complicated for some rural people who occasionally stop there. They are apt to complain to Statler maids when sheets are changed every day. This is not only wasteful, they say, but sheets sleep better after they have been used a few times.

There is another type of guest who is all too familiar with hotels, or vice versa. Some of these, usually women, develop traits that drive the housekeeping department crazy, and win for these guests unenviable reputations. One of them is known around the Statler circuit as "The Blind Buster." It is usually not longer than thirty minutes after she has moved into a room before she has pulled a Venetian blind loose from its moorings or maimed it in some way. Another one has an affection for three-cornered coffee tables, used in some Statler rooms. If she gets a room without one, she annoys the housekeeping department until one is brought. Some guests, immediately they check into a room, will strip covers off the beds, and toss the clean towels from the rack into the tub. Then they will demand that new bed linen be brought and the beds remade under their inspection, and that fresh towels be brought immediately from the laundry. And there are still other guests who are afraid of germs. They insist on the housekeeper supplying them with sufficient clean towels to cover the beds, furniture and the floors.

The most exasperating experiences the housekeeping department has with male guests is when sex rears its ugly head. When a guest is inflamed with whisky, maids sometimes have to flee for their honor, regardless of their age, color or marital status. Then there are times, generally during conventions, when a guest may become befogged with strong drink, and wander out into the corridor in a nude state, presumably looking for the bathroom. An experienced maid, upon encountering this situation, will throw a sheet over the guest and attempt to steer him back to where he came from.

One time in Detroit, a maid who had come on duty early one morning, opened her linen closet and found standing inside it a naked man. It turned out he'd got out of bed two-thirds asleep an hour or so before, and, instead of opening the door to his bathroom, had gone through the door into the corridor. When he was awake enough to realize where he was, he was standing in the corridor unclad. The shock of this realization rendered him so he could not remember his room number or the direction from which he had come. He heard some early-rising guests chatting around the corner, coming in his direction, so he ducked into a door that was cracked open. This proved to be the linen closet, where he remained too embarrassed to emerge until the maid found him there.

There are generally some old-timers among the maids, who have no home ties, and live on the service floor of the hotels so as to be available if an emergency arises. Once during an American

Legion convention in St. Louis, one of these maids went to sleep, neglecting to lock her door—a serious oversight at such a time. Next morning she awakened to find a large Legionnaire asleep in bed with her. He was fully dressed in his uniform, cap and medals, and still carried a walking stick. It turned out he couldn't find his room early that morning. He walked into the first door he found unlocked, and lay down upon the first convenient place.

It is partly because of the unpredictable situations and the nerve-shattering experiences they encounter—if the maid happens to be a nervous type—that hotels have more trouble keeping maids than any other type of employee, except dishwashers. Anybody knows why dishwashers are discontented. The Boston Statler once conducted a scientific study to determine what type of woman made the most desirable housemaid, and found that, in general, they are women in their forties or fifties, who have had some experience such as practical nursing and who are married or have been. In spite of the high average of turnover, if a maid lasts at her job for the first year, she is apt to become fascinated with the excitement and strangeness of such a career, and stay on the rest of her working life. Some of Statler's oldest employees, in point of service, are housemaids.

One maid is usually assigned a block of sixteen rooms to put in order during her eight-hour day. She is paid about thirty-five dollars a week, as contrasted with ten to fifteen dollars a week hotel maids were paid in New York thirty years ago. They were usually paid less elsewhere. In slack seasons when the hotel isn't full, the management can usually cut down the size of its staff of maids in a painless way by suggesting that any maids who would like to take a few weeks off without pay may do so. There are usually enough of them who wish to do this so nobody has to be let go who would like to keep on working.

This rather fluid working arrangement is one of the appeals, but the majority of the old-timers are drawn to the work by the atmosphere of excitement that seeps up from the dining rooms and banquets downstairs into the maid's world of linen closets and vacuum cleaners. When the hotel has a celebrity as a guest, most of the maids find occasion to get on his floor sometime during the day. When the Duke of Windsor was stopping at the Cleveland

Statler some time ago, housekeepers had to take up posts on his floor to shoo the maids back to their work on rooms of less glamorous guests.

There are other forms of excitement having nothing to do with celebrities or the crazy antics performed by some guests. The maids at the St. Louis Statler still talk about a Peeping Tom who was abroad in that house years ago. They like to tell about the elaborate plan that was laid to catch him and why it failed.

It started when some of the maids began to notice small holes drilled just under the lock plate in some guest-room doors, and informed Howard Busch, Resident Manager, who cautioned them to secrecy and laid a plan of strategy. Busch announced, falsely but convincingly, that a group of models from a prominent New York agency would arrive at the hotel the following evening, and would occupy a certain suite. Suspecting that the offender might be an employee, he circulated bulletins to all departments telling them of the models' anticipated arrival, and where they would be quartered. He asked everyone to stand ready to give them the finest of "Statler Service." He then stationed two detectives in a room across the hall to watch for the Peeping Tom to rise to the bait.

Actually, no models ever arrived. A couple of policewomen, who did not look at all like models, occupied the suite. But almost everyone in the house had the impression that the place was loaded with females of cover-girl character. The peeper was not bagged that night, probably because he could not operate on account of the crowded conditions of surrounding corridors. Male members of all departments—bellboys, assistant managers, porters, waiters, engineers—were up and down the corridors most of the night, presumably to be ready in case any of the models should suddenly require something or other. The maids relate with great merriment that even "Old Man Bates," the night auditor, who hadn't been above the lobby level in twenty years, was seen in the corridor in the vicinity of the suite no fewer than five times that evening.

Occasionally hotel housemaids have startling encounters with various strange pets that guests smuggle into their rooms. In St. Louis, a maid reached over to pick up some soiled towels in a corner of a bathroom, and grasped a large tropical snake. Another maid in the same hotel turned on the hot water into a bathtub, preparatory to washing the tub, but failed to look back of the shower curtain before turning the tap. Presently she heard loud splashings and gruntings back of the curtain. She took a look, and there was a sizable alligator having a hard time with the hot water. In New York, a maid was horrified upon entering a bedroom one morning to find a small child asleep in bed with a cheetah. Fortunately, the child's parents arrived back at the room from breakfast about that time and explained that the child always slept with this animal. Another time, a maid stripped some soiled linen off a bed and chucked it down the linen chute, without knowing a small monkey was asleep under the folds of the sheets. He smothered in the chute, and the owner sued the hotel.

Perhaps the most spectacular performance ever given by a pet smuggled into a Statler guest room was the case of a small monkey that a soldier home from the Pacific brought secretly into his room in the St. Louis house. The soldier left the monkey tied, while he went out for several hours. The monkey slipped his leash, and proceeded to the bathroom, with the apparent idea of brushing his teeth, as he'd seen the soldier do. The monkey had learned about turning on a water tap, but, unfortunately, he knew nothing about turning one off.

The housekeeping department became aware of the animal's project an hour or so later when floods of water began coursing down the corridors of that floor and chunks of water-soaked plaster began falling from ceilings of rooms on the floor below. When the plumbers located the guilty room, they found the monkey sitting on the edge of the bathtub, which was overflowing from both taps going full blast. The monkey's mouth was covered with lather, and he was waving gaily the soldier's toothbrush.

Except for seeing-eye dogs, most Statler hotels allow no pets on the guest-room floors. But, as with most rules, there are exceptions, as when Mrs. Donald W. Twigg, wife of a U.S. Naval attaché at Ankara, Turkey, wrote the New York Statler for reservations for herself, her daughter, Susan, and their dog, a Harlequin Great Dane named Loki. The hotel replied that it was reserving a double room for Mrs. Twigg and daughter, and the dog would be accommodated in the kennels. When he arrived, Loki stood seven feet high, as he reared upon the room desk. They couldn't get him into a kennel cage in the house, and he was allowed to stay in the room with the two ladies.

Mrs. Twigg and daughter made out better in this situation than did United States Supreme Court Justice William O. Douglas, a brother of Arthur Douglas, president of the Hotels Statler Company, when the Justice attempted to check into the Muehlbach Hotel in Kansas City with his dog. Barney Allis, owner of the Muehlbach, had been apprised of the Justice's anticipated arrival by some Statler people, and Mr. Allis had a large suite scrubbed, repainted and redecorated for Justice Douglas' arrival. He instructed his staff to see that the Justice should want for nothing— all the staff, that is, except the night manager, who was not aware even that the Justice was expected.

Naturally he was on duty when Justice Douglas arrived with his police dog. The night manager, who wasn't feeling very well that evening, told the Justice curtly that no dogs were allowed in that hotel, and he'd better go someplace else. Kansas City was crowded that night, and the Justice and dog were finally able to find unattractive lodgings in a mean, drafty hotel on a side street, where they sojourned during their stay in Kansas City. Meanwhile, at the big Muehlbach suite, the fruit, which the management had sent up for the Justice's enjoyment, grew softer, the ice melted and the flowers withered, while the management wondered what in the world had happened to Justice Douglas.

Many dog lovers object to leaving their pets in hotel kennels, fearing they will become contaminated with vermin left by former occupants. To guard against this, the kennels in the New York Statler, which are situated in the baggage room on the mezzanine floor, are cleaned and sterilized after each occupant vacates a cage. This has always proved adequate as a sanitary measure, except in one instance.

That happened just after the war ended, when some Army nurses arrived at the Statler fresh from Europe with some European mongrels they'd brought back as pets. These dogs, which were quartered in the kennels, were a lean and hungry lot, but nobody realized they were infested with large numbers of the hungriest of vermin from war-torn, starving Europe. These vermin had grown tired of gnawing upon the bony beasts they infested. For, once in the hotel's kennels, they deserted the European dogs and spread over the baggage room in search of new meat.

They were particularly attracted to a couple of well-fed French poodles, from the polite region of Greenwich, Connecticut. The poodles had been brought into New York by their owners, two well-to-do matrons of Greenwich, who had planned to stay at the Statler while showing their dogs at the Westminster Kennel Club's annual dog show in Madison Square Garden. But when the dog show opened next day, the poodles were unable to appear. They had been bitten so savagely that they required medical attention. The owners, who suffered severe bites about their own ankles, had some hard things to say to the chief baggageman, in charge of the kennels. On the other hand, the Army nurses commented when they were ready to leave that their dogs looked happier than when they had arrived.

It is partly because the best-behaved dog in the world at home may become nervous in a hotel atmosphere and howl day and night, and partly as a precaution against their bringing vermin into guest rooms that Statler hotels have their restrictions against pets on guest floors. A good many people resent this, but it appears that, among hotel frequenters, there are more bug-haters than dog-lovers.

In years gone by, the bedbug caused more woe, perhaps, than any other factor in hotelkeeping, affecting all hotels now and then, regardless of how expensive their rates or exclusive their clientele. Since the discovery of DDT, the bed bug has become almost extinct, and most people have forgotten there ever were such creatures. The New York Statler, with 3,400 mattresses in use, received only three bedbug complaints last year, and they turned out to be false alarms.

But even now, with the bedbug definitely on the run, a mattress is torn apart and examined under a magnifying glass every time even an imaginary bedbug is reported. The man in charge of this exhilarating work at the New York house is Jacob Adams, who has been mattress maker there for years. Adams is a well-rounded merry-faced man, in his latter sixties, who usually takes the role of Santa Claus at the Christmas parties for employee's children.

Adams' real job is to rebuild every mattress in the hotel at least once every five years. This involves removing some forty pounds of "Super Extra Drawings," meaning the best horse-tail hairs, and putting them through a machine that picks and tosses them to make them airy and crisp. Another apparatus blows the dirt out, and another sterilizes the horsehair, which is then built around 900 pairs of springs, in the case of double mattresses, and encased in ten yards of ticking.

Besides this regular work, Adams has to do frequent repair jobs on burned and wet mattresses. This tends to embitter him toward humanity in general, which he claims hasn't proper respect for mattresses. In the New York house an average of three mattresses come down each month that have been burned, usually by guests who fall asleep while smoking. The bed-wetting problem is even more common. Over a weekend, with a holiday crowd that may take a cocktail now and then in the house, Adams has received as many as fifteen wet mattresses from the housekeeping department.

"Men, women," Adams often grumbles. "One is as bad as the other. It seems to me that grown people could learn to hold their water. I have had to rebuild only two wet baby mattresses in the last five years."

The guest is charged for burned mattresses according to the amount of repair work that has to be done. Adams has a standing charge of ten dollars that he sends to the cashier for all wet mattresses, because all of them have to be unpacked and the horsehair cleaned and re-sterilized. New ticking is always used because urine stains will not come out. Another occasion when a mattress is torn apart, cleaned, sterilized and rebuilt is when a guest dies in bed.

When a guest dies in a hotel room, regardless of the cause, it is usually the hotel's policy to keep it as secret as possible from the other guests, for obvious reasons. The death is also kept quiet around the housemaids, because some of them will never go in a room again if they know somebody has died there. A hotel, full of people, noise, music and activity, would seem to be the least likely of all places as a haunt for spirits. But some maids—usually the older Negro women, who came from back in the country years ago—believe the spirits will stay on in a room where there was death—particularly late on winter nights when the corridors are quiet, and the wind whistles about the high cornices.

At the Cleveland Statler, there is one old housemaid who refuses to enter two rooms, day or night, for this reason, although she will pass by them in a half gallop along the corridor when it is daylight. Another maid is worried about one room, where she once found a man who had done himself in. She will go in to clean the room during the day, if another maid or a housekeeper goes with her, but she wouldn't think of going in alone during the day, or under any circumstances at night.

And there is still another maid in the same hotel who refuses to get off the service elevator on the eighth floor at any time. Once when she did get off on that floor, thinking it was the seventh, she dashed down the service stairway so fast that she fell and sprained her ankle.

The thing that bothers this woman is an eighth-floor corner suite, where a guest from Akron, Ohio, died one night years ago. They found his body next morning, slumped in an easy chair where he had died reading his home-town newspaper, which was lying across his knees. His death didn't disturb this maid at the time, although she had been present when the body was discovered. It wasn't until one night the following winter that something happened—at least, she thinks it happened—that has kept her off the eighth floor ever since.

It was nearly midnight, and a storm was blowing off Lake Erie. The wind was howling under the eaves, shaking the windows and rattling the doors. This maid, who was on night duty, passed along the eighth-floor corridor in front of the locked door of the corner suite. It was then that she heard, above the noises of the storm— or so she told the night housekeeper a few minutes later—a noise inside the suite that sounded like somebody turning the pages of a newspaper.

Of course, everybody knew it was her imagination, because the suite had been vacant that night. But a few old-time maids still whisper among themselves that on the following morning another maid, who was sent to the suite to dust, found a crumpled newspaper lying on the floor in front of an easy chair. Now, a newspaper is likely to be found lying around any Statler suite. The

Statlers deliver a fresh newspaper to every guest every morning, and the boys frequently make a mistake and stick a newspaper under a door of an unoccupied room.

In Cleveland every morning the guests receive copies of the Cleveland *Plain Dealer*. But the paper the maid found on the floor of the corner suite, they say, was a copy of the Akron *Beacon-Journal* for the day before.

15

"Largest Hotel in the World"

Ellsworth M. Statler—who began to dream of himself as the operator in New York of "the world's largest hotel" back when he was
a bellhop hustling ice water in the old McLure House in Wheeling,
West Virginia, in the latter 1870's—finally realized his dream about
forty years later with the completion of the Hotel Pennsylvania.
Statler was lessor of this immense place from the day it opened, but
his company did not own it, nor did it bear his name, until twenty
years after Statler's death.

The Hotel Pennsylvania—now the New York Statler—is a squar-
ish, soot-stained, blocklike citadel rising into the heavy gray hu-
midity that shrouds the island of Manhattan. At its feet threshes
the traffic that preys upon the railroad station and the garment
center of the world hard by. The hotel spreads its façade along
the entire block from Thirty-second to Thirty-third Streets and
extends eastward halfway over the long block between Seventh
Avenue and Broadway. It has always been one of the most profitable
large hotels in the world.

This is not saying too much for the New York Statler, because
most of the very huge hotels were not successful, and went through
various stages of reorganization and bankruptcy until the war came,
and the hotel business entered a boom that persists up to the

present. The Pennsylvania had heavy going during the depths of the depression of the early 1930's, but it survived intact, which is more than can be said of most large hotels. It was not until 1948 that the Pennsylvania, having paid all of its debts from the depression, found itself healthy and thriving and owing no man, firm or corporation.

It was then that Arthur Douglas negotiated a deal that bought the Pennsylvania from the railroad, and named the big house after the Old Man, who had dreamed of it back among his water pitchers and the derby-hatted, stogie-smoking drummers who patronized the old McLure House. This was highly appropriate and fitting because the big hotel on Seventh Avenue was now inhabited by the largest number of the most prosperous drummers that any hotel is likely ever to house.

When it opened in 1919, the Pennsylvania, with 2,200 rooms, was the largest hotel in the world. It kept that distinction for nine years until completion in Chicago of the Stevens Hotel, which has about 2,700 rooms but claims 3,000. Actually the Stevens, which has small rooms, is only slightly larger than the Pennsylvania in cubic content. Both hotels are exceeded slightly in cubic size by the Waldorf-Astoria in New York and the Palmer House in Chicago.

Since it opened, the New York Statler, nee Pennsylvania, has made more money perhaps than any hotel in New York. It now probably runs second in gross business only to the Waldorf, which, considering its rent and debts that it is still paying off, has never made much of a profit. From its opening up to the depression, the Pennsylvania made several million dollars a year profit. In recent years, it has had the highest occupancy of any big commercial hotel in the big town. In 1951, the New York Statler was the only large hotel in New York that had better business than during the year previous, and the only one that kept its occupancy average as high as ninety per cent.

The hotel was conceived by Thomas W. Hulme, then general real-estate agent for the Pennsylvania Railroad, as a vehicle for increasing property values in the vicinity of the fine new Pennsylvania Station, completed in 1911. At that time it was surrounded, unfortunately, by blocks of dismal boarding houses and blank-faced warehouses. The big hotel was conceived as a means of lifting this gloomy neighborhood to a level that the railroad considered befitting its fine new terminal.

The railroad owned a large block just east of its new terminal and decided to build a 1,000-room hotel there to lease to an operator named F. J. Matchette. Statler, who was building his St. Louis house at the time, did not hear of the project until too late to try for the lease.

However, Matchette talked the railroad into building a hotel more than twice the size originally contemplated. The railroad felt it should not risk a project of this magnitude to only one lessor, and brought Statler in as an associate. Before the hotel building was started, Matchette retired on a stock-sharing agreement, and Statler became sole operator of the $12,000,000 project.

A tunnel was built from the hotel into the Pennsylvania terminal, with a connection to the new Seventh Avenue subway. The house was situated some distance back from the street to allow for a wide sidewalk, on which it was hoped crowds of well-to-do people one day would promenade.

That is about what happened. Properties thereabout doubled in value before the hotel was eight years old. The Pennsylvania Station area, while it never became as swanky as that around Grand Central, developed into a section of great commercial importance, with Macy's, Gimbel's and Saks department stores nearby. Other hotels, such as the New Yorker and Governor Clinton were built, and the world's most important garment center grew up along Seventh Avenue.

When the big hotel opened, the postwar slump had set in, and it seemed problematical whether it would be profitable. But because of its proximity to the Pennsylvania Station and because of Statler's management, it was a success from the beginning. It remained more than ninety per cent occupied from its opening until the depression set in, so that Statler's New York hotel operating company was able to pay the annual rental of $1,000,000, and have a profit of $2,000,000 to 3,000,000 each year.

This left Statler with opportunity and confidence to continue his hotel-building career. He next built in Buffalo, where he wanted to construct a grander edifice than the old Buffalo Statler. In 1920 he bought the site of the old President Millard Fillmore home at the foot of Delaware Avenue, and, in 1923, opened there an 1,100-room hotel, which was the most luxurious of all the Statlers built during the Old Man's lifetime, with the possible exception of his last house, the Boston Statler.

The new Buffalo Statler was built by the Old Man probably as a sort of monument to himself. It had more rooms than all the other hotels in Buffalo combined. There was some talk that the Old Man would not like any monument to himself that was not profitable, which it was believed the new Buffalo hotel might not be. Some considered it too large for Buffalo, but the hotel has always done well. It not only marks the center of Buffalo. It practically is Buffalo, and from the Statler emit most of the civic projects, community movements and social affairs of that city.

Statler had bought property across the street from the Boston Common for his hotel there in 1920, but high building costs delayed the start of the hotel until 1925. He proceeded then against the advice of his board, but Statler said he was going to build the Boston house if it broke the company. The Boston Statler with 1,300 rooms, the largest hotel in New England, opened in 1928, not long before the arrival of the depression, which was to ruin the hotel business. But Statler did not live to see that sad era.

As it turned out, his Boston house, being brand new, impressive and popular in Bean Town, made more profits during the depression than any other hotel in Statler's organization. It was one of the principal factors that allowed the Statler Company, even with its guiding genius dead, to survive the panic, which wiped out the other three big hotel chains of the land, and drove four out of every five hotels in America into bankruptcy.

E. M. Statler died of pneumonia April 16, 1928 at the age of sixty-five, after a brief illness. He is survived by his widow, Mrs. Alice Seidler Statler, who had been his secretary prior to their marriage in 1927, when she was thirty-four. A year and a half before, Statler's first wife had died. She was the former Mary Manderbach, of Akron, whom Statler had married in 1894, just before he left Wheeling to begin his adventures with his restaurant in Buffalo. They had no children, and three of the four children they had adopted had died tragically before Statler did. The only child remaining is Ellsworth Statler, Jr., who breeds horses in

Southern California and has never taken an active part in the company.

Mrs. Statler became chairman of the board upon her husband's death. She was succeeded some years later by J. L. Hennessy, who had started under Statler as a steward. He resigned in 1948, and was succeeded by William L. Marcy, a Buffalo attorney who had married Mrs. Katherine Statler, widow of Milton Statler, one of the Old Man's adopted sons. The late Frank A. McKowne, who had been Statler's secretary, was named president of the company in 1928. McKowne retired in 1945, and was succeeded by Arthur Douglas, who had been directing most of the organization's policies for several years, and who is still president of the Statler Company.

Mr. Statler had always run his hotels as a one-man show, and so, when he died, nobody was around who could properly succeed him. The executives and the board of directors managed to keep the company out of receivership, but allowed the hotels to run down, delayed maintenance and cut out national advertising. Thus, the Statler Company, which had pioneered for twenty years, suddenly found itself back in the pack along with the ordinary run of hotels.

Mrs. Statler was unhappy about the disintegrated state of the company's operations and deteriorating morale. In 1936, she secured two new directors—her legal adviser, Arthur Ballantine, a partner in the distinguished old law firm, Root, Clark, Buckner & Ballantine —and her financial adviser, Bayard Pope, chairman of the board of the Marine Midland Trust Co., of New York. They, with William Marcy, who had become a director, decided that maintenance had gone to pot; some managers were not competent, and there was not proper co-operation between the executive offices and the individual hotels. They decided that what the company needed most of all was an aggressive head, who had imagination and enthusiasm.

The man they chose, principally on Ballantine's recommendation, turned out to be Douglas, who took, at first, the post of secretary-treasurer, but became the executive vice-president a year later, in 1938. Arthur Douglas, who was thirty-six then, is a native of Yakima, Washington. He had worked his way through Whitman College and Columbia University's Law School as a tutor (his most famous student being José Ferrer, the actor), and had joined the Root,

Clark, etc., law firm. During the previous ten years he had been representing that law firm in the South, where he had charge of reorganizing 120 office buildings, garages, theaters, apartment buildings and hotels that went into bankruptcy following the Florida hurricane of 1926 and later during the depression.

Douglas and the new board set about with plans that resulted in the studio bed and radical redecoration of Statler guest rooms. They built new dining rooms, and remodeled the bars with chromium, leather and neon, as opposed to the early-century decor, which ran to tiled floors, paneling, a battery of spittoons and ornate mirrors.

They rearranged the hotel lobby floors to allow more space for shop and store rentals. Statler's income from store rentals, concessions and the like now amounts to about $2,225,000 a year, including $100,000 a year from pay toilets.

Another project of Douglas and the new board was to get rid of some extraneous properties held by the company in various cities, on the books for $10,000,000. Douglas sold them for over $5,000,-000, writing off half the loss on paper to Government taxes. The principal idea in getting rid of the properties, he says, was to "put the company back into the hotel business," so that all of its thought and energies could be aimed at hotel betterment.

The company now went back into national advertising with one of the most successful programs of magazine display in advertising history. Statler's principal advertisements are a full page each month in *Time, Life, The Saturday Evening Post,* etc. Research surveys show that the Statler advertisement is always either the first or second most-read of all the advertisements in the issue of each of these magazines. The Statler advertisements take the form of a somewhat sophisticated comic strip, with five panel drawings, by Tony Barlow, showing some type of guest being profoundly impressed with the splendors and comforts of Statler. These pictures, each accompanied by a four-line verse, have become about as well known to the light-reading public as Blondie and Li'l Abner.

Statler, for the past fifteen years, has had experts figuring ways to eliminate duplication of employees' efforts so that, while the number of guests was increasing by 200 per cent and income by

300 per cent, the number of Statler employees increased only about eighteen per cent.

If the increase in employees had been anywhere near in proportion to the increase in business, what with the increase in wage scales, Statler would now be broke. As it is, efficiency, plus, of course, good business during the war and postwar years, has increased the market price of Statler stock from eighty cents to about twenty-two dollars a share. Of the Statler stock, incidentally, about forty-five per cent is held by members of the Statler family and in Statler trusts. The remainder is owned by some 2,000 investors, including a good many hotel men not otherwise connected with Statler.

In order to increase efficiency in its operations, save materials, standardize purchasing and prevent lost motion, the new management abandoned the existing policy under which individual hotels were run more or less independently. The firm assembled in usable form all the information its people had been learning about the operation of hotels over the years, and printed it in fool-proof directives, which range all the way from how to handle the press to an eight-page treatise on how to make coffee. Every employee is expected to study the rules for his department so he will know the Statler-approved way of serving a mackerel or making a bed. In the food department, representatives such as J. M. Faussone, executive chef, or Miss Mildred Haugh, director of food supervisors, travel from house to house to see that the sauerbraten in Cleveland tastes as good as that in St. Louis, or that the Washington Statler does not pay more than it should for beef bones.

John C. Hevenor, a vice-president, spends most of his time traveling among the houses thinking up new ways to eliminate lost motion. In this regard, Hevenor and W. R. Leber, in charge of engineering, have perfected a remarkable system for conserving time and materials in Statler's maintenance, repair and engineering matters. There is great opportunity for savings in this field, since the company spends around nine cents a year of every dollar income on repairs and maintenance.

The New York Statler's engineering department receives about 23,000 trouble calls a month. Most common of complaints are those about leaky faucets, but calls are brisk on noisy toilets, particularly those that whistle, and on noisy radiators. Building Superintendent W. J. Buckley is convinced some guests sit in a pose like Rodin's Thinker, straining to hear a slight radiator clank.

Every now and then the hotel plumbers have to go into the pipes to get a diamond ring somebody has let go down the basin drain, or a platinum dental bridge they have accidentally flushed down the toilet. These are usually fished out of a trap, built for that purpose in the drains of that bathroom. Occasionally, valuables get past that into the house trap in the basement. When that is opened, the engineers always remove, in addition to the valuable they are seeking, anywhere from 15,000 to 45,000 used razor blades that guests have flushed away.

The engineering department of the New York Statler carries an inventory of $65,000 worth of plumbing and electrical parts, carpenters' materials and various hardware. When not busy on jobs about the house, the electricians, plumbers, and carpenters are required to spend their time salvaging parts. When a plumbing valve is replaced, usually not more than one or two of its thirty-odd parts are ruined. The other parts are removed, reconditioned, and put into the stock. This is in contrast to what happens in many hotels, where a whole valve may be tossed into a barrel, and eventually thrown away.

The engineering executives know that it takes an average of twenty-five minutes to make an ordinary electrical repair and forty minutes for an average plumbing trouble order. When engineering employees in one of the hotels begin to climb above these time averages on house jobs, the company looks into the reasons why.

Besides these meticulous matters of cost saving, the new board of directors and Douglas attacked the lethargy that had settled over the organization since the founder's death. They thought it would be healthy for the company to have some new projects and challenges. They wanted to build a new hotel, even though nobody else had considered doing such a ridiculous thing since the onset of the depression. But it takes some time to get a new hotel started —one that is properly planned and thought out, at least—and while this was in process, the directors got the company a new project in the Hotel William Penn in Pittsburgh.

The Statler Company contracted to manage this 1,500-room house, largest between New York and Chicago, for a flat fee of $140,000 a year. This did not represent very much money, but it was a new project, and Douglas was anxious to get the company thinking in terms of new projects. Statler considered buying the William Penn, but never made an offer. The arrangement of the house never completely suited Statler's thinkers, for one thing, and the stock was so widely scattered that the hotel could not have been bought in one deal. The firm withdrew from this operation in January, 1952.

Management of the William Penn by Statler began in 1940, and within a year and a half, Statler opened its new 850-room Washington house, which has proved to be perhaps the most financially successful hotel of its size in the country.

In 1948, Statler bought the Hotel Pennsylvania for $14,500,000. Since the depression, Statler had been receiving about $200,000 a year profit from the Pennsylvania Railroad for operating the hotel for the ten years prior to purchasing the property. During the first year Statler owned the Pennsylvania, its profit was $1,460,000.

On January 1, 1949 when the Hotel Pennsylvania's name was changed to Statler, New York newspapers speculated that it would cost $400,000 to re-equip the hotel with silver, linens, blankets and such bearing the new name. It probably would have cost that, except the name was changed on the marquee and stationery and that was about all. The company knew it would not have Pennsylvania-labeled inventory on its hands for very long.

"Consumption," which is a polite word in hotel circles for theft by guests, would take care of silver, linens and blankets that bore the old name, and the company could make its replacements with new Statler-monogrammed stock gradually as a regular operational expense. All large hotels have to make allowances in their operational budgets for thefts by guests. It is difficult to understand why, but highly respected, responsible businessmen—who wouldn't dream of shoplifting—will slip away from a hotel with a thirty-dollar silver coffee pot, and brag about it at home.

Not long ago, a man, annoyed at the New York Statler because he did not get a reservation on a certain date, wrote: "I have been a steady Statler customer for twenty years, and I have the towels at home to prove it."

Statler executives were most flabbergasted when a salesman

showed up at their offices one day with a large sample case of silver, including used tableware bearing the name, Hotel Pennsylvania. He wanted to sell Statler back some of its own stolen silver. He was also prepared to sell silver bearing the names of the Waldorf-Astoria, Astor, Ritz-Carlton, Commodore, St. Regis and New Yorker hotels.

"Consumption" also includes breakage, such as Statler had in one recent typical year of 152,000 cups, 69,000 saucers, 165,000 plates, 270,000 water glasses, 170,000 highball glasses, 219,000 whisky glasses, 41,000 champagne glasses and 85,000 cocktail glasses. Some guests even try to steal glasses, such as one who claimed that the dozen Statler-style cordial glasses a housemaid started to remove from her luggage were her own. She said she always carried a dozen glasses or so around in her suitcase.

Most of the glass consumption is broken, but the 200,000 face towels the company loses in a typical year are mainly stolen by guests. So are the 67,000 bath towels, the 62,000 pillow cases, the 43,000 bedsheets, the 3,200 blankets, the 2,900 bedspreads, the 13,-500 tablecloths, and the biggest loss of all, 340,000 napkins.

Shortly after Raymond McSoley was sent from Boston to manage the Cleveland Statler in 1945, he and Mrs. McSoley were invited to a cocktail party and buffet supper one evening in the home of some prominent Clevelanders. There were a large number of guests present, and the hostess, in making her rounds, came to McSoley. "I know you are new in Cleveland," she said, "but what is it you do?"

McSoley said he was the new manager of the Hotel Statler. Whereupon an expression of chagrin crossed the hostess' face, and well it might. The napkin that McSoley had been handed with his plate and teacup was a salmon-colored fabric that anybody familiar with a certain hotel chain would have recognized immediately as a Statler room-service napkin.

In the silver department, Statler's losses a year run to some 75,000 knives and forks, 16,000 oyster forks and 138,000 spoons. Demitasse spoons have a great appeal to souvenir collectors, even to hotel men themselves. Once when the New York Statler was host at a luncheon for hotel executives from other companies, the hotel discovered, when the guests had departed, that 116 demitasse spoons had gone along with them. This caused Statler officials to mutter things like "Et tu, Brute."

Occasionally one of the Statlers will receive a shipment of a few dozen, perhaps, faded old Statler towels from some former guest who has gotten religion, and repented from taking ways. Women, the company has found, are much worse about taking towels than men. Once in a while somebody tries to walk out of a dining room carrying a champagne bucket under a coat or a silver sugar bowl in a hat. One time the Washington Statler's officers stopped a man making off down L Street with one of the lobby chairs. People even steal Gideon Bibles. Mrs. Sarah Hippe, executive housekeeper at the Detroit Statler, reports that around 100 Bibles are taken every year.

Hotels are handicapped in trying to recover articles taken by the guests because a "stop thief" attitude is hardly in line with the best traditions of hospitality. Statler usually pursues a subtle line, as the management of the Detroit house did once when three college girls, who belonged to prominent families, spent a weekend there, and left with three coffeepots, each worth about thirty dollars.

The hotel sent telegrams to each of the girls' homes saying that the coffeepots were missing, but implying that the management believed someone else had taken them. The girls' co-operation was requested in trying to recall any questionable-looking characters they may have seen on their floor. The telegrams fell into the hands of their parents, as the hotel management had calculated would happen. The missing coffeepots were sent back by return mail along with a note saying it was hoped the management would understand that the episode was a thoughtless schoolgirl prank.

Probably the smartest decision the Statler people ever made on the spur of the moment to rescue its property occurred around 1940 at the Hotel Pennsylvania, which was filled with a football crowd in town to see the Army-Notre Dame game. It was a bitter cold day, and the management was perturbed to see people leaving early for the Yankee Stadium, most of them taking along a pair of robe blankets from their rooms. It was a pretty sure bet that most of the blankets, which cost the hotel around eighteen dollars a pair, would never get back.

The management didn't think it would look very well if they started wresting blankets out of the hands of guests. At the same time, it was hard to just stand there and see the hotel's property carried away. Then one of the hotel officials had a flash inspiration. He had all the hotel's extra new blankets brought down, and stacked in piles in the lobby. Bellboys were stationed at each stack and instructed to offer blankets to everyone leaving the hotel who appeared to be bound for the game.

That put an entirely different psychological slant on the blanket-taking situation. Since the hotel had been thoughtful enough to offer one a blanket, one would not think of abusing such hospitality. It was a matter of honor. The crowd leaving for the game that day had a warm glow of gratitude in its heart toward the Hotel Pennsylvania. And almost every one of the blankets was back in its room that night.

16

It's as Good as Money

The old Waldorf-Astoria, haunt of many of the nation's millionaires of the Gay Nineties era, used to claim the distinction of inaugurating among hotels the practice of cashing checks for guests and patrons, or, as they say in the industry, the Waldorf "put hotels in the banking business." There are plenty of hotel men who do not regard this as a distinction, exactly—more like a nuisance. That is because much of the public has got the idea that hotels are anxious to hand out cash to anybody who can produce, as evidence of financial stability, nothing more than the ability to write his name and, of course, to breathe.

Somebody who never spent a nickel there in his life will walk into a hotel, often during a weekend or at night when banks are closed, and present his check for a hundred dollars or so. When the hotel doesn't cash it, he is apt to fly into a righteous rage, as though he had been denied the right of free speech or admission to church. There are other characters—who wouldn't think of entering a bank, except at night with a jimmy and crepe-soled shoes—who will stride confidently up to a credit manager of a hotel as though they owned the place.

Among businessmen, respectable but unknown to the hotel, probably out-of-town bankers are the most incensed when their personal checks are not honored immediately. Hotel credit managers say that, in their own banks, these men probably require a stranger's birth certificate, fingerprints and a letter from his pastor before they will cash his check. But they expect hotels to cash their checks when about the only evidence of affluence they can produce at the moment is a well-developed belly.

When the hotel demurs about cashing his check on flimsy identification, a banker, like many other businessmen in a similar position, is apt to fling at the credit manager a familiar cry: "That's what you are in business for, isn't it!" Sometimes credit managers get to believe that they are the only persons laboring under the archaic notion that hotels are in business to sell rooms, entertainment, food and whisky.

Each year, about $10,000,000 is lost on bogus checks in the United States. Hotels and restaurants are among the principal victims. In a year, the Statler Company cashes some 700,000 checks for about $40,000,000. Its losses average about seventeen cents for every $1,000 worth of business the company does.

Bad checks fall into four general categories: forgeries, no-accounts, accounts-closed and insufficient funds, of which the latter are the most prevalent. Most I.S.F. checks, however, are collected eventually.

The majority of forgeries are done through use of credentials that have been lost or stolen. Naturally, in Statler hotels, the best identification is the company's credit card. Around 350,000 of these are issued each year, which is the largest list of hotel credit-card holders in the world. Statler credit cards are honored by most other hotels, some of them as far away as Turkey or Japan. This is probably because Statler is more careful than most hotels about who gets a credit card in the first place, and infinitely more thorough about keeping check on its cards once they have been issued.

Holders of Statler credit cards are instructed to wire the company collect immediately their cards are lost or stolen. There have been instances when a card fell into the hands of some crook, who has flown from one Statler city to another to cash as many checks as possible before the company learned the card had left the original holder. If it is in order, a Statler card automatically entitles the holder to get cash up to $100, in addition to his hotel bill, although he does not need to be registered in the hotel for it to be honored. Before cashing the check, the cashier compares the signature on the credit card with that on the check. She also consults a master credit-card file to be sure that card has not been canceled for any reason. If the holder wishes to get more than $100, he has to see somebody in the credit department.

Persons without credit cards, who wish to cash personal checks, rely most often for identification upon their Social Security card. Actually this is of no value whatever as an identification because Social Security rolls are kept so confidential that nobody, including the F.B.I., can get at them to check up. Furthermore, no investigation is made of Social Security applicants so that, if he wishes, a person might have as many Social Security cards as he could think up names to call himself. The second most popular type of identification is the driver's license, which isn't of much use either. Few cities or states trouble to check on exactly to whom they are issuing a driver's license. Some people use credit cards issued by other hotels, but Statler credit managers seldom set much store by them, since they frequently do not contain the name of the card holder, or the year it was issued and almost never the signature of the holder.

What burns people most of all is when a hotel declines to honor a cashier's check. "It's as good as money. You know that, don't you?" most people are inclined to shout at such a time. But, whether they know it or not, cashier's checks can be, and often are, counterfeited. The same is true with checks bearing the name of some large business concern. One bad-check artist was discovered in the Cleveland Statler after a housemaid had noticed a strange-looking mechanical apparatus in his room, which she reported to the chief house officer. It turned out to be a press for printing fake cashier's checks. This man had only to look into the Dun & Bradstreet directory, get the name of the cashier of some remote bank, print up a check on some forms he had, sign the cashier's name, and he was in business.

Some years ago, there was run to earth at the Buffalo Statler a gentleman who had bilked hotels of thousands of dollars over a decade or more according to this interesting system:

He gave as his home, say, Chicago, where he kept a respectable bank balance in, say, the Tenth National Bank, but he lived mostly in hotels about the country. After a week in a hotel, he would explain to the credit manager that he was going to check out the following day, and wished a give a check for the amount of his bill, plus several hundred dollars extra. He would say he knew the hotel would likely want to investigate his account before cashing a check for that amount. He would give as reference the Tenth National Bank, of Chicago, and suggest that the credit manager communicate with the bank. This was done, and the bank reported favorably.

The next day this man presented his check, drawn on a regular Tenth National Bank form, and the credit manager would immediately approve it by initialing it in one corner. This man, however, would not take the check immediately to the cashier, but to his room, where he had equipment for eradicating the bank's name from the check, then printing in the name of a nonexistent bank, say, the Twentieth National Bank of Chicago. He would then take the check, still bearing the hotel credit manager's o.k., to the cashier, who would cash it without question. By the time the check got back to the hotel from the Chicago Clearing House, which stated there was no such bank as the Twentieth National, the man would be in another hotel in some distant city preparing to work the same deal on some unsuspecting credit manager there.

Charlie Heidler, night manager of the Cleveland Statler, was fooled once by a different version of the same trick when he approved a personal check for a man giving his name as, say, John Brown, of Rochester, New York. Now the nature of their duties, which consist of dealing with humanity in the late evening when many people in hotels are at their worst, influences many night managers to become suspicious of all human motives. Heidler approved the man Brown's check only after being confronted with overwhelming evidence that here was a sterling character. These identifications included membership cards in leading clubs, civic organizations and fraternal groups. There were clippings from newspapers, showing Brown in company with the mayor, the president of the Chamber of Commerce, prominent churchmen and other important people participating in uplifting civic occasions in Brown's home town, where he was in the clothing business.

Nevertheless, when Heidler noticed that Brown did not take his check to the cashier immediately after it had been approved, he instructed the cashier not to honor a check signed by John Brown, when it was presented, but to send Brown back to him.

The man, John Brown, was never sent to the assistant manager's desk, nor did the cashier cash a check signed by that name. However, about ten days later, the hotel auditor informed Heidler that a check he had approved for one Harry Maxwell had come back from a Rochester bank marked "No Account." Heidler could remember approving no check for anybody by that name, but when he saw it, he recognized it immediately as the check he had approved for John Brown, highly respected citizen of Rochester and local civic leader.

As it developed later, the man was all that in his home town, under the name of John Brown. However, he was wanted by hotels all over the country for cashing checks under the name of Harry Maxwell and other aliases. He had a scientific system for eradicating the signature of John Brown, after his checks had been initialed by the credit departments of hotels, impressed by the civic stature of John Brown. He would then re-sign the check with the name of some nonexistent depositor. After long extradition proceedings, the Cleveland Statler was able to bring him to trial in Ohio.

During the recent war, a number of hotels had experiences with young men, not in the armed services, but who purchased Army or Navy officers' uniforms for themselves, procured some imposing medals for valor, and traveled about the land impressing a lot of people in lecture halls and night clubs. They generally chose to live in luxury in hotels, often with funds procured through cashing bogus checks at hotels, which were anxious to accommodate returned heroes.

An example of this type was a fake Navy lieutenant commander, exposed while a guest at the Detroit Statler. He had created a stir in that city with accounts of his personal prowess and some penetrating interpretations of the strategy of the war in the Pacific in his remarks before some luncheon groups and in newspaper interviews. But he looked familiar to Charlie Thompkins, chief house officer at the Statler, and he asked the Shore Patrol to investigate. It turned out Thompkins had seen an F.B.I. photograph of the man, made back before he grew the nice mustache he sported in Detroit. He was wanted by the F.B.I. for impersonating an officer. He was a civilian tailor from Brooklyn, who had never been nearer the Pacific than St. Louis. He said he had bought his uniform and embarked on the career of a returned hero to impress girls.

At night and on weekends, when the credit manager is generally off duty, the responsibility for approving guests' checks is up to the assistant managers on the floor, who are guided pretty much by instinct. Frank Bennett, who has been an assistant manager at the Cleveland Statler for thirty years, says he can't explain what it is, but he, or almost any other experienced assistant manager, will approve a $100 check without a second look at one man, but they will hesitate over a $5 check for some other man, although the assistant manager has never seen or heard of either party before, and there is no particular difference in their looks.

Almost every time a check comes back that he, or any old-time assistant manager has approved, according to Bennett, it generally turns out to be one they did not feel right about, although the man who gave it may have had plenty of identification, with nothing tangible wrong with his appearance. Once after he approved a man's check, feeling that maybe he shouldn't, Bennett watched the man absently while he went over to the cashier's desk and got his money. Then he walked over to the Western Union desk and sent a telegram. After he had left, Bennett learned from the Western Union operator that the wire had been sent to a small city in Canada, which the assistant manager noted on a slip of paper and stuck away in his drawer.

In about two weeks the check, which had been drawn on a bank in New York, came back, marked "No Account." When the hotel tried to communicate with the man at the address under which he had registered, that address turned out to be false. It turned out that his home was actually in Canada at the address where he had sent the wire, which Bennett had noted. When the hotel wrote to him there, the man sent the fifty dollars to cover the check in a hurry, apparently in the hope of escaping the embarrassment of legal action in his home town.

Another case of Bennett's following his instinct was when a man, registered in the hotel and loaded with identification credentials, presented a check which Bennett refused to approve. He doesn't know why. Thirty minutes after this man had gone, promising that Statler hotels would never enjoy his patronage again, a second man hurried down to report that his room had been entered a short time before, and all of his identification credentials stolen. He described these to Bennett, who recognized them, from what the man said, as the same set of credentials that had been offered a half hour before by the man whose check he would not cash.

The most frequent type of character who gives hotels checks drawn on banks in which he has no account is a youngish fellow between twenty-five and thirty-five, well-dressed and nice-looking. In these times, he is apt to be a war casualty, suffering from some form of mental upset. Frequently, these men will write letters to themselves and attempt to use them as credentials. These letters are usually written on the stationery of some large business concern, and signed with the name of one of its officials, who appears to be on intimate terms with the man who has the letter.

Another popular device is the hurried approach, in the hope of catching the credit manager off balance. Such a procedure goes something like this: A man will rush into the credit office, in a "time-is-the-essence" manner, slap his check on the credit manager's desk, glance at his watch, and say in effect: "Here, please cash this. . . . I've got to catch a plane. . . . I know everybody who amounts to anything in the hotel. . . . I'm a close friend of the manager (giving the manager's nickname, if he has one). . . . He'd OK it in a minute if he were here . . . such a bother, and please hurry."

Still another method is the "broken-hearted approach," calculated to arouse such sympathy in a credit manager's breast that he will approve a check against his better judgment. In this role, the check casher enters the office softly as a tragic figure, frequently clutching—if not exactly a letter-edged-in-black—a telegram, which states that a near and dear member of the family is dying at home. These messages invariably arrive after banking hours. The recipient, of course, was not expecting such a tragic turn of events and is without cash at the moment. He appeals to the credit manager's humanitarian instincts to cash his check so he may have funds for transportation to the bedside before it is too late.

After getting stuck with worthless checks from a few characters such as the foregoing, credit managers grow to suspect anybody they do not know intimately who is anxious to cash a check in a hurry. Yet, it appears to many people, including employees of hotels who are in other departments, that a credit manager must be a heartless wretch, indeed, to turn down such soul-rending pleas. Once, in an effort to establish some point along these lines, the staff of the Boston Statler, at an employees' Christmas party, contrived to have their credit manager, E. H. Morris, served a plate of octopus meat, without his knowing what it was. The staff was delighted when the credit manager ate the octopus with relish, thereby establishing, to the staff's satisfaction at least, that credit managers thrive on strange and frightful fare.

There are times, of course, when credit managers, like almost everybody else, are carried away with passion in the case of some person who has proved to be an unusual trial. In such cases, the credit manager may take rash and radical steps, as happened once in the New York Statler when the credit manager flew into a rage when he got back two checks that a woman guest in the house had given him. This woman had not had the grace to flee before her checks returned, but was still residing in the hotel, blithely signing her meal checks when she had nothing with which to pay her bill.

The credit manager, accompanied by a house officer and carrying the two phony checks, advanced angrily upon her room. The woman was in the bathroom when they arrived, and refused to come out. Whereupon, the credit manager confiscated her belongings, and left instructions for her to leave the hotel immediately before he really got mad. The woman was unable to do this, since the credit office had all her clothing. The credit manager was, therefore, forced to relent to the extent of releasing one outfit so she could be gone.

By and large, however, credit managers are pretty much like other people. Some credit managers are, in fact, gentle people, who are soft-spoken, and considerate, among them Mr. A. G. Abbott, credit manager of the Washington Statler.

He looks more like a gentle, scholarly college professor than like the savage character that many people suppose credit managers to be. In his spare time, Mr. Abbott studies the science of sound as a hobby, and has recently completed a book-length manuscript upon that technical subject. He has also written a book on color and color tones. At this writing, he was having difficulty finding a publisher because, according to the publishing houses he had contacted, his works are too highbrow for the general reading public.

When a man unknown to him and without particularly convincing credentials approaches him with a personal check, Mr. Abbott goes about the matter in a scientific manner to determine if this man conforms in any respects to a pattern into which worthless check passers generally fall. This pattern, which the Washington credit manager has developed over the years of dealing with such persons, include some of the following points:

What about his appearance? Does he look like a businessman, a gentleman of leisure, an employee of a large concern or a race-track character. But, most important, *does he look like what he says he is?*

Then, how does he come in? Is he agitated and in a hurry? Does he have his personal checks? Is the amount he wishes to get reasonable? What the man says and the way he says it have a strong bearing on his case.

People who are trying to put something over are inclined to talk too much, make irrelevant remarks and try to get too familiar. Persons whose worthless check passing results from some form of mental unbalance, in particular, are apt to give themselves away by telling the credit manager all about their business and private and personal affairs. The hotel has no interest in this whatever, except that such disclosures tend to establish such a person as one who will bear watching.

If a credit manager suspects the authenticity of a check that purports to have been issued by a large business concern, he often notes the amount for which it has been drawn. This is to see whether, if it does happen to be forged, it would fall under the state's felony statutes, punishable by a long prison term, or whether the amount would confine it to a misdemeanor, punishable by a light stretch or a fine. If a check forged for fifty dollars or more becomes a felony in that state, a suspected check is much more apt to be forged if it is for slightly under fifty dollars.

Credit managers have found that another sound procedure in the case of company checks suspected of being fraudulent is to compare the signature on the hotel's registration card of the man wishing to have it cashed with the signature on the check purporting to be that of the company's paying officer. Occasionally the two signatures are in the same handwriting.

Hotel credit managers often warm up for the day by saying "No," in a pleasant way, to one of several faithful local characters, afflicted by drink who've been showing up for years early in the morning with red eyes, rumpled clothing, unshaven faces and monumental cases of the shakes. They haven't been a guest in a decent hotel in decades and nobody has cashed one of their checks in modern memory. But they keep coming back, year in and year out, presenting to the credit manager a check form filled out in a shaky scrawl that is as illegible as the check is worthless.

A sadder and more serious problem occurs when guests who have been good customers of the hotel for years suddenly take up drinking, or lose their job or their reason. Frequently, some traveling salesman who has been stopping at Statler hotels for twenty years will lose his job. He says nothing about this to the hotels, but keeps traveling from city to city, stopping in the hotels as he always did, as he looks for another connection. If he gets one, everything is fine. But, more frequently, his checks begin coming back one day marked "I.S.F."

Certain hotel check problems and procedures are typical of individual cities. In Detroit, for instance, where most people think a lot about automobiles, a good customer of the hotel is likely to want a check cashed for $2,000 to $3,000 over a weekend when the banks are closed, so he can make a quick car deal. But probably the most interesting of the individual city situations are those that the Washington Statler has with the "Big Deal Boys."

This type will sail into Washington with a big idea, but frequently very little cash. He needs a plushy hotel background in order to impress properly those to whom he hopes to sell his idea. The Statler, where a good many important people like to stay and where the President frequently comes, is ideal for this purpose.

"The Big Deal" is perhaps more characteristic of Washington in these times than the New Deal. A typical "Big Deal Boy" is likely to come to the national capital under circumstances something like these: Every now and then, the Government publishes a list of products it will wish to purchase over the next year or so as information to producers who may wish to submit bids. An "operator" in another city, after reading these lists, may get an idea that some small makers of products might, by combining their efforts, turn out in large quantities some materials the Government wishes to purchase. He will call a meeting of these producers, find out if they believe they could do this, and, if so, what commission they will give him if he secures for them such a contract.

He then advances upon Washington, gets a suite at the Statler, if he can arrange it, and starts in to make the proper impression by entertaining people he believes can help him get the contract. This calls for a lot of steak, lobster, crêpes Suzette, hors d'oeuvres, cold cuts, setups and strong and mild drink, mainly Scotch whisky and champagne.

All this outpouring of plenty is calculated, not only to please the palates of the proper people, but to impress them with the promoter's good address. The reputation for glamour of the Washington Statler and the company's high repute tend to encompass such a man—or so he hopes. That is probably the impression that gets out to a certain degree, since the hotel apparently approves of him and trusts him. After all, he is stopping there, and the hotel is extending credit.

The truth may be, however, that the hotel knows very little about its open-handed guest, whose intentions may be high but whose finances may be low. If his big deal pans out, he will enjoy great affluence; if it does not, he may have to take desperate measures, such as giving the hotel a bum check, in order to get out of town. It is the credit manager's responsibility to try to evaluate such a situation, and see that the man doesn't get in too deeply at the hotel. This is a complicated problem, since the credit manager knows the preponderance of the hotel's customers are completely reliable. Thus, he has to be doubly careful not to insult a reliable patron in an effort to protect the house from characters who are not.

In spite of all they have learned about human nature, most hotel credit managers will admit that an expert sharper can usually take them the first time, but seldom more than once. Chances are that they will bag him sooner or later. One of the smoothest of bad-check operators, who took in many hotels, was a former steward of a prominent girls' school. After losing his job there, he preyed upon hotels by pretending to arrange for a large student group from his former place of employment to stop in these hotels for a week during the summer vacation. He was so convincing about it that none of the hotels he approached ever thought it necessary to check with officials of the school he claimed to represent.

The hotels' sales departments were so anxious to get this good business, in the middle of the summer, that they gave the former steward all sorts of polite and solicitous attention. Besides that, he was highly convincing in his role as arranger of summer tours for elegant young ladies. He drew upon his past experiences in arranging a small banquet at the hotel for the visiting undergraduates and for a good number of prominent local matrons, who were alumnae of the school.

He was careful to eliminate all fried foods and various rich dishes from the proposed menus, and have substituted wholesome, health-giving dishes of herbs and greens. He also gave close attention to the location and arrangements of the rooms the visiting undergraduates were to occupy. He saw that these were not too costly, not too small, not too near the elevator shafts, but located where the young ladies could come and go with the least possible contact with male guests in the house.

This was all very proper and convincing to the sales-department representative, who by this time had made all sorts of concessions, in the hotel's name, on behalf of the young ladies, and had taken thousands of words of notes. Therefore, when the arranger mentioned that he would appreciate the hotel cashing his personal check for $200, the man from the sales department ushered him into the credit office, introduced him to the credit manager, and saw that he got his funds immediately.

The girls, of course, never arrived at the hotel, but the man's check came back there as a permanent resident. He worked his scheme upon numerous hotels along the eastern seaboard, but he finally came to grief in the New York Statler. The Washington Statler, which had fallen for his scheme, sent a detailed description of the man and his *modus operandi* to other houses in the organization.

Therefore, when he arrived eventually at the sales offices in the New York Statler, he was recognized by a sales representative, who asked him to have a seat for a few minutes. The hotel man then sped out to look for a policeman. His exit was so hurried, in fact, that the former steward suspected he was discovered, and took a hurried departure. He was followed by two secretaries and a bell-boy, who joined in the movement out of curiosity. They raised such a clamor that a police squad car pursued the man, and captured him on Seventh Avenue near Times Square.

But just because the New York Statler happened to nab this in-dividual is no indication that this house was too smart to fall for the same sort of scheme. One time a crafty operator arranged an imaginary banquet there for six hundred persons at eight dollars a plate, in addition to a couple of large luncheons and a cocktail party, which were to occur about four days later.

The New York sales department believed in him so strongly that it threw its weight around among Broadway ticket agencies to pro-cure for members of the organization 130 tickets to Hellzapoppin, then popular on the Great White Way. The hotel even paid for these tickets, expecting to collect from members of the organization.

But neither the banquet, the luncheons nor the cocktail party ever took place. After the hotel had cashed his bogus check for $100, the man disappeared and has never been heard of since in the region of Seventh Avenue and Thirty-third Street. Fortunately, the hotel suspected that something was wrong before it prepared the food for the banquet, but it was too late to dispose of all those theater tickets, which were forgotten in all the confusion until about two hours before curtain time.

And so it came to pass that the audience attending Hellzapoppin that night had a large representation of Statler Hotel employees— bellboys, porters, housemaids, engineers, cooks, dishwashers, wait-ers and house detectives—who seldom attend Broadway produc-tions. They had been amazed, upon getting off work that evening, to receive offers of free tickets, courtesy of the hotel management.

17

Glamour on Sixteenth Street

Except for the old Waldorf-Astoria that opened in New York in 1893, the Hotel Statler, which was opened in Washington, D. C., exactly fifty years later, has had more influence upon the thinking of hotel men than any single structure that has been built since American innkeeping graduated from the roadside tavern.

The old Waldorf set the style in atmosphere that the better hotels tried to copy for thirty-five years. Then, like a charming old lady who has stayed up too late, it bowed out hastily in 1929 just ahead of the financial debacle that ended the era that the old Waldorf-Astoria typified.

The Washington Statler, conceived during the tense time preceding the last war and completed in the midst of the war boom in the national capital, has become to many people who were there a sort of symbol of the excitement and glitter, the abundance of military brass, the mysterious rumors, the late parties and the clamor for sleeping space, thick steaks and good whisky that was wartime Washington.

The Statler is all mixed up in the memories that the Wacs and the Waves and the Washington-based military and the small businessmen, angling for Government contracts, took home to Sauk Center and Dubuque along with their moth-balled old uniforms and tired old brief cases. For if the Pentagon was the center of the Washington war effort, the new Statler hotel was the stronghold of the teeming social affairs and the hopped-up efforts to live today for tomorrow you may die.

Architecturally the Washington Statler is the most striking example among American hotels of the trend toward simplicity in appearance and increased efficiency in function. It was the first large commercial hotel that changed from the form that had been in vogue for half a century to the modern concept, with simple lines, wide picture windows, glass walls, and lobbies and public rooms designed more for utilitarian purposes than columned splendor.

It was the first modern type air-conditioned hotel. It inaugurated horizontal windows, and was the first hotel to make wide usage of studio beds, which are being copied widely, not only in this country, but in Central and South America. According to one prominent architect, upon his return from a visit to South America, the first thing a person notices when he enters a hotel architect's office down there is a worn-out copy of a special issue in 1943 of *The Hotel Monthly*, which devoted fifty-five pages to describing the Washington Statler. It predicted the Washington house would have "a profound effect on the future of hotel construction."

As with any change, the public reaction to the Washington Statler has not been entirely favorable. Some people hold that it is too cold and impersonal, like a Federal housing project. But most guests think it is wonderful, and go to all sorts of lengths to try to get rooms there.

Most hotel men are envious of its operational setup. Statler officials and experts put the results of their thirty-five years of operational experiences into the Washington house plans. They asked employees, from managers down to pot wallopers, to make suggestions about arrangements of their various departments in the new building, and adopted the suggestions that made sense.

The result is a hotel that can operate with extreme economy, so that the Washington Statler has been one of the most profitable hotels in the country during a period of great hotel prosperity. The Washington Statler has an income of only slightly more than a third of the Waldorf's. Yet, it has been showing a profit annually of almost three times that of the palace on Park Avenue.

In view of the dramatic success the Washington Statler has enjoyed ever since it opened, it seems queer now to reflect on the trouble the company had getting the project started.

Some Statler directors were against it when the hotel was proposed in 1938. They felt the company had better be content with its existing hotels, particularly since the hotel business was still in sad shape from the depression. But Arthur F. Douglas, who was executive vice-president of the company at the time, felt that building a new hotel in Washington would shoot some life into the Statler organization, which had been stagnant since the death of E. M. Statler ten years before.

Nobody was interested in lending anybody money who was nuts enough to want to build a hotel. The big insurance companies had invested heavily in the hotel building boom of the 1920's. Then they lost heavily when most of the hotels they had financed went broke during the depression. Insurance companies were sick of hotels. They did not care to lend money even to the Statler Company, which had emerged from the depression intact. The Metropolitan Life Insurance Company agreed cautiously to lend up to $2,000,000 for the Washington house. But Statler needed to borrow at least $5,000,000. The hotel was expected to cost $8,000,000.

Then one Saturday night, Arthur Douglas attended a Gridiron Club dinner, where he was introduced to Jesse Jones, chairman of the Reconstruction Finance Corporation. Jones, who had long been a friend of the Statler executive's brother, Associate Justice William O. Douglas, asked Arthur Douglas what he did.

"I," said Douglas, "am in the hotel business. I am with the Statler Company, and I'd just like to say that we would love the best in the world to be able to build a new hotel here in Washington. We would build one where they could throw a real Gridiron dinner, if somebody would just lend us the money."

Jones told Douglas to come by his office on Monday, and the R.F.C. would lend him five million dollars. He added that Washington needed a hotel such as the Statler people would operate, and predicted—correctly, as it turned out—that, within two years after the hotel opened, the R.F.C. would dispose of the mortgage to a private investor at a good profit. That happened about as he said. The Aetna Life Insurance Company was so impressed by Statler's Washington operation that it refinanced the 4 per cent R.F.C. loan for 3½ per cent, and the R.F.C. was paid $50,000 for allowing the life insurance company to do so.

The site chosen was near the White House on Sixteenth Street between K and L Streets; construction began early in 1941. Statler quickly encountered difficulties with the Washington zoning laws that limit the height of buildings, and which several times almost stopped the job. As it was, in order to get in sufficient facilities to handle the big Washington functions, the number of rooms was limited to 850. The company would have preferred to build at least 1,000 rooms. But while the number of rooms had to be limited, the company devoted larger areas to dining rooms and public spaces than any other Washington hotel had.

To get as many rooms as they did, ceilings of guest rooms were built several inches lower than usual, and furniture was designed to give the rooms the illusion of being higher than they were. This turned out rather fortunately, since it was found that in an air-conditioned hotel, the lower ceilings work just as well, and that much useless wall space is eliminated to help offset high building costs.

Statler had anticipated the wartime material shortages, and when the hotel site had been bought, the company began laying in its steel, laundry equipment, linen, hardware, kitchen and air-conditioning equipment. Even then, when the war arrived, the company had a terrible time persuading the Government to allow it to use some of its own equipment that had been built and stored for two years.

The company had planned to make a great thing of its aluminum window frames, the first ever used in a hotel, but about the time they were ready for installing, the drive for scrap aluminum began. With the late F. H. LaGuardia, chairman of the drive, screaming that somebody's old teakettle would win the war, Statler did not consider it politic to hang all that aluminum on the outside of its building, located, as it was, just five blocks from the White House. So the company sighed sadly, and threw $75,000 worth of fine aluminum window frames upon the stockpile.

This turned out to be unnecessary because the frames were never used in the war effort in the first place, and the Statler people got blamed for being unpatriotic with aluminum anyway. This happened after a truck loaded with aluminum for the Pentagon Building broke down in front of where the Statler was being built. Some newspaper columnists heard of it being there, assumed it was for the Statler, and proclaimed it to the world.

The biggest setback came in the fall of 1941 when nine floors of steel framework had been erected, and wooden forms for the concrete had been built up to the fourth floor. Several carloads of lumber, which was stacked on the ground, caught fire one Sunday afternoon. It was one of Washington's most spectacular fires in years, and it just about ruined the Washington Statler forever.

Actually, it ruined 290 heavy steel beams, and new steel was unobtainable. The Government had put a priority on every piece of steel that was to be rolled for the next year and a half. Statler officials were about ready to give up for the duration, and write off as a loss the $6,000,000 they had already put into their hotel-to-be.

But the American Bridge Company, which was erecting the steel, began to comb all the small steelyards in the country and to canvas the second-hand dealers in that precious commodity. They came up with an assortment of odd beams of various lengths and descriptions, but of sufficient strength for the purpose. These were sawed in proper lengths and fabricated into the framework. And so, after six weeks delay, work resumed, and hopes brightened somewhat for the Statler, but heavy going was still ahead.

Fires seemed to haunt the project. Several months after the first one, two trucks loaded with new and hard-to-replace furniture for the hotel burned on a nearby parking lot. When fires were not invading the place, officers of the Army and Navy were. They had their eyes on the hotel as a possible WAC or WAVE roost. Generals and admirals were as thick as carpenters about the nearly finished building. They would walk through the lobby and public rooms admiring things. Arthur Douglas, hiding in what was to be the credit manager's office, viewed the visits of the military with foreboding.

For a while it appeared that the Washington-based military was as anxious to capture the new Statler as the Pacific-based forces were to take Guadalcanal. Then one Friday, just a week before the hotel was to accept its first guests, a young junior-grade naval lieutenant strode into the manager's office, and announced that he was taking over the hotel as territory of the United States Navy. He didn't actually raise a flag, but he made it clear that his orders were from higher up, and if the Statler people resisted, he would, on the following Monday, return with condemnation papers.

Douglas, who was about ready to strike his colors and resign from the company at this point, managed to get in touch with the late James V. Forrestal, then Under-Secretary of the Navy. Forrestal had not, until then, been apprised of this piece of naval strategy, and, fortunately for Statler, he took an unenthusiastic view of it.

Forrestal appeared to feel that seizing the fine new hotel might give the impression that the Navy was more at home in the cocktail lounge than on the bounding main. Besides, there had been criticism in some quarters about the military taking over the Vanderbucks Arms and such for WAC or WAVE quarters when the Y.W.C.A. would have served the purposes better.

And so, on January 18, 1943, the Washington Statler accepted its first guests in 250 rooms of the still uncompleted hotel. But even as the cash register began to ring, the Statler people ran into more troubles. The maids, who were preparing the new rooms, found that the mattresses would not fit the beds. They were about four inches too short.

They had been stored for two years on their ends, so that their own weight had caused them to collapse, like accordions. The management hired a crew of husky workmen, and armed them with clubs. They set about beating the mattresses unmercifully. By evening they had been beaten out until they were long enough to fit the beds.

The management got its last big scare on January 30, 1943 when the Embassy Room, the big swanky dining room, was to have its grand opening. A large delegation from Hollywood and Broadway were present, including Robert Young, Laraine Day, Dennis Morgan, Loretta Young, Roy Rogers, Fred Waring, Edgar Bergen, Janet Blair, James Cagney, Abbott and Costello and Lawrence Tibbett.

It looked like a very large evening, except for one minor matter; the Embassy Room had no chairs. With half of Hollywood on hand, the Washington Statler had no place for the celebrities to sit. The Embassy Room chairs were en route from New York by truck, but

an ice storm had enfolded the land between Washington and Philadelphia, and the drivers had decided the roads were too slippery to
proceed further. They had taken refuge in a bar somewhere in
Delaware when the Statler officials got in touch with them by telephone, and offered a twenty-five-dollar bonus to each truck if they
made it into Washington with the chairs in time for the room's
opening.

The affair was to start at 6:00 P.M., and at ten minutes past five,
the trucks rolled in. The management put every available employee
into a line from the trucks' tailgates in through a side door, through
the lobby and into the Embassy Room. They passed chairs hand to
hand like a bucket brigade fighting a fire. Ten minutes before the
room was scheduled to open, the chairs were in place.

From that night on the Embassy Room of the Washington Statler
has been one of the bright entertainment spots of the nation, much
to the surprise of the Statler Company. Before the Statler was built
there, the national capital had never supported a swanky night spot.
Therefore, when the company was planning its Washington house,
it did not count on its Embassy Room becoming to Washington
what a combination of the Copacabana and the Stork Club would
be in New York.

In fact, the company had intended its Embassy Room to be only
half as large as it is. The half of the room nearest the entrance had
been planned as a cocktail lounge, separate from the dining room.
However, it had been arranged so that a heavy curtain, separating
the two, could be moved, and the two rooms thrown together on
fiesta nights every now and then.

The two rooms were thrown together for opening night because
of the big first-night crowd. Furthermore, Xavier Cugat and his
orchestra were entertaining and any sensible management would
arrange to have them in the largest room possible, considering the
size of Cugat's outfit and all the noise it makes. But after opening
night, the entire room filled up every night, and business in the
Embassy Room has remained so excellent ever since 1943 that the
big curtain, which would have cut it in half, has never been drawn.

The Embassy Room has since featured regularly such high-
bracket entertainers as Dorothy Shay, Carl Brisson, Victor Borge,
Guy Lombardo and Hildegarde. These entertainers also appear

occasionally in the other Statler houses, but Washington has them most often. Lesser-known entertainers, performing in other Statler houses, are constantly besieging John B. Grande, Statler vice-president in charge of food and entertainment, to put them in the Embassy Room—at much bigger money, of course.

As a defense mechanism, Grande is said to have adopted a policy, whenever he is in one of the Statler supper rooms, of gripping his nose, as though he smelled something unpleasant. This is calculated to forestall entertainers from getting a too-exalted view of their own art.

Hotels seldom make very much profit from their entertainment room when one of the more costly stars is performing there. It takes an awful lot of dinners to pay some entertainer $5,000 a week on top of all the food and service expenses. However, the expensive acts give a hotel publicity and prestige, and add to the aura of gaiety and sparkle that the general public likes to associate with life in hotels.

Until the Embassy Room came along, the chief entertainment spot in the Statler organization was the Café Rouge of the New York Statler, formerly the Hotel Pennsylvania, which has been renowned as a citadel of the dance since that hotel opened in 1919.

The Pennsylvania Hotel was completed at about the time the rage for big dance bands was beginning. The late Mr. Statler opened the hotel with Vincent Lopez' orchestra for entertainment, and that house has stuck exclusively with big bands ever since. Italian waiters and captains in the dining room, who have the ear for fine music inherent in their race, view some of these musical aggregations with mixed emotions. They suffer dreadfully from all that noise, but they love the big crowds—and tips—that the big bands draw to the Café Rouge.

During one of his Pennsylvania Hotel engagements in the 1930's, when he introduced the "Big Apple" there, Benny Goodman asked Julius, the craggily handsome and distinguished assistant headwaiter, what he thought of music à la Goodman. Julius, an old-timer in his field, replied: "It stinks! It's awful! But God bless you for those beautiful crowds."

When building their Washington house, the Statler people had their eyes on the big, semiofficial social events, particularly the two

annual dinners of the Gridiron Club, an organization of newspapermen who present skits ridiculing various national and international
personalities and happenings. The Gridiron affairs are attended by
the President, the top crust of Washington officialdom, most of the
people currently figuring in the news and prominent figures from
all over the world. Accounts of Gridiron doings are carried at length
in most large newspapers, and Statler yearned to be in on this
prestige and publicity.

The Gridiron dinners had been held for years in the Willard
Hotel, across the street from the National Press Club, but facilities
there were not well adapted to stage presentations. Statler built its
Presidential Ballroom with the Gridiron Club specifically in mind.

Dressing rooms were included, and, at the suggestion of Gridiron
officials, blueprints were changed at the last minute to eliminate a
balcony. A mirrored wall was substituted for a wall of windows that
had been planned to look out over L Street, after it was pointed
out that the Secret Service does not approve of windows and balconies in rooms the President frequents.

For a week before a function is held that the President will attend, the Secret Service meets with the hotel personnel to work out
exactly where the President will be at various times during the
evening, where photographs will be made and when, who will have
charge of escorting the President about the hotel and so on. The
S.S. checks to see that no waiters or kitchen help with known subversive tendencies work that night.

After the new Statler was built, the Gridiron Club, White House
Correspondents Association, White House Photographers, Radio
Correspondents, Women's Press Club and such have held their
affairs there. The same waiter, Angelo Keperis, has served the
President and the three persons sitting to his right at every function
the President has attended in the hotel since these affairs have been
held there. Also, the same waiter, Max Reuss, has flanked the
President, serving the person on his left, usually the Chief Justice,
and the three or four persons to his left.

Waiter Keperis, a short, bald, grinning man, who doesn't hear
very well, reports that Mr. Truman is an easy man to please at table.
He eats what everyone else does, but prefers his meat well done.
"Cooked to death," according to Chef Emil Buisson, who always

puts a sprig of greenery on top of the President's serving so the waiter will be sure which is his.

In spite of all these pains, there have been times when an error was made in serving the President, of all people. When Joseph Short, of the Baltimore *Sun*, was appointed the President's Press Secretary to succeed the late Charles G. Ross, Short was promptly stricken with stomach ulcers, an affliction that goes with his job. Not long after that, the Statler was arranging the first big dinner the President was to attend since Short became secretary, and Short telephoned the hotel to say he could eat only clear consommé and a dish of custard, under doctor's orders.

Unfortunately, the hotel got the impression that Short was ordering this meal for the President. Some radio commentators heard about it in some way, and sent forth tidings that the President's stomach was acting up. On the night of the dinner, the President was served a bowl of clear consommé and a dish of custard, while his secretary got the steak dinner.

Short, a self-effacing individual, went ahead and ate the heavy food rather than cause any trouble, and the President managed to worry down the clear consommé. But when the dish of custard was set before him, Mr. Truman rebelled. He gave the custard a scornful look, and announced that he was hungry, and in perfect health. He said, for goodness sake, take that gooey stuff away, and bring him some meat and potatoes.

When Mr. Roosevelt was President, the Statler's chef usually made a special plate for him from ingredients sent over from the White House. But Mr. Truman eats almost anything, and has a bigger appetite than his predecessor, according to Waiter Keperis, who says Mr. Truman also laughs louder at the show. The President usually has one roll with his meal, seldom touches wine, and wants the coffee pot left at his elbow after the meal so he can help himself.

There are always 548 guests at the Gridiron dinner, where terrapin Maryland is always served. The rest of the menu may vary, but the terrapin is a must. The terrapin cost the hotel about three dollars each, and it takes twenty-three dozen to serve the party.

The skits are sometimes rough on the prominent people being roasted on the gridiron, but they also took a lot out of Henry Rising, building superintendent of the Washington Statler until he was transferred to the Los Angeles Statler, while it was being built. It was his job for years to supervise the building of the sets, which were usually designed by Jim Berryman, cartoonist with the Washington *Evening Star*. It is not every hotel building superintendent who has to dash off now and then a stage set that resembles a prop in a Ziegfeld finale, as Rising did for the United Nations Club show.

The Presidential Ballroom, scene of this hilarity, is as good an example as any of the architectural and functional differences between the Washington Statler and most of its predecessors. Traditionally, a hotel ballroom has a stuffy formality, with columns, vaulted ceilings, balconies, mirrors, chandeliers and galleries. They are pretty changeless, no matter whether the occasion is the Junior League ball or a display of the latest coffins at an undertaker's convention.

The Presidential Ballroom is extremely plain, except for a sculptured American eagle on the ceiling and some simple sculptures over the doors of the same hue as the oyster-white walls. There is no set stage, but a portable one that can be made any size and set up at any place in the room desired. The room has a lighting setup comparable to a large theater.

In fact, the room depends entirely for its decorations upon lights, cold cathode of white, red, blue, green, yellow and other colors. The architects felt that a more convincing effect could be produced through lighting than by stringing tinsel and setting up cardboard scenery and potted flora. Certainly, it is instantaneous and no added expense to change the atmosphere from romantic moonlight for a dance to a bright, efficient, showroom for displaying, say, some new refrigerators. The only weakness in the whole idea is that the hotel's lighting men have to be pretty careful with some of their color combinations, which may tend to give persons attending a gay party the color of zombies.

When the Washington Statler opened, it had perhaps ten times as many applications for permanent quarters, business and residential, as there were rooms in the house. Among the prominent firms and individuals applying for office or living quarters were the Coca-Cola Company, James F. Byrnes, the Ford Motor Company, the late Justice Frank Murphy, Armour & Company, Senator Herbert

H. Lehman of New York, various other congressmen and senators, the late Harry Hopkins and The Saturday Evening Post. The hotel didn't have the space for any of these people or corporations.

There was also a great push by concessionaires and shopowners to operate in the shop and store space the hotel lobby afforded. The pickings are always good for shopkeepers in the Washington Statler, but during the war, business for them was fabulous. According to Miss Margaret Graham, who runs the men's haberdashery shop in the Statler, it wasn't unusual for one of the big spender's bills for clothes, flowers, candy and perfume to run to $600 to $700 a week. Most of the big spenders were representing manufacturers. They charged these items on their hotel bills, and sent them in as "expenses." Some of them bought so much that it was embarrassing to the shopkeepers, who knew, of course, that they were spending money that was not their own.

But this rosy existence of the boys with the expense accounts, their wives and women—who lived in a cloud of hard-to-get Scotch and steaks, perfumes, furs and flowers—is gone. Every now and then, one of the former big spenders will show up around the Washington Statler. His suit may be shiny in the seat and across the shoulders. He no longer wears a thirty-five dollar hand-painted necktie, and he frequently wants one of the shopkeepers to cash his check, usually for twenty-five dollars. These men don't try the hotel credit department any more. The credit manager knows their checks have been coming back ever since 1946.

About four-thirty o'clock each afternoon, the wartime cocktail set would descend upon the Washington Statler in a swirl of mink and high brass uniforms. They always overflowed the veranda, filled the glass-walled front lobby, and occasionally spilled out into Sixteenth Street. But people looking for rooms were on hand at all hours, including after midnight.

With the hotel jam-packed and shaking with war excitement, crowds of people who had no place to stay eddied back and forth in front of the registration desk. Practically every hotel in the country had all the war business it was able to handle, but the Washington Statler was the apex of war-crowded conditions. The people who applied there daily for rooms could scarcely have been bedded down in the Pentagon. The line waiting at the room desk was so long one night that a man toward the rear walked over to the Western Union desk, and sent a telegram to the room clerk. He figured it would go through all the telegraph channels and be delivered to the room desk before he got there.

The room situation at the Washington Statler has quieted down now, of course, but the demand remains so great that the hotel has never accepted permanent guests. It is probably the only hotel in the country that has observed the seven-day-stay limit ever since the close of the war. People resort to all kinds of schemes to get reservations there. They send the hotel photographs of themselves and their families, write their room needs in jingle form, send in Statler advertisements clipped from magazines with their letters, call the hotel long distance from the West Coast and from ships at sea, or they may get their congressman or senator to bring pressure.

Except for one week, the Washington Statler has been ninety-five per cent occupied since it was built. The reason it has not been a hundred per cent occupied is that rooms must be taken out of service for painting and redecoration. The week it was not full was in January, 1949, when President Truman was inaugurated. There had been tremendous advance publicity saying that every inch of living space in Washington was taken that week. People were reported bedding down as far away as Philadelphia. So those who came for the big affair thought it was useless to try the hotels, and the Statler was only forty-five per cent occupied.

Aside from handling more prominent figures and celebrities than any other Statler house, the Washington Statler has to grapple with other special problems. For one thing, citizens of Washington are highly flag conscious. In front of the hotel on a clipped lawn along Sixteenth Street, the hotel has two large flagpoles, from which United States flags are generally flown.

However, if the hotel's flag custodian is one minute after sundown getting the flags down, the switchboard gets numerous calls from people who demand to know if the Statler is not aware of proper flag etiquette. "And if one of the flags happens to touch the grass when it is being raised or lowered," one hotel official has pointed out, "some indignant old D.A.R., who is sure to be passing at that moment, will come in and give us a very hard time."

The hotel occasionally has trouble getting special flags large enough to go well on its big flagpoles. When some foreign dignitary comes to Washington, the District of Columbia usually distributes flags to most of the prominent buildings along with banners saying "Viva el Presidente" and such sentiments. But the five-by-ten foot flags the District gives away are not large enough for the Statler flagpoles.

When President Auriol, of France, was given a big Washington reception in the spring of 1951, the Statler had a large French flag flown across from Paris, since a proper flag was not available in Washington. When it arrived, the hotel's flag custodian was interested to note that it was stamped, "Made in New York." When General MacArthur's reception was held in Washington last summer, and he stopped at the Statler, the hotel asked the Pentagon to send over a large five-star general's flag. After the reception was over and General MacArthur had gone, the hotel learned that the flag the military had sent was actually General Omar N. Bradley's flag, who many believed was responsible for General MacArthur's being relieved of his command.

Even Hollywood has joined in to help impress the general public that the Washington Statler is one of the land's chief glamour spots. The motion picture, *Born Yesterday,* was written and also laid in the Washington Statler, but the films overplayed Statler's splendor, as the movies often do. They built a set representing a Statler suite that was more expansive and ornate, perhaps, than anything this side of the Taj Mahal.

People still show up daily at the hotel, asking to be allowed a look at this wonderful suite. For a while after the picture came out, the hotel management was embarrassed by this. The Presidential suite was nowhere near as gorgeous as what had been shown in the movies. But the visitors were deeply impressed anyhow.

In fact, the Washington Statler is not a luxurious hotel. It is a good, comfortable commercial hotel that has become the most glamorous thing in Washington principally because it is the first commercial hotel that has departed from the old hotel-building tradition, established before the First World War. The Washington Statler is one of the few large hotels anywhere—and it was the first—that reflects with its glass walls, efficient arrangements and absence of adornment the type of age in which the world is living today.

An example of how the hotel has caught the national fancy is a two-column, front-page story once carried in the Lynchburg, Virginia, *News* concerning the adventures of one Arnold Silverman, local jeweler, who got to spend a night in the Presidential suite by accident, so to speak. He arrived at the Statler with a reservation, but all the rooms were occupied except the big 1240 suite. So he and Mrs. Silverman were put up there for the night at the price they would have had to pay for an ordinary double room.

In an interview with one of the writers for the Lynchburg *News*, Mr. Silverman, in describing their night in the suite, expressed pretty well the way that a good many people have come to regard the Washington Statler:

"Ah those lamps," Silverman said. "Those gorgeous decorations. The beautiful sun deck. It was all like a dream—a beautiful, beautiful dream."

18

They're All Dirty

An important reason why the Hotels Statler Company, Inc., chose
Washington, D. C., to locate its first new hotel since the death of
the firm's founder was its belief that Washington had no hotel well
designed to handle large conventions. This was true even though
the national capital was a natural convention center with all sorts
of drawing attractions ranging from the country's most famous
monuments for dead heroes to the lusty and living New Deal and
Franklin Delano Roosevelt.

The Statler became an important factor in Washington's increased
convention activities, which in 1939, a normal before-Statler year,
amounted to 125 conventions with 50,000 delegates, who spent
$3,500,000. In 1949, a normal after-Statler year, Washington had
216 conventions with 120,000 delegates, who left $12,750,000 with
Washington's business concerns, of which the greatest single bene-
ficiary was the Washington Statler.

An estimated one-fourth of the entire Statler organization's gross income—about $50,000,000 for 1949, a normal year—comes from convention delegates. In view of these facts, a person can easily see why Statler—and most other hotels as well—knock themselves out being nice to conventions, even though most of the hotel's other patrons take an extremely critical view of all conventions—other than their own annual affair, of course. Probably nothing can so infuriate a traveling man as to be informed that no rooms are available because a convention is in the house.

The Statler organization keeps up-to-date dossiers on some 2,000 national groups that hold conventions attended by 100 or more delegates. Conventions with fewer delegates than that hardly make it worth a large hotel's while to reserve public rooms and provide free meeting space. The choice conventions are the big ones, such as the American Medical Association, American Bar Association, American Dental Association and the United States Chamber of Commerce. But the red carpet is rolled out with éclat for lesser-known groups such as the Guild of Banjoists, Mandolinists and Guitarists, the Grand Lodge of the Ladies Auxiliary of the Order of Scottish Clans, the Mystic Order of the Veiled Prophets of the Enchanted Realm, Ancient Order of Hibernians in America, American Ichthyologists and Herpetologists and the International Concatenated Order of Hoo-Hoo.

The rowdy conventions, often those of veterans or fraternal groups, are a trial to hotel staffs, which sometimes have to condition themselves physically and psychologically to cope with unpredictable situations. The Statlers' security steps include removing from rooms all wastebaskets, which are handy as missiles and as water containers for dropping out of high windows upon the passing populace. For the latter reason, corners are snipped from paper laundry bags in guest rooms. Ink wells, coat hangers, telephone directories and other possible missiles are removed. So are the pillows, which are not returned to the rooms until late at night when the guests are weary and not as impulsive as they are earlier in the day.

A goose-feather pillow, when ripped open, becomes the hydrogen bomb of all hotel equipment. Carpets and all the furniture are removed from the lobby because guests, particularly if they are the

American Legion, will wish to make fires in the middle of the lobby floor, recalling possibly their grim, gay days of 1918 when they warmed corned beef over campfires.

Probably the quietest and best-behaved of all conventions is the On Leong Merchants Association, a group of Chinese businessmen who meet almost every year in one of the Statlers. They never make any newspaper headlines, but, on the other hand, neither do they undertake to destroy the hotel. The On Leongs retire early, and do not keep other guests awake all night with resounding story and song. They never get drunk, or ask for unusual services, or try to cash bum checks, or chase the housemaids around the corridors, or run out of money before paying their bill. When the convention is over, its secretary, armed with a big roll of money, visits the cashier and pays for everybody.

Most conventions go unnoticed in the columns of large metropolitan newspapers. To rate a spread on page one in the *New York Times* a convention in these times would have to be the occasion for the revelation of a cure for some dread disease, or the announcement of a great new weapon of war, or the disclosure of some vast sociological movement.

So far as treatment of the colorful, human-interest overtones of conventions are concerned, these are likely to resemble an event reported in the St. Louis newspapers, during an American Legion convention in that city: Miss Frankie Beamer, a stenographer, had filed suit for $25,000 against the American Legion, the Hotel Statler and the City of St. Louis. Her complaint was that, while she was in the Statler lobby, some playful Legionnaires fired a small cannon there, startling her so that she leaped into the air and fractured her tibia. She sued the Legion because its members had perpetrated this deed, the Statler because it happened in its lobby, and the City of St. Louis for allowing the Legion in town at all.

There are now about 19,000 national groups in America that hold conventions. These range from an association of nudists, who have some understandable difficulties finding hotels that will accept their business, on up to the Church of God, about whom hotels are not too happy either. Too many delegates of the latter take an uncompromising view of certain frivolities demanded by most guests, as one Church of God delegate did when he heard a radio playing

in the Cleveland Statler. He told the management that he regarded
radios as sinful, and unless all of them in the hotel were shut off
immediately, he would take his business elsewhere.

Some national groups seem to exist for the sole purpose of holding a convention every year. If newspapers attempted to cover fully
all conventions that are held, their columns would contain little
else. For the convention, in our time, has grown into an amazing
part of current Americana, constituted, as it is, of hot air, hoopla
and hangovers, of broiled-chicken banquets, toastmasters and bore-
dom. Most of all, conventions have become a national excuse to go
some place and blow off some steam.

The Statler people were among the first to realize the great business potentialities for hotels that existed in the rise of the conventioning habit among Americans. Statler became the first hotel
company to organize a sales department to sell its hotels and their
services to conventioning groups. This department, developed and
headed by Howard F. Dugan, vice-president in charge of sales
and advertising, is mainly responsible for the fact that Statler en-
tertains more conventions than anybody else.

The company has about fifty salesmen in all, located in each city
where there is a Statler hotel and in Chicago. The salesmen keep
an ear to the ground to learn what cities a group is considering
for its convention two or three years hence. (Large conventions are
generally scheduled that far in advance.) A first-class convention
salesman needs to have qualities of an international spy to learn
the inside dope. He must have a willingness to be defeated upon
the golf course by the proper people, and he needs a cast-iron
stomach to be able to triumph in his sales arguments when the
question of selecting a convention city resolves itself into a drinking
session.

The sales departments keep in touch with secretaries of trade
associations, which hold large conventions. Statler salesmen cultivate these men, since the permanent secretary of such a group
is generally the boss of the convention. Thus, trade-association
secretaries are regarded as slightly sacred by Statler salesmen.
Some secretaries of very large groups are presented by the company
with Gold Cards, a magic credential around a Statler hotel that
entitles the bearer to almost every privilege short of shooting the
manager.

When angling for a convention to come to his hotel, the salesman agrees that the hotel will furnish a certain large number of rooms for housing the delegates and public rooms sufficient for all the scheduled meetings, dinners, committee sessions and usually a suite to serve as headquarters for the executive secretary. When the convention arrives, this salesman becomes "Mr. Statler" to the group. He sees that it is provided with signs, and that necessary printing is done. He sees to the making or mounting of display models of buildings, ships or mountain ranges. He sees that the convention officials have typewriters, stenographers, telephones, mimeographing machines, dictating equipment, flowers or entertainers. He is on call to help members get checks cashed, or to hand an eye-opener to some prominent official of the group, who is having trouble arising in the morning after a hard night.

Once during a convention of scientists at the New York Statler, arrangements had to be made for Dr. J. R. Dunning, of Columbia University, to bring in equipment necessary to explode a miniature atomic bomb there. In the Washington Statler, arrangements were made for reception of one of the first broadcasts of live color television. This was for members of the American Urological Society to witness some operations being performed in local hospitals.

Once in St. Louis, arrangements were made for the International Association of Bridge, Structural and Ornamental Iron Workers to cash $200,000 worth of expense checks for their delegates during a three-hour period one Friday afternoon. This involved bringing in a portable vault, filled with money, from a local bank. It was accompanied by two bank guards, three policemen, three cashiers and the bank manager.

In Buffalo, it was only by exercising great firmness that Manager Theodore Krueger restrained officials of an insurance convention from putting on a life-saving demonstration with the Buffalo Fire Department rescuing a live woman from a fifteenth-floor window of the Buffalo Statler. Krueger, who had visions of somebody slipping and the remains of the lady spread out on the sidewalk in front of his hotel, finally prevailed on them to use a dummy, but the convention people were not happy about it.

At one convention in the Washington Statler, a twenty-five-foot model of the cruiser, *Juneau*, was built in the lobby. For the International Apple Association meeting there one summer, eight large apple trees were groomed for months ahead of the convention so they would be in the full splendor of their bloom when it came time to set them in tubs of earth in the lobby. After the convention was over, some members of the hotel staff removed the trees, and planted them in their own back yards, where they are still doing very well.

The sales departments, before booking an organization whose origins and purposes they do not know, always make a check to see if they are Communist-backed or otherwise subversive. Statler sales departments also have to be on the lookout when certain male convention groups mention that at one dinner session they want "absolute privacy." This may well mean that the entertainment being planned involves some young women disrobing. The Statler Company regards such entertainment as beneath the dignity of their houses.

Another duty of the sales department is to guard against rings of crooked gamblers, who sometimes haunt large conventions. These men often make contact with delegates by boarding trains on which they know delegates are en route to the convention city. It is easy to become friendly with the delegates, who are often in a relaxed mood and liberal in their estimation of strangers. By the time they reach the convention city, they are all old pals. The delegates may procure for the gamblers guest badges, and register them as their guests.

The gamblers will strike some night when a group of convention-ers is gathered in some suite, and somebody suggests a game of dice. Occasionally, along toward dawn, some delegate, smarter than the rest, will examine the dice of the men who are doing all the winning—and whom nobody seems to know very well—and find the dice are loaded. The hotel officers are then called in, but the affair usually ends by the gamblers making restitution and getting out of town. Neither the hotel nor the organization wants the publicity that would arise from calling police. The luggage of some gamblers who follow conventions has been found to contain as high as 100 pairs of dice—all crooked.

Another parasite that preys upon conventions is the professional moocher. He is an ingratiating individual who manages to mingle with the guests as though he were a delegate, and walk into all the free cocktail parties and dinners. He can consume great amounts of food and drink, and his ego is refreshed, for some queer reason, through posing as a prominent convention-goer.

Sales departments have also to be forever on guard against booking more conventions at a time than the house can handle. Frequently there are dozens of organizations that want to hold their conventions in the same hotel the same week. The worst week of the year for that is when baseball's World Series is being played in October, one of the biggest convention months.

When a baseball team representing one of the Statler cities is leading the league on July 4, many business firms will write the Statler there with the idea of arranging their convention to coincide with the World Series, if it is played there. Others want to engage large blocks of rooms so that they can reward their prize salesmen with trips to the Series. The hotel probably is already scheduled with conventions, and, as far as the local baseball team is concerned, it hasn't won the pennant yet by a long shot.

Yet, a good many disappointed sales managers of firms, whose representatives stop regularly at the Statler, get pretty sore about this. The hotel may find rooms for some of them, but then the team may not be in the Series at all, or, even if it is, the people who have managed to get rooms may not be able to get tickets. In either case, the people for whom the rooms have been engaged do not show up that week. They seldom notify the hotel that they are not coming. This situation has been particularly trying to the Boston Statler because of the Boston Red Sox team. It has won only one pennant, but has been threatening to win almost every year since the end of the last war. From the hotel's standpoint, that is worse than winning.

The most desirable of large conventions are divided into two general types: First, the scholarly and dignified conventions that are apt to make news, and get the hotel much choice publicity, but which are seldom great spenders of money. Second, the convention that seldom makes the headlines, but whose delegates and guests flood the coffers of the house with cash.

One of the most desirable of all conventions is the American Trucking Association, with 2,200 delegates, mainly owners and operators of fleets of trucks. They never do anything very newsworthy, but they do spend a lot of money with the hotel. The big truck, machinery and tire manufacturers give elaborate suite parties, with abundant refreshments. At a three-day convention, this group may spend from $150,000 to $200,000.

On the other hand, the National Education Association, attended by about the same number as the truckers' convention, is apt to make a lot of news. But its delegates, who are more interested in scholarly things than in making whoopee, will spend considerably less. Organizations like the Daughters of the American Revolution bring the hotel prestige, but do not spend much money either, except with the stand that sells picture postcards.

"They buy postcards and stamps all day long and until the stand closes at night—thousands and thousands of them," Miss Margaret Graham, who runs the haberdashery shop in the Washington Statler, has observed. "Once in a while one of them will think of her husband back home, and buy a tie for him from me—an inexpensive tie, that is."

There are conventions that do not bring a hotel any particular prestige, and whose delegates do not spend much money, but which do create a lot of noise. These gatherings have been well described by the permanent lady guest in the Cleveland Statler whom we have quoted before.

"I call these 'Overall Conventions,'" she was saying not long ago. "They are the fellows who go trooping into the Café Rouge—they wouldn't spend the money to go to the Terrace Room—in their shirt sleeves and without neckties. When they find they can't get in without a coat and tie, they're insulted. 'Why in hell can't I get in without a jacket?' they'll say. 'I'm with the convention, ain't I? What the devil kind of sissy joint you folks think you're running anyway?'

"Then, in a happier mood, they'll stand in a bunch out in the middle of the lobby, falling all over each other with playfulness. They'll slap one another on the back, and poke this and that one in the ribs. Then they'll see one of their members just arriving at the hotel. They haven't seen him since last year. This is really great, the way they greet him.

"'God damn, boy, are you getting fat. Look at that gut! And with that loud go-to-hell shirt on, too!' They will then punch this fellow in the belly a few times, and if his wife is along, they'll make a great to-do about kissing her. She is a big triple-chinned character in a light, flowered dress, with short sleeves and her fat arms flared out like pregnant liverwursts. All these guys will pat her behind, and say how they think they will trade off their wives for her."

In the experience of most large hotels, two of the most exasperating conventions of all are the American Legion and the Woman's Christian Temperance Union.

The Legion's high jinks are too well-known to dwell upon here. However, it may not be generally known that the hotels occasionally have to defend the Legionnaires during a convention. This is something like the proverbial "Man Bites Dog."

Such a situation arose during the Legion's national convention in New York in 1947, with headquarters at the Statler. One day a newspaper photographer posed a Legionnaire from Asheville, North Carolina, with some pretty girls in front of the hotel, and made their picture. This was used by his paper in New York. One of the wire photographic services picked it up, and it was printed in the paper in Asheville, where the man's wife saw it, and promptly flew into a rage.

She wired her husband to come home immediately, else she was boarding the next train to New York, and would bring him home by the ear. The hotel, at this man's request, sent his wife a lengthy telegram, explaining that it was all a newspaper gag. James H. McCabe, the manager, promised if she would let her husband stay until the convention ended, the hotel would see to it that he behaved himself.

Probably the most exasperating and dangerous pastime of the American Legion, in convention assembled, is dropping sacks filled with water from high hotel windows upon the passing populace below. One of the most notable instances of this occurred during one of the Legion's early conventions in St. Louis. Sacks of water were being released from a high window in the Statler upon pedestrians on Washington Avenue in front of the hotel with uncanny accuracy. Almost all of them were direct hits or near misses. The puzzling thing was that, in spite of a double watch by police and house officers, they could not detect the guilty window. To drop water bombs that effectively should have required a lot of leaning out the window and sighting, but nobody was doing this.

When police finally caught on, it turned out to be a plot of several Legionnaires, who were surveyors in private life. One or two men had been posted in a high room of the Hotel Lenox, across Washington Avenue from the Statler. Another lookout post had been established across the street from the Statler, but about a block west of it on Washington Avenue. Another had been located a block east of the Statler on Washington, and still another around the corner on Ninth Street.

These observers used their surveyors' instruments to take bearings on persons walking along the street, who would pass the Statler. They had means of determining the wind direction and force. They used trigonometry and logarithms to calculate the speed of the victim, and determine the instant he would probably be under the bombardier's window two or three minutes before he got there.

They signaled this data to the lookout post in the window across from the bombing window in the Statler. Everybody's watches were synchronized. The final lookout post signaled to the bombardier in the Statler the instant he should release his bag. All this man had to do was lift the bag over the windowsill, exposing only his hand for an instant, and release his destruction.

While the Woman's Christian Temperance Union has always been a stout advocate of water as a beverage, they have never been known to drop it in bags out of hotel windows with the idea of hitting people on the head. There are, however, some other complications in being a host to a W.C.T.U. powwow. The main one is pretty well covered in a letter received by the Boston Statler several weeks before that body held its annual national convention there in the summer of 1951. This letter, from one of the W.C.T.U. state presidents, said:

Gentleman: I am planning to attend the national W.C.T.U. convention in August. I prefer to be at convention headquarters, but I want to know whether you sell or serve alcoholic liquors. Trusting that you do not, I want to reserve space for three persons in dormitories. To the contrary, if you do sell liquors, I will appreciate your supplying the names of nearby hotels which do not.

The Boston Statler was at a loss here. Not only does the hotel sell and serve alcoholic liquors, it knew of no hotel that did not, and it had no dormitories.

One of the greatest strokes any of the Statlers ever struck in connection with the W.C.T.U. occurred at the Cleveland house when the state W.C.T.U. was having its annual convention in the fall when the football season was going on. Aside from the delegates, the house was filled largely with a crowd intending to attend a football game on Saturday. As usual, there was considerable imbibing of alcoholic liquors among this group, which celebrated until a late hour Friday night.

The W.C.T.U., at its session the following day, deplored this outburst of riotous living, and denounced the Statler because it harbored "drunken hooligans." The body had about resolved to hold its convention next year at another hotel in Cleveland, instead of the Statler. But before the vote was taken, word of this reached Richard McLain, then sales manager of the Cleveland Statler.

McLain hurried to the meeting, and persuaded two or three of the state temperance leaders to accompany him to this other Cleveland hotel. By that time it was late in the afternoon, and the cocktail hour had arrived. It was the custom of this rival Cleveland hotel to place some tables and chairs in one corner of its lobby, off from the cocktail bar, where some of its more proper and decorous lady patrons might sit in the cool of the evening and sip sherry, away from the confusion in the bar, while they discussed literature and art. It was this group that McLain had in mind when he entered the lobby with the W.C.T.U. leaders at his heels. Pointing an indignant finger at this sedate circle, he said: "In our hotel, at least we confine drinking to the bars. We can't control what guests do in their rooms. But here, as you can plainly see, you ladies will have to walk through a saloon to get to and from your meetings."

The ladies, horrified by this prospect, hurried back to the closing session of their convention, which voted at the last minute that the Ohio convention of the W.C.T.U. would be held again in the Cleveland Statler the following year. As for McLain, he has been promoted to resident manager of the Statler in Detroit.

Perhaps the conventions that provoke the most amused comment around the Statlers are the annual gatherings of the Dames of

——, a female branch of a large male organization. The permanent lady resident of the Cleveland Statler who sits in the lobby and observes such things once described this convention as follows:

"The Dames of ——," she said, "come from I don't know where, arriving by Greyhound bus, I think. They have wholesome, kindly, good-humored faces, clear and unspoiled and shining. Most of them have red hands that are big and lumpy. They've worked hard raising their children. In a way, they are kind of cute. They are middle-aged and past. Their children have grown up, and this is the one chance they get during the year to get out and dress up, and amount to something on their own.

"When they arrive here, they've all been to the beauty parlor. You can tell by their hairdos. Their coiffures are combed and pasted down in ringlets so tight and so close to their heads that a tornado wouldn't ruffle a hair. It's got to be that way, because the hairdos have to last three days.

"When they come down to dinner the first night, they have all put on their uniforms—long white dresses that drag on the floor. They wear these all the time they are appearing in public here in the hotel. We call them the 'Night Gown Brigade.' They swish around the lobby as important as queens fixing to step up on their thrones, holding their dresses out of the way of their feet, and running off in all directions as though they had somewhere important to go.

"They don't get drunk, and when they do take a drink in one of the restaurants, they'll more than likely have it served in a teacup. But if some of them get rooms near yours upstairs, there is hell to pay all night. When they get up to their rooms, right after checking in, they've all got to visit one another. They get out of their traveling clothes and into some nice frilly gingham housecoats they've bought new for the convention. That way they feel free. . . . 'Oh Mary, was I glad to get out of my girdle. . . .' and all that stuff.

"All night long they are as frisky as colts, locking one another out of their rooms and cute things like that. The telephone department takes an awful beating. They're forever calling one another in their rooms. . . . 'Oh, Ethel, what are you wearing in your hair tonight to dinner? . . .'

"The elevator operators take a going-over, too. One of the girls will get one foot in the elevator and the other on the floor, and then she'll see one of her pals coming. . . . 'Oh, Lucille, have you got the key? No. I'll wait for you here in the elevator. . . . What, operator, you can't wait? . . . Well, Lucille, I'll just ride down, and wait for you in the lobby. . . . What, operator? You say you're going up?'

"As I say, these women are kind of cute. In a way we sort of hate to see them go when the big doings are over. It will be a whole year before they get off from home again and back to the Statler. You can see that in their faces when they are checking out.

"But while they are with us, it is pretty hard on some who live upstairs. There is that eternal giggling all night, and running up and down the corridors and slamming of doors, and much calling for irons and ironing boards to press those damn long white dresses. . . . And, oh my God Almighty, you ought to hear them struggling with them girdles."

Occasionally, a convention will draw delegates from rural sections, who have never stopped in a big hotel before. They have been known to arrive with hampers containing a three- or four-day supply of food. At mealtimes, they may repair to the mezzanine balcony. There they will consume their ham or chicken sandwiches and sweet gherkins, while relaxing in the easy chairs, gazing comfortably across the upper spaces of the lobby, as they drop their crumbs fastidiously in ash trays.

Some convention delegates, unaccustomed to hotels, insist on cleaning their own rooms. They shoo the maids away, or else send them to fetch brooms and dust cloths. One time in St. Louis, a group of farmers from Arkansas, attending some convention or other there, approached the Statler room clerk as they were preparing to go out early in the evening. They asked for a key to the hotel's front door, pointing out it would be midnight or later when they got back.

However, as a rule, most convention delegates remain in the hotel at night, and conduct their celebrations there, exasperating nondelegates attempting to get some sleep. Rather than cleaning their own rooms, they often leave them in a condition that requires wall washing and a new paint job.

Timmy O'Fallon, a one-time Boston policeman who got a job in

his retirement as a lobby man in the Boston Statler, once described
the convention situation pretty well during a convention there of
the Knights of Columbus. Timmy, an ardent Catholic, admired this
body profoundly. But one morning, as he puttered about the lobby
with his broom and dustpan among the legs of the conventioning
Knights, who were dropping cigar ashes, chewing gum wrappers
and the like about the carpets, he was muttering unintelligible
words of unhappiness. Walter Carney, the front office manager,
heard this in passing, and asked Timmy what he was mumbling
about.

"I was just a-sayin' to meself," the Irishman replied, "that it
makes no difference whither they are the stoorpid Mairsons or the
glooorious Knights of Columbus, THEY'RE ALL DURRRTY."

19

The Diplomatic Laundryman

When General Eisenhower came home in triumph after the last war in Europe, he was greeted officially in the national capital with a parade and other festivities, attended by a good portion of the residents of Washington, including the 100 employees in the laundry of the new Statler Hotel there. The District of Columbia had probably made elaborate arrangements for this occasion, but the General's welcome was entirely spontaneous, as far as the Statler laundry help was concerned. It was so spontaneous, in fact, that the management didn't know they were out celebrating until the housekeeping staff went to prepare the rooms for a couple of thousand guests, and found that no fresh sheets or towels had come up from the basement that day.

This presented an awkward situation; the great soldier and several score of other bigwigs were among the hotel's guests. The management was aghast at the thought of such people having to sleep between dirty, used sheets, and dry themselves upon damp old towels. So a group of employees and executives, including some of the assistant managers in their carnations and striped pants, went down to try and run the laundry. Their knowledge of laundry equipment and procedure was slight, but their spirit was commendable. Manager Herbert C. Blunck presided at an ironing machine, and the housekeeper, Mrs. Alice Druley, had charge of a tumbler. The work they turned out was somewhat below standard, being creased and torn a bit here and there, but it was clean, and—perhaps most important of all—none of the guests knew anything had gone wrong.

All this had come to pass because the Statler's laundry superintendent, who was celebrating the day liquidly, became so enthused that he told all his workers to take the rest of the day off, and go wave their hats at the General. They went willingly enough, and the superintendent wandered away or went to sleep before he got around to telling the management what he had done.

The shortage of labor during the war was felt more intensely by hotels than most other businesses because of the high proportion of human help a hotel requires. Most hotels that tried to keep their service up to standard during the war were forced to keep much larger staffs than ordinarily. All the Statlers had trouble maintaining "Statler Service," which the organization had been boasting about for several generations. This was particularly true in the Washington house, which opened after the war had begun and had no nucleus of old, seasoned employees, except a few who were sent there from other hotels in the organization.

The Washington laundry had to worry along with a skeleton force of old Statler employees, augmented by castoffs from industry, the WPA and others, who had come to the city from the farms in the neighboring states. They were often earnest and hard-working, but they hadn't been around much, and their idea of a laundry was an iron pot sitting over an open fire by the side of a stream someplace.

Among this group was a girl from Virginia named Ruby. She was a hard worker with more than average intelligence, so the superintendent—not the same man who later dismissed the force to celebrate Eisenhower's arrival—put her in charge of the machine that prints laundry marks upon the guests' clothing. The hotel, although in operation, was still under construction at the time, and new equipment was being added every day. One of the last gadgets to be installed was the Teleautograph—a mechanical system for sending messages from the general offices to various departments. The operator writes upon it a message, which is transmitted by electrical impulses throughout the building to receiving devices, where the message is recorded on rolls of paper by a mechanical writing arm.

The laundry's Teleautograph receiver was installed late one night, when none of the laundry force was on duty. It was located in the small room where Ruby worked. Ruby, who had never heard of anything of the sort in her life, was marking some shirts about eight o'clock the next morning when the little box, which she had noticed when she'd first come in, clicked a couple of times, and began writing a row of figures. The girl dropped her work, and retreated to the far side of the room, where she regarded the thing bug-eyed until it stopped writing. Then she crept up on it, got her work, and went to the other end of the room, where she resumed her marking. Presently the thing began to write again. This time it wrote words, which was too much for Ruby. She dropped her work, grabbed her hat, and was fast leaving her hotel career, when the superintendent overtook her at the employees' entrance.

"This place," Ruby announced, "is hanted, and I don't want nothing to do with no hants." The superintendent tried to explain that the device was mechanical and not a spiritual affair, but Ruby said it reminded her of the handwriting on the wall that Daniel saw in the Bible. She was finally persuaded to stay after the superintendent had the operator in the general offices send down a message on the Teleautograph, which said: "Dear Ruby: Don't be afraid of me. I am no ghost. I'm just a machine, and I'm here to help you do your work better. . . . [signed] Mr. Statler."

The problem of coping with spirits crops up every now and then with laundry employees. One time in Buffalo, a Negro woman head checker died, and the superintendent undertook to promote her assistant to that post. The assistant never did accept the better job, fearing that the dead woman's spirit would return and trouble her, if she took the vacant place. "I works hard here all day," the woman explained, "and I need my nights for sleeping. I can't expect to get my rest, if I'm going to be fussing around all night with a ghost."

Occasionally one of the laundries gets an employee who claims to be something of a spirit himself. Among these was a self-styled preacher employed in the Buffalo laundry, who contended he was divine, sanctified and untouchable. His most alarming trait was, however, his steadfast refusal to take a bath. He said that a divine person, such as he, couldn't afford to let water run off his holy body into sewers. The superintendent finally persuaded him to bathe in the waters of Lake Erie. Several employees at the laundry went down to the lakeside to watch this ritual, which occurred in the fall of the year. The man emerged from the icy waters shivering and chattering. He announced that he had suddenly received a call to go back to full-time preaching. So he went away, and they have never seen or heard of him since around the laundry of the Buffalo Statler.

Ghosts and spirits are not, however, the principal problems with which employees in Statler laundries have to grapple. The guests are. One guest, who happens to be feeling in either a mean or an absent-minded mood, can cause a hotel laundry more grief than all the spirit world combined since the time of Banquo. A guest whose mind is upon other things may casually send down items of great value in his soiled laundry. Within a short time he is likely to burst wildly into the laundry in a state of intense excitement, demanding that everything be stopped instantly until whatever he has sent down by accident has been recovered.

Usually these items have already been retrieved from the guest's bundle by the checkers, and never get into the machines. But occasionally all equipment has to be halted while the employees paw through hundreds of shirts looking, for instance, for a couple of large diamonds, which one guest in the New York Statler once left in his shirt pocket.

Another guest in New York came into the laundry shouting that he had left $250 in the pocket of his sport shirt. The checker had missed catching that as the shirt went by, but they found the money tumbling around among several hundred shirts and some washing powder.

One morning in St. Louis, Laundry Superintendent Frank King happened to glance into a bundle that had been sent down by an Oklahoma school superintendent, and found $3,000 lying around in some soiled socks. There was the time in Cleveland when a man telephoned the laundry to say he had left two $1 bills in one of his pockets, and they'd damn well better still be there when his clothes were returned. With a sly note of triumph in his voice, Superintendent Matt Brady told the man that he was mistaken: There were not two $1 bills in the pockets—there were two $10 bills. "I don't want two $10 bills," this surprising customer shouted, "I want my two $1 bills or nothing."

Guests sometimes send down woolen suits of clothes, bedroom slippers, overcoats and even felt hats, which they apparently expect to be laundered. When there are child guests in the house at vacation time, the laundry may expect stuffed dogs or elephants or rag dolls. One little girl in Cleveland once sent down her white live poodle to be laundered. And once in Detroit, Jim Londos' manager sent the Statler laundry a wrestling mat. The laundry did this unusual job in the interest of sportsmanship, after the wrestler's manager had explained that they hadn't been able to locate a clean wrestling mat in all Detroit, and Jim wouldn't wrestle on a soiled one.

The Statler laundries have never arrived at an exact science for laundering some foreign garments such as Hindu turbans, Arab burnooses and the pantaloons worn by Hindu women, which the hotels receive every now and then. Although almost everything in the Statler system is standardized, in laundries and everywhere else, the handling of these exotic garments is left pretty much up to the individual initiative of the employees.

The best customers hotel laundries have are regular commercial travelers. They like the one-day service, which allows them to operate with a relatively small amount of haberdashery. But probably the biggest reason for their superior patronage is that they are aware that hotels have laundries—a fact with which many people apparently are not acquainted. Whenever a Statler fills up with a convention crowd, the guest laundry immediately drops off. Most people attending conventions bring along enough clean clothing so they do not need to have anything laundered while they are away from home. Probably the worst of all hotel laundry customers are professional people, such as doctors and teachers. Among Statler guests, Monday is the biggest washday, as it is everywhere else. Friday is next biggest.

The Statler laundries patch, darn, sew on buttons and make all minor repairs. A Statler laundry stocks seven different shades of woolen thread to darn wool socks alone. The great specialty of Statler laundries, however, is their method of finishing shirts, folded into an eight-by-ten-inch package and sealed in cellophane. This method was perfected by Albert Halstead, laundry superintendent for the Statler system, and has been in use since 1939. The size of the shirt makes it convenient for packing, and the cellophane protects it in a suitcase. A good many men favor this method of doing shirts so strongly that they always send their things to Statler laundries, whether they are guests in the hotels or not.

One man who had been touring Europe for a number of weeks landed at the New York Statler with enough soiled linen to fill a sixteen-bushel laundry truck. He had refused to have his laundry done over there. One loyal customer of the St. Louis Statler is Colonel Clark Hungerford, president of the Frisco Railroad. His laundry arrives now and then by mail from wherever about the globe he happens to be, and when he is home in St. Louis, his chauffeur brings down and picks up laundry via limousine.

While the guest laundry provides most of the excitement, Statler maintains laundries primarily to handle the house's work. About ninety per cent of the laundry's effort is with hotel linens and employees' uniforms, which amount to about ten pounds a day for every room in the house.

Miscellaneous house items include caps and sweatcloths for cooks, cooks' trousers, and collars, cuffs and headbands for maids.

When laundry is lost, most people are fairly honest about their losses, although there are some graphic exceptions. Not long ago in Cleveland, one man complained so savagely about some garments he said the laundry had lost that the superintendent asked the manager's office to look up his guest history. They found that he was a character for whom the Cleveland Statler and other hotels had been looking for ten years for passing worthless checks.

One time in Buffalo, a large package of laundry was delivered into the Servidor of room 938 on a Thursday evening, according to the laundry's records, but the next day the couple occupying the room said it had not arrived. Occasionally, laundry is placed in a Servidor in the wrong room by mistake, so all the 1100 rooms in that hotel were checked, but the package was not found. Finally, on E. M. Statler's tenet that "the customer is always right," the hotel paid the sixty dollars the man and his wife said the lost laundry was worth.

Three years later, Albert Vega, the superintendent who had handled the sixty-dollar loss at Buffalo, was sent out to St. Louis to take charge temporarily. A day or so after he got there, the laundry received a complaint about a missing bundle that Vega recalled was almost identical to the one in Buffalo three years before.

He went upstairs to see the people who reported the loss, and as soon as he stepped into the room, he recognized the same couple to whom he had paid the sixty dollars in Buffalo three years before. And they recognized him. "I understand," said Vega, fixing the pair with a savage eye, "that you have lost some more laundry."

"Oh no," the woman replied brightly, reaching under the bed, and bringing out a large laundry box, "we've just found it. It was under here."

Like practically every operation in a hotel, the laundry occasionally requires diplomacy, and Mr. Vega, a Mexican by birth who teaches Spanish at night at the University of Buffalo, is one of Statler's better diplomats in the laundry field. One time, the Buffalo laundry received a man's dress shirt that had apparently been through an interesting evening. Inscribed across its stiff bosom in ink and lipstick were various intimate phrases such as "I love you" and "You are wonderful." There were also pictures of hearts and cupid's bows.

Vega telephoned the guest who had sent it down to explain that the laundry probably could not get all of this art and literature off his shirt without destroying the fabric. The man said to do the best they could. He said it really didn't matter too much.

His attitude at the time seemed quite placid, considering the fact that late that afternoon, after the laundry had been delivered, the man telephoned Vega in a great rage, shouting that the laundry had sent him the wrong dress shirt. The superintendent tried to explain over the phone that the laundry had not been able to get the marks out of the shirt, and had to send it back with the arrows and "Honeys" still discernible. But the man demanded that Vega come to his room at once.

When he got there, the guest swung open the door and faced him. He was waving one arm angrily in the air, but with the other hand was slipping a $10 bill into the palm of the surprised superintendent. There was a woman in the room, who Vega quickly guessed was not the same who had worked on the guest's shirt from the night before. In fact, the lady present was the guest's wife, who, it developed, had arrived at the hotel to join her husband unexpectedly that afternoon. She had been putting away his laundry when she saw the shirt front with its faded, but still legible, inscriptions of endearment.

"What do you mean by sending me this ridiculous garment?" the guest bellowed at Vega. "This isn't my shirt."

"I'm delighted that you called, sir," replied Vega solicitously and without hesitation. "I have been looking everywhere for that particular shirt. There has been a terrible mistake. Another guest, who now has your shirt, has been very angry with me because I could not find his shirt, which you have. Now, if you will give it to me, everything can be straightened out quickly."

As Vega bowed out into the hall, the guest followed him, and whispered, "I don't give a damn what you do with the shirt, but make this look genuine."

An hour later Vega telephoned the room, and the man's wife answered. He explained that the mythical guest who had her husband's shirt had checked out with the shirt before he, Vega, could make the exchange. Now, he went on, the hotel would have to pay for her husband's shirt. After a quick conference with her husband, the lady said $7.50 would be satisfactory. Vega said that amount would be credited to her husband on his bill.

"We really ought to charge the hotel more than $7.50 for that shirt," the lady said before she hung up. "It was beautifully made. You can't get that material any more. And it had great sentimental value. . . ."

20

The Comptometer in the Kitchen

Once during the summer of 1951, Arthur F. Douglas was dining in the wilds of Vermont at a village inn, where they loaded down the table with every kind of food available thereabouts every day at dinner, and let the guests fall to and help themselves—a type of restaurant procedure that most people who live around New York imagine went out of existence about the time of "Tippecanoe and Tyler Too."

Douglas, who has dwelt around New York for a good many years in intimate association with the restaurant business, was confounded that the inn could provide all the food a guest could eat for a dollar. After dinner, he asked the proprietor, a shirt-sleeved rustic, if he could give him an idea of what his food costs were per dollar sales. The man looked at Douglas curiously, as though he had addressed him in Zulu, and asked him to please repeat that question.

Fifteen minutes later, when the innkeeper had begun to grasp what the Statler president was driving at, he said he had never heard of such a thing in his life, and hoped he never did again. "When the hotel business gets so hard up that I have to keep books on the food I'm feeding my guests," he added, "that's when I am pulling out of the hotel business, and taking up some other line of work."

It was hard to tell which was the more amazed: the Vermonter, upon learning that large hotels have to keep account of their food costs to remain solvent, or Douglas to find that any hotel or inn on earth could get along that didn't.

Yet, food cost accounting, or "food controls," in the hotel business is a fairly recent thing. E. M. Statler originated a system of his own to keep records of his food costs when he opened his first permanent hotel in Buffalo in 1907, but the majority of hotels at the time, including the large ones, kept no books, aside from signatures and entries on the guest register. Prices guests paid for food were set largely by tradition or according to the disposition of the hotel owner.

In 1918, when the Hotel Pennsylvania was being built for him in New York, Mr. Statler had Horwath & Horwath, the noted hotel accountants, set up a food-control system for that house, which was later installed in his other hotels. The company still uses this system as a basis, but has added so many touches of its own that Statler's food controls have for a long time had the reputation of being the most intricate and effective in the industry.

For one thing, Statler appears to have achieved better co-operation in this regard than most other hotel companies have from its chefs—ordinarily a temperamental clique of creative artists, who refuse to be bothered with profit-and-loss figures. It has been said that, next to the cooking ranges, the most important piece of equipment in a Statler kitchen is the adding machine.

There is a saying throughout the rest of the industry that Statler cost experts, keeping a gimlet eye on the ever-changing food markets, stand ready at all times to revise the entire menu price structure of the organization each time rhubarb or rutabagas jump a couple of points in either direction. One rival hotel operator says he wouldn't think of sending back to the kitchen some dish that didn't suit him, when he is dining at the Statler. If he did, he says he would hear, in his imagination, calculators and Comptometers clashing all the way from New York to St. Louis as Statler's food department readjusted its records, prices and estimates in consideration of this single rejected plate of corned beef and cabbage.

Food control means simply a hotel's system of determining the cost of feeding its customers, what its customers like to eat and what prices the house ought to put on its menus to make its desired profit. When he started in business, Mr. Statler's idea of a profit that was fair, both to his hotels and their customers, was fifteen per cent, and the organization has kept a fifteen per cent profit as its goal ever since.

To make this profit, the Statler people have found they have to ask three times as much for a meal as the food actually costs. If the chop, string beans and potatoes on a luncheon cost the hotel sixty cents at the market, the proper price on the menu should be $1.80. Outside of the one-third that goes to paying for the raw materials, one-third or more of this price is absorbed by wages to everyone concerned in its preparation and serving. The final third goes to paying for light, heat and power used in the food department, replacement of its equipment, maintenance of that part of the building it occupies and to the hoped-for but not often realized fifteen per cent profit to the house.

High meat prices in these times, however, have made it impractical for the hotels to charge always exactly three times what the raw materials cost. This is likely to set the price of meat items on the menu higher than the company likes to charge or its customers wish to pay. Therefore, the hotels often set the price of meat entrees lower than the formula to produce their desired profit, and depend on other items, usually fish or fowl, to make up for the profit they did not make on meat.

In June, 1951, the Statler in Cleveland was paying $1.07 for every serving of roast beef, when trimmed. In figuring the cost on the menu, the company adds to the meat cost the cost of the accompanying vegetables, about fifteen cents a serving, and the cooking materials—salt, pepper, oils and spices—amounting to about five cents, making the raw materials for a roast-beef luncheon cost the hotel $1.27. When this is multiplied by three, the price on the menu, according to the Statler formula, should be $3.81 to pay all the costs of preparing and serving and give the desired profit.

However, the company felt this was more than the customer should be charged. So the price of a roast beef luncheon at the Cleveland Statler that month was set at $3.15, or sixty-six cents lower than it should have been for the company to make its fifteen per cent profit. In fact, on every serving of roast beef that month, it took a loss.

But, while the Cleveland Statler was losing money on roast beef in June, 1951, it was making back part of the loss on turkey steaks, which are sliced sections of turkey breast breaded and fried and a popular item in Cleveland. At the time, the hotel was paying about forty cents a steak. It costs two cents to bread and fry each steak. Adding to this the cost of the meat and the accompanying vegetables brings the cost per steak to the hotel to sixty-one cents. Multiplying this by three gives a price of $1.83, according to the formula. However, turkey-steak luncheons at the Cleveland Statler that month were priced at $2.15. This was thirty-two cents above the formula, and so, for every two turkey steaks the hotel sold, it made back what it lost on one serving of roast beef.

The company expects its hotels to make a better profit on food during the winter than in summer, when the restaurant business, particularly banquet sales, falls off. The fewer dinners, the greater the chances for food waste. Besides, it requires almost as much light, power and cooking pots to prepare for two thousand as for four thousand. Therefore, the Statler policy will allow its houses to let their food costs per dollar sales go as high as thirty-four or thirty-five cents during the summer. They are expected to counteract this, and get the annual average down to thirty-three cents, by cutting costs per dollar sales to as low as thirty-two or thirty-one cents during the winter.

Just how much they will cut costs or allow them to rise is not left to the individual hotels. Each month the executive offices in New York sends to every hotel the cost figure it is expected to maintain that month. This figure is based upon that hotel's food cost record so far that year, modified by local eating habits existing in that city, which the company knows about through keeping records over the years.

If, for one month, a hotel is called on to cut its food costs one or two cents under what its costs were for the preceding month, individual stewards are not allowed to lower their quality standards in purchasing, nor are the chefs allowed to cook mainly hash. The stewards are expected to take advantage of market conditions, and buy as many provisions as practical that are in abundant supply at that season and reasonable in price, while the chefs are expected to create from these supplies dishes that are popular in that city.

But the world's best bookkeeping will not make a food department prosperous unless the chef knows how much food to prepare and what the clientele likes to eat. The amount to prepare depends partly on the time of the year, while tastes vary in the various cities. Generally, however, most Statler cooking, as with the majority of large hotels, follows the French style, as expounded by Auguste Escoffier. This is opposed to the Italian school of cooking, which is strong on garlic, thyme, rosemary and heavy spices; or the English school, which has very little spice and is usually considered too flat by Americans; or the German school, which is livelier than English cooking but too heavy for most American tastes. The French kitchen combines the Northern and Southern European cooking styles, and is more delicate than Italian cooking, but tastier than either English or German.

Although French cooking is the basis of their kitchens, the Statler hotels vary their dishes and methods of preparation in deference to tastes in the individual cities. Clam chowder at the Boston Statler is always made New England style, with cream, while the hotels in Cleveland, Detroit and St. Louis serve no clam chowder but the Manhattan type, with tomatoes and vegetables. Their customers do not recognize the New England style. The other houses in the organization serve both kinds. The New York and St. Louis customers like more German-type foods than those of the other houses, while such items as kidneys and beef tongue are confined mainly to the New York house.

Boston has the reputation of being the leading seafood town, but seafood is probably more popular in the Midwestern cities because there it still has a certain novelty appeal. It has not been so many years since it was the custom in Cleveland for a person having lobster at a good hotel or restaurant to pick out his live lobster before it went to the kitchen, and carve his initials on its shell. That way he was sure, when it was served, that it was the same lobster he had picked out alive.

The St. Louis Statler is the only one in the organization that regularly puts pie on the dinner menu or catfish on any menu—many St. Louis eating habits being of Southern origin—while Boston is the

only Statler where fish is more popular for breakfast than bacon
and eggs, or where a guest can get a baked-bean sandwich.

In figuring the amounts of food to prepare, the Statlers have
found that, during the spring, fall and winter, eighty per cent of
their guests will eat breakfast in the hotel, forty-five per cent luncheon and sixty-one per cent dinner. These figures do not apply during
the summer, when there are many tourists in the houses. Tourists
usually haven't as much money to spend as businessmen on expense
accounts, who make up the bulk of the Statler trade the remainder
of the year, and tourists are more apt to take their meals at the
cafeteria down the street.

The same is true when the house is full of convention delegates
who are paying their own way, and regard hotel food as too high.
The weather also can have a bearing on the chef's calculations. On
a Monday night, for instance, when the dinner business is not ordinarily very rushing, the dining room may overflow if the weather
turns off stormy.

Figuring out what to serve for breakfast—the New York Statler
serves at least 1,000 breakfasts every day of the year—is no problem because more people have orange juice, toast and coffee than
all other breakfast selections combined. For luncheon and dinner,
Chef Reinhold Keller, of the New York house, always makes his
menus two days in advance to give the steward plenty of time to
purchase all necessary supplies.

A basic luncheon menu at the New York hotel will include a fish
entree, an egg dish, one or two broiled dishes (usually chops), a
roast dish (maybe leg of lamb), a gravy or potted dish (beef à la
mode or American pot roast perhaps), two light entrees (stuffed
green peppers or chicken cutlet), three different large sandwiches
(such as a Statler Special made of sliced cold turkey on rye with
lettuce and tomatoes, stuffed eggs and Russian dressing), and about
three salads, such as chef's salad bowl, a fruit salad and a combination fruit salad.

For any week-day luncheon during the fall, winter or spring,
Chef Keller knows that if he offers the following entrees on the
menu, each will appeal to about the following number of customers:
corned beef and cabbage, 180 to 200 takers, so he always buys
twelve briskets of corned beef; leg of lamb, 180 customers, so he

buys eighteen legs of lamb; fillet of sole, 160 takers; shirred eggs and sausage, 110 takers; scrambled eggs and Canadian bacon, 180 to 220; Spanish omelet, 175; lamb chops, 200 to 220; charcoal-broiled hamburger steak, 250 to 270; Irish lamb stew, 215; and cold seafood plate, 150 customers, if the plate contains shrimp, crab and lobster; otherwise, only half as many takers.

At dinner, roast beef is the most popular item on the menu, considering that it is usually the most expensive, and 100 to 125 diners will order it. About the same number will order the small *filet mignon.* If turkey is on the menu, 220 will order that; 200 will order chicken, and ninety to 100 will take duck—twice that many if the duck is boned. Around sixty persons will order fish, unless it is charcoal-broiled salmon, which will double fish entree sales.

The most popular expensive dessert is Statler ice-cream pie. In a day, from 200 to 250 portions will be consumed, while about 100 prefer Statler cheesecake. Among the simpler, less expensive desserts, apple pie is most popular—500 to 600 portions a day. Steamed fig pudding will be accepted by 250 diners, and chocolate éclairs by from 80 to 100. Fruit pies are far more popular than custard pies. Aside from apple, the most in demand are blueberry, raisin and cherry.

The reason such a large bite is taken from the sale of hotel food to pay for upkeep of the kitchens and equipment and salaries of food department employees is that hotels need more and larger kitchens and more employees to perform all the varied services and varieties of food a hotel is expected to offer than are necessary at the Automat, which prepares a simple, limited menu, and sets the food out on some shelves.

The New York Statler has, in all, eight kitchens: the main kitchen, which serves the Manhattan Room, room service and the Café Rouge (the latter only in the evening), and the coffee-shop kitchen, both one floor level below the lobby; the Café Rouge kitchen on the main floor, which serves the hotel's largest dining room at noon; an employees' kitchen on the mezzanine; a banquet kitchen on the first floor, serving the main ballroom; a smaller kitchen just above it to serve the upper ballroom; a kitchen on the eighteenth floor to serve the Keystone Room, and a serving kitchen on the nineteenth floor for the Penn Top. Two other kitchens in the house have been eliminated, but the eight still operating contain over $1,000,000 worth of equipment, which must be maintained all the time, and replaced occasionally.

Chef Keller has his office in the main kitchen, one of the largest kitchens in the world with 25,000 square feet of floor space.

Not counting extras, the chef's staff is made up of: nine bakers, ten pastry bakers, four ice-cream chefs, nine butchers, twelve cold-meat cooks (*garde-manger*), nine roast cooks, twelve sauce cooks, nine fry cooks, six vegetable girls, four soup cooks, four banquet chefs, eight pot washers and four cleaners. Nine out of ten cooks are foreign-born, including the chef, who comes from Germany. The majority of the cooks are German, Italian or French, mainly because Americans aren't as good in the kitchen as Europeans are.

Next to the chef, the head sauce cook is regarded as the senior man in the kitchen, and most chefs are former sauce cooks. Sauce cookery is considered the most expert of all forms, since it is concerned with gravies, sauces, broiled and poached fish, and any of those items can go terribly wrong. The head cold-meat man is next to the sauce cook. He is a decorator, as well as a cook, and handles the special meat salads, such as lobster or chicken. He makes all the cold-meat sauces.

Next to him is the fry cook. His particular art is handling the fancy fried dishes, mainly potatoes. There are twenty-six different ways of fixing potatoes that the Statler kitchens consider day in-and-out routine. These include potato pancakes, potatoes au gratin, parsleyed, French friend, mashed, cottage fried, home fried, cro-quettes, kloesse, potato puffs, boiled, hashed-brown, lyonnaise, long branch, country and American fried.

The titles of the other kitchen employees are pretty well self-explanatory, except that the roasters and broilers handle all the steaks, chops and roasts. The butcher has three men assigned to meats which are boiled, while three other butchers are assigned to boiling shrimps, salmon and other fish that are served cold. The few fish that are fried are handled by the fry cook.

When preparing banquets, the New York Statler prefers to pay its regular kitchen force to work overtime, and hire as few as pos-sible extra cooks. The regular staff has better cooks, for one thing, and the use of his regulars permits the chef to better co-ordinate his banquet menu with the items being served in the restaurants. For a banquet, the kitchen usually prepares ten per cent more food than is needed to feed the exact number the sponsors have guaranteed will attend. As an extra precaution, the chef always includes on his regular dinner menu the same kind of soup and the same entree that are being served at the banquet. If over ten per cent more people than had been expected attend the banquet, the kitchen can take care of them. If less attend than had been expected, the food that would have been left over can be absorbed in the hotel restaurants.

In preparing a banquet, as is the case with regular menus, the chef knows about how much people will eat and how they like their food prepared, and is governed accordingly. If the banquet entree is chicken, the cooks begin roasting it two hours before dinner, because almost everybody likes chicken well done, except for a few gourmets, who insist that chicken is better when juicy and rare. If the entree is steak, that goes on the fire always when the soup is served. If the entree is roast beef, it is usually served rare, unless the waiters are instructed to the contrary, because seventy-five per cent of people like roast beef that way.

Incidentally, people are more persnickety about their roast beef than anything else the Statlers serve. Diners often claim their roast is too rare, or too done or too fat. The latter complaint always annoys the roast cooks, because, if the roast were not fat, it would be tasteless and tough, and the customers would complain more loudly than ever. The fat is generally in the center of the cut, and if it were removed, it would leave an unsightly hole, and they wouldn't like that, either.

The largest banquets the Statler people have ever served have been the annual Jefferson-Jackson Day dinners of the national Democratic party, held at Washington's National Guard Armory, where about 5,500 of the faithful come to eat a steak dinner at $100 a plate and listen to war cries uttered by their party chieftains. *Time* Magazine has described it as: "A combination revival meeting and war dance . . . calculated to terrorize and stupefy the G.O.P. . . . It is almost comparable to the Burning of Rome."

It is highly possible that the Republican party has not been as uneasy about these formidable feasts as have been the banquet departments of the Washington Statler and the Mayflower Hotels, which combine forces to prepare the food and serve it. The wrath of a prominent Democrat is a frightful thing to behold, when his steak is served overdone or cold; and this event brings together more prominent Democrats—or, as a matter of fact, more *people*— to eat a complete dinner under the same roof than is known to have occurred elsewhere in history. The hotels' catering problems are complicated by the fact that the Washington Armory has no kitchens, making it necessary for the food to be cooked in the hotels, about two miles away, and hauled to the scene.

The menu at the first dinner at the Armory, in 1950, was: Texas pink grapefruit, celery and green olives, broiled *filet mignon bordelaise, pommes rissoles,* string beans *provençale,* lettuce hearts with Roquefort dressing, fancy ice cream, *petits fours,* demitasse. The Statler supplies the gear for the tables occupying the two acres of Armory floor to the President's right, while the Mayflower takes care of equipping the two acres to his left. Each hotel supplies 275 waiters, as well as forty captains, thirty cooks and twenty-five stewards. The service is directed by Jack Wechsler, executive maître d'hôtel of the Statler Company, who operates large boards equipped with colored lights that signal when waiters are to serve or clear the tables.

The supply problem, however, was regarded as a simple thing at the time the first dinner was being planned, compared with the question of how to get the steaks all that distance from the hotel kitchens to the Armory and serve them hot and fit to eat. The problem was finally solved by the hotels' building twelve service kitchens at the Armory, each equipped with a large charcoal heater that would maintain a steady temperature high enough to cook slowly the 475 steaks each would hold.

As finally executed, the plan involved searing half the steaks in the Statler and half in the Mayflower kitchens, starting at ten o'clock the morning of the dinner, and getting the undone steaks into the heaters at the Armory by 3:00 P.M. For the next three hours, until the dinner hours at 6:00 P.M., they cooked slowly, and were served hot, pink on the inside, crusty brown on the outside, as steaks should be.

This schedule was arrived at by trial and error over several weeks of rehearsal prior to the dinner. Democratic party and hotel officials sat in as guinea pigs at the rehearsals, and ate great quantities of burnt and raw flesh until the formula was finally perfected.

As it turned out, the steaks won more acclaim, in dispatches of the press, than the speeches did, but unknown to the newsmen, there were several near calamities. The steaks were ordered from New York, and were to have been delivered to the hotels the afternoon of the day preceding the dinner. But somehow—a Republican plot was never proved—they were quietly set off the train on a remote and deserted freight platform on the outskirts of Washington. It took Mr. Wechsler until the following morning to locate them. If the steaks had not been found, the President and his colleagues might have had to sup on hot dogs, and the Democratic party would have suffered the most dastardly misfortune since the defeat of Samuel J. Tilden for President in 1876.

During the dinner, all went well with but two exceptions. One captain of waiters failed to see the signal for serving the first course, and his block of waiters walked in late. Then, between the clearing of the first course and the serving of the steaks—the most critical phase of the operation—Senator Herbert R. O'Conor (Dem.-Md.) headed a group of 200 Democrats who, in the words of Director of Service Wechsler, "stomped out in the middle of the floor in front of the President, and started hollering about the next election." It almost threw out of gear the precision timing, but the Senator and his men were shooed off the floor in time.

The Democratic party kept for its war chest $90 of the $100 per cover, and the hotels got only $10 per plate, which was hardly enough for them to make much money, considering all their effort and extra expense. It was a case of service costs getting out of hand, in Statler bookkeeping terms. But every newspaper, news magazine, news service, radio and television network and newsreel in the land carried lengthy treatments of the affair, with particular praise for the hotels' food and service. The general reaction was pretty well summed up by *Time* Magazine, which said:

Despite the confusion and the roaring babble set off by the throngs on the floor and in the galleries, the dinner was deftly served. The serving men, who had been drilled as meticulously as a troop of light cavalry, charged forth to clear or to serve. To the unconcealed awe of all, the filet mignon arrived hot!

For press notices like that, the Statler Company could afford to forget costs per dollar sales just this once.

21

No Speech Is Worth an
Eight-Dollar Steak

One time, during the latter 1940's, a certain pigeon attained widespread renown, through reports of the press and radio, because he took up residence in the lobby of the Hotel Statler in New York. He caused such confusion and chagrin among the staff and guests of that establishment that he became, during the three days it took to evict him, the most distinguished pigeon in all of New York, a city of millions of pigeons.

The pigeon came to be in the lobby, in the first place, through the following circumstances: Certain foreign-born and Jewish peoples often celebrate a wedding in a large hotel, where they spend thousands of dollars for great displays of food, drink and flowers and for dancing that lasts far into the night. The wedding ceremony or the entertainment that follows frequently includes some ancient ritual. Among some families of Greek descent one of these rituals is the releasing of lovebirds or, preferably, doves when the wedding cake is cut. This is supposed to portend a peaceful life of wedded bliss.

It happened, then, that once when a big Greek wedding was being planned for the New York Statler, the celebrants couldn't find doves, so they settled for half a dozen pigeons, and released them in the ballroom—unknown to the management—when the wedding cake was cut. Unfortunately, they had neglected to tie long ribbons about the birds' legs so that they could be retrieved after their part in the ceremony. The party was over at a late hour, long after the pigeons had gone quietly to roost on some high molding near the ballroom ceiling.

They were still perched there early the next morning, and were unnoticed by housemen who cleaned the ballroom. However, that afternoon when functionaries of the banquet department came to set up for a large dinner, the birds had become obvious in various ways. Five of them were quickly captured from their perch on the chandelier when spotlights were shone in their eyes, blinding them temporarily. But the sixth, a robust and adventuresome bird, managed to escape to the lobby.

The New York Statler has an immense, rectangular lobby with a towering ceiling. The floor is generally crowded with people, but crowds were noticeably slim during the three days the pigeon held forth. Sometimes, when people ventured across from one side to the other, they had to duck desperately as the pigeon soared across in a sort of diving swoop. At all times, guests and employees had to keep a weather eye aloft for obvious reasons.

The hotel sent its employees up fire ladders to try to stun the bird with long poles. The lights were turned off, and efforts were made to blind the pigeon with spotlights. Men were sent up in mechanical hoists, and tried to nab him in butterfly nets. An air rifle was procured from Gimbel's department store nearby, but the shooting idea was quickly abandoned out of deference to the ornamental plaster work.

Finally, the pigeon was bagged by means of a trap, devised and operated by an employee named Albert "Wimpy" Fimbel, a wall washer, chairman of the Employees' Recreational Committee, the leading checker player of the hotel, and holder of the hamburger-eating championship of Hudson County, New Jersey.

A wedding celebration is probably the only type of hotel function in these materialistic times that would rate enough care and attention from those giving the party to warrant all that trouble. Almost every other kind of function, public and private, held in hotels nowadays, is painfully simple compared with the elaborate displays of fine food and drink that characterized such occasions in years gone by.

Some Jewish families have looked forward to and saved money toward a memorable wedding party for years, and they will talk about it for years afterward over creased old menus and pressed flowers from the bride's bouquet and petrified pieces of wedding cake, in their gold-initialed boxes.

The wedding of the daughter is frequently the high point of the generation for a family, so no expense must be spared and nothing must go wrong. Some Jewish families who are not wealthy will save enough to have an elaborate wedding, even hotel employees themselves. One time at the New York Statler, a gentle-eyed Jewish banquet waiter, who had worked there eighteen years, asked Jules Gallina, maître d'hôtel, if Gallina had any objection to his having his daughter's wedding and party at the Statler, where he had worked so long. Gallina said he didn't if the waiter thought he could afford it. The waiter then promptly paid in advance $2,300, the actual cost of the party to the hotel, which probably represented for him ten years of savings.

But the most of the big weddings are given by wealthy families, and can easily cost $10,000 to $15,000 for one night. Such affairs naturally delight the hotel's money counters. They are also pleasing to the maître d'hôtel, who is bored with supervising dull business-club luncheons with their eternal soup, entree, vegetables and dessert. Weddings give him an opportunity to demonstrate his art to the fullest.

For reasons of propriety and etiquette, a hotel can't exactly go out and solicit wedding business. It must wait for the party to come to the hotel. Then, the system is to put on such a wonderful show that all the guests who have daughters not yet married will think favorably of the Statler as the place to get it done. The best years are those when daughters of several wealthy families are getting married, and each family is out to beat the parties the others threw. At a time like that, expense becomes no consideration, and the maître d'hôtel and his banquet department exist in a rosy world, consisting of champagne cases, floral designs, seating plans and money.

Celebrated for his organizational abilities and attention to detail when arranging large weddings is the maître d'hôtel of the Boston Statler, Maurice Ribert, or "Mr. Maurice," as he is known to the mamas and papas of the brides, who meet with him to select the wines and menus for buffet, dinner and breakfast, and decide upon the music and floral decorations. The menu is most important of all, because prodigious amounts of food and drink are consumed at these affairs. At one wedding in the Boston Statler a few years ago, the 475 guests consumed an average of twenty-five pieces of hors d'oeuvres per person; fifty cases of champagne, or just over a quart per guest; ten cases of whisky and an average of four glasses of liqueurs per person, in addition to food and wines served at the table during dinner and breakfast.

An affair of this size will occupy the hotel's entire mezzanine. It will usually get under way at 6:30 P.M. in the Georgian Room, which has been carpeted in green, and adorned with floral decorations costing a thousand dollars or so. A green-covered platform has been built at one end with an altar and a concealed microphone for the rabbi. The guests begin arriving half an hour ahead of time, and are admitted through both the ballroom and side lobby entrances by doormen, wearing white gloves for the occasion. The entrances have been scrubbed so that the marble glows and the brass shines, and new lights are installed in the marquee, which has had all its glass washed and polished. The hotel alerts the garage that handles its parking to have a double force of men on duty so there will be no delay getting automobiles from the entrances.

Inside, two bellmen, wearing white gloves, stand at all stairways leading from the lobby to the mezzanine to direct guests to the Georgian Room. When all the guests have arrived, these bellmen will move to the mezzanine. When the ceremony is over, they will direct guests from the parlor, where the receiving line is receiving and the bride is being kissed amid the popping of photographers' flashbulbs, to that section of the floor where the serious eating and drinking are to start.

A security patrol, consisting of one city policeman in uniform, a city fireman in uniform and five hotel house officers in uniform, is stationed at various strategic spots to keep an eye open for thieves and gate crashers. These may include persons anxious to get a free meal and a lot to drink without an invitation, or footpads who have an eye on the fur coats and costly gems worn by some of the wealthier women guests. There are also such persons as local bartenders, whom the father of the bride may have invited in a weak moment while in his cups, without consulting the bride and her mother. Each member of the security patrol is paid $1.50 an hour by the hotel, which is later reimbursed by the bride's father.

Five cooks, in all, are paid six dollars each to carve the sturgeon and smoked salmon, which are prominent on the buffets. Included besides are: Beluga caviar, slices of rye and flute bread, lobsters sautéed in butter, cold shrimps with cocktail sauce, fresh shrimps with butter and lemon sauce, assorted *canapés,* fish balls with cocktail sauce, baked oysters casino, stuffed celery, and assorted hot *bouchées.*

The dinner, which costs ten dollars per guest and includes a thick soup, broiled squab chicken, baked fish with almonds, an elaborate salad course and several gravies and sauces, begins at 9:15 in the ballroom. About fifty tables, seating ten persons each, have been set with the hotel's fancy blue-and-gold china, and a centerpiece of flowers is on each. A special table for the bridal party is built on a slightly raised dais. Two orchestras alternate in playing the dinner music and for dancing. One orchestra has twenty-five men, the other eighteen. The host has provided, through the hotel, supper for the musicians: a sandwich and a half, coffee and ice cream for each man, at $2.50.

The culmination of the dinner is the entrance of the four-tier wedding cake, which cost seventy-five dollars. The waiters withdraw from the room. All the lights go out, except a bright spot, which centers upon the bride as she confronts, with knife in hand, the cake. There is a roll of drums. The bride plunges the knife into the cake, then draws it forth. (Applause.) Instantly the waiters file back into the room bearing flaming servings of ice cream that flicker in the dark like a miniature torchlight procession. (More applause.)

After the bride has cut the initial slice, the cake is wheeled into the kitchen, where the cutting is finished by experts. The cake is served with the demitasse on the mezzanine foyer, which, during the dinner, has been adorned with trellises of blossoms and banks of greenery. Rolling bars have been brought, from which guests are served brandy, benedictine, Cointreau, chartreuse, crème de menthe, grand marnier and drambuie. Fifteen waiters are required to serve the wedding cake and the demitasses.

Meanwhile, a corps of housemen and waiters are preparing the grand ballroom for the dancing. Tables are pushed closer together to enlarge the dance floor, while tablecloths are changed from white to blue, except the bride's table, which remains white. The dancing continues until 1:30 A.M., when breakfast is served. When breakfast is over, the guests start to leave, full to the throats and thinking about a lot of things. They get their wraps from the checkroom—no tipping tonight; the host has paid the concessionaire eighty dollars for this service. They pick up a piece of the wedding cake, neatly boxed on a handy table, to take home as a souvenir, and down the special elevator to wait at the entrance for their cars, being summoned by the doormen in white gloves.

Mr. Maurice, the maître d'hôtel, is by now worn down to his nervous energy. His joints ache and his full-dress shirt front is gouging at his Adam's apple. It has been a big production, and a thousand things could have gone wrong. Yet, nothing serious did, except several guests got sick, a couple of fights were narrowly averted, at least half a dozen gate crashers tried to get by the guards, soup was spilled on two guests and gravy upon four others. The soiled garments will be cleaned at the hotel's expense. Like most showmen, Mr. Maurice believes this is the best production he has ever staged, and, tired as he will be at work tomorrow, he will feel better than most of the wedding guests.

Aside from wedding celebrations, most big dinners in hotels in these times are run-of-the-mill: shrimp or fruit cocktail, soup (usually tomato), entree, green peas and potatoes, ice cream and coffee. If the entree is chicken at the New York Statler, the dinner costs $4.50; turkey (the most popular), $5; a regular steak, $7; or $8 if it is a *filet mignon*.

There is more money for the banquet departments of hotels now than during the fine dining era of the past, because three or four times as many dinners are given now. But they remain mostly routine, whether for an important convention or the reception of a hero, or whether they are given by Gimbel's or Macy's department stores as a reward to some employees for superior feats of salesmanship. In the old days, a banquet was a great event to be talked about long afterward, and great attention was given to the choice of foods and the arrangement of service. A typical convention banquet menu of the New York Statler of thirty years ago was: caviar, consommé, boneless frog legs, sweetbreads (Eugenie), sherbet, *filet mignon,* vegetables, cold Virginia ham with *pâté de foie gras,* fancy ice cream with spun sugar, coffee and cordials.

A dinner like that placed the chef and the maître d'hôtel on their mettle. It was a challenge to prepare and serve. Nowadays, when any group strays from the usual dull pattern, the maître d'hôtel is amazed and overjoyed, as was Mr. Gallina some time ago when the North American College of Rome alumni (a Catholic clerical organization) in arranging a dinner, ordered Persian melon Proscuite (melon wrapped in thin ham slices) instead of the usual shrimp cocktail; boneless stuffed squab chicken, instead of the usual sliced roast chicken; and potatoes Olivelle (small round potatoes with onions) and green peas *bonne femme* (peas with pork) instead of the usual boiled potatoes and listless boiled green peas.

Perhaps the most staggering blow Gallina's professional pride ever sustained was when the secretary of a trade association, whose members are noted as spenders, was arranging their banquet for 1,375 persons during the association's annual convention at the New York Statler. This group had ordered $3,000 worth of whisky, but when it came time to arrange the dinner, the secretary said to the maître d'hôtel, "I believe we will just take the $4.50 chicken dinner. By that time, the boys will be so drunk they won't know what they're eating anyway."

Experiences like that discourage maîtres d'hôtel, causing them to wonder if it is worth the trouble to describe to persons arranging banquets the wonders their departments could perform, if given the opportunity. But in at least one Statler hotel—the Cleveland house—the enthusiasm for the grand old days of dining still flames as brightly in the breast of the maître d'hôtel as it ever did in that era when saddle of Rocky Mountain sheep, diamond-backed terrapin and ruddy duck were served amid soft candlelight, to the accompaniment of rich old wines in dusty bottles.

This man, Francis Santi, was thirty-eight years old when he became maître d'hôtel in 1950, and too young to remember much about the era he reveres. But he was schooled and inspired in such things by his father, Ferderico Santi, who was maître d'hôtel at the Cleveland house for thirty years until his death.

The elder Santi had a head and a disposition like a Caesar, and he may have suffered from delusions of grandeur now and then. But he was to elegant dining in Cleveland what Oscar of the Waldorf had been around New York some years earlier.

The banquets he arranged used to feature French, or separate service for each guest, which is unheard of at banquets nowadays. Most of the dinners Santi supervised were notable for floral displays and niceties like jeweled tablecloths, also the finest plate and china in the Statler organization. Then, as the 1920's and prohibition wore on, his banquets became less ornate. Even Mr. Santi could not arouse in his customers the enthusiasm over fine dishes and elaborate displays that were his passion.

He spent the last twenty-five years of his life bemoaning the passing of the era of elegant dining, and hopefully predicting its return. Sometimes when a prominent group was planning a dinner, they would tell Mr. Santi they wanted *filet mignon,* baked Alaska —the best, at eight dollars a cover. "But," somebody would remember, "you've got to serve it in forty-five minutes. We're going on the air at nine P.M."

In the privacy of his office, Mr. Santi would explode. "Poof! It is ridiculous. They want I should serve in forty-five minutes. In all history of words, no speech has ever been worth an eight-dollar steak."

The old gentleman carefully educated his son, Francis, to carry on with the fine dining idea in Cleveland when he left off. He sent Francis to college in Italy four years, then two years to hotel school in Switzerland, and saw to it that the boy worked for years in food departments of well-known European hotels. So when the old Santi died, while visiting his birthplace at Florence, Francis stepped into his place.

Francis Santi is not ordinarily an impressive man. He is gangling, and his sport coat is often rumpled. His collar and tie get askew, his hair may be falling over his forehead, and he wears thick-lensed spectacles. But when Francis gets into his uniform, tails and shirt front, behind a vessel of flaming brandies in a dark room, he undergoes a startling change. No symphony conductor, interpreting the most delicate passages from Chopin, ever wielded the baton with gestures of more refined elegance than those with which Francis Santi waves his long-handled spoons.

"It is, or should be, the enthusiasm of the maître d'hôtel," Santi, the Younger was remarking some time ago, "to undertake the unusual in giving 'Personalized Service' at small and medium-sized affairs for the satisfaction and delight of his patrons. 'Personalized Service' means the partial preparation in view of the patrons' own eyes, as the saying goes, of fine foods. That is the old-line theory and practice of this profession to which I have the honor to belong. . . .

"A steak is a steak, as a point of fact, as the saying goes. There is very little I can do to enhance the steak, except to produce it with the French service. But from the point of view of certain fowl, I can make an impressive display by the proper carving of it before the guests, and serving it with the wild rice and, perhaps, the bottoms of artichoke hearts, sauté.

"There are certain salads that can be prepared in the dining room to the great visual satisfaction of the guests. A Princesse salad—no. With that, you slice the head of lettuce. Then you add the spears of asparagus, a slice of tomato, a piece of pimento, then dressing. This is best prepared in the kitchen.

"But we can suggest to the guest a Caesar salad. For this, a wooden bowl and the wooden spoons are brought into the dining room for the preparation. There is the combination of the lettuces . . . the wine vinegar . . . the raw eggs . . . the imported olive oil . . . the garlic rye bread cubes . . . the sections of anchovies . . . the salt in its silver container . . . the pepper in its mill . . . the watermelon rind . . . the lemon juice . . . the grated Parmesan cheese . . . your sections of tomato. All this can be gracefully assembled before the eyes of the guests with a certain degree of showmanship. Yes, showmanship, I believe, is the essence of this profession.

"I have served here a banquet of five hundred persons with flaming cherries jubilee. This may be done in an arresting manner, involving much showmanship. We have the five hundred dessert plates, the five hundred napkins, the five hundred individual ice blocks, the five hundred glass nappies and the five hundred individual molds of ice cream. There are four stations with chafing dishes, where the cherries are fired with brandy and rum. You must have split-second timing here of the flaming of the cherries to coincide with the entry into the room, in the hands of trained waiters, of the five hundred dessert plates, the five hundred napkins, the five hundred individual ice blocks, the five hundred glass nappies and the five hundred individual molds of ice cream. Every guest must be served at approximately the same time to achieve the desired effect. It is all highly technical.

"One of the most delightful offerings of all foods is the 'Roast Pheasant *en Plumage* (Autumn Festival Presentation).' For this, the feathers are plucked from the pheasant with the greatest care. A sandwich loaf of bread is French fried to create upon it a crust. The feathers and the head are wired upon this in a most natural manner, and the wings are spread to heroic proportions. Under this plumage and its supporting framework is placed a roast pheasant, which is then mounted among the vines of grape, the October leaves and the vegetables of autumn . . . the glowing pumpkin, the russet apple, the golden pear, the yellow leaves of the maple, the sober brown of oak.

"After the presentation has been wheeled about the room for the inspection of the guests, the remainder of the roast pheasants are brought into the room in chafing dishes, and, due to the fact that only the breast is generally used, because of its tenderness, the breast is carved before the guests, and served, half of a breast to each guest, with the appropriate garnishes.

"I must say that it requires much salesmanship—if I am allowed the use of this word—on my part to convince my patrons that they should take advantage of this type of personalized service. If I am fortunate in a year, perhaps one group out of every ten will accept some of the personalized services my department is equipped to perform.

"My task is even harder with wines. I am forever battling with my honorable customers to persuade them to truly appreciate the bearing that wines have upon foods. One enhances the other; brings out the hidden flavors of both. At times it seems a bit discouraging—a losing fight, because they will not be convinced. Except for a bit of champagne to toast the bride at weddings, most of them will not have wine at all."

22

The Vanishing Profession

E. M. Statler gave a lot of thought during his lifetime to how the custom of tipping might be abolished. But, since tipping is something bigger than any one industry and is grounded upon basic human behavior, he concluded that he alone was not a powerful enough man to kill it, although he regarded tipping as sinister, to say nothing of being stupid and ridiculous.

He once made a strong experiment against the practice in his hotel checkrooms and dining rooms, but it didn't work. In spite of all the signs and instructions to the contrary, customers still insisted on handing a dime or a quarter or a dollar to the girl behind the counter when she gave them their hat or to the waiter for his service. Statler finally gave up his crusade, and published reluctantly in his Statler Hotel Service Code that he did not believe a hotel could be maintained on a tipless basis, because some people would tip in spite of all the rules.

"But," he added to his customers, "please do not tip unless you feel like it. If you tip, let your tipping be the yielding to a genuine desire, not conforming to an outrageous custom."

Statler spent a lot of money developing the Servidor and installing them in his hotels. They eliminate the necessity of the guests' coming in contact with and tipping the service employees.

Servidors are now used in many hotels outside the Statler organization, but the first ones in the world were installed in the Pennsylvania Hotel in New York.

Before his death, Statler was considering a plan to serve meals via Servidor—breakfasts, at least. His idea was a "packaged breakfast," a simple meal a guest might order by telephone at night. It would consist, perhaps, of cold fruit juice in a thermos jug, toast or rolls kept warm in a special container, jelly or marmalade, and hot coffee in a thermos. This would be enclosed in a package and delivered at the hour named into the Servidor in the guest's door. A guest could have his breakfast in the dining room or the coffee shop, if he chose, but Statler figured that the "packaged breakfast" would save guests time and trouble, and would, of course, eliminate the necessity of tipping at breakfast time.

Statler died before he put this into effect, and the organization has not pushed the idea since. The company still does what it can to live up to the old man's operational proverb—"Tip grafters get short shrift here"—by keeping investigators traveling from hotel to hotel. Their duties include handing out meager tips to employees, and observing their reactions. If a bellboy or porter registers outward disgust at the size of the tip, he is reported to the management.

But, neither Mr. Statler nor anybody else has ever been able to do much about the traditional principles of tipping in hotel dining rooms. That is all tied up with human vanity, pride and snobbery. If Statler had been able to revolutionize dining-room tipping— which would have amounted to readjusting human nature—by now he would be recognized easily as the greatest reformer in the history of the world, instead of just the greatest reformer in the history of the hotel business.

Recently, as a luncheon a gentleman was giving in the Embassy Room of the Washington Statler was ending and the guests were having their coffee, a waiter in charge of that table whispered a prophecy to Kurt Moss, the headwaiter. He said he'd give Moss every penny over ten per cent that this man tipped the waiters for serving his seventy-five-dollar party. Sure enough, when the bill was settled, the tip was exactly $7.50. The waiter had figured what it would be when he had observed the host urge upon one of his guests the last piece of cake, and, when the guest said he couldn't eat any more, the host had consumed it himself. It is an axiom among waiters that anybody who can't stand to see food he is paying for go back to the kitchen is not a good tipper.

In days gone by, ten per cent of the bill was regarded as the proper tip, but tipping, like everything else, has undergone inflation. A guest can still get by with tipping ten per cent without being considered a "stiff," provided the waiter is good-natured and hasn't worked too hard serving him. A "stiff" is the most scurrilous word in the waiters' vocabulary, and refers to an individual who tips poorly, or not at all. Nowadays, a tip of fifteen per cent is usually regarded as *de rigueur*, and, of course, twenty per cent is still better.

When an old-time waiter sees a guest sit down at his table, he generally knows within a couple of minutes—often before the guest takes his seat—approximately what his tip will be, and the waiter governs his service accordingly. He bases his estimates upon the guest's appearance and behavior, which waiters have been observing ever since humans began to eat at tables, and waiters to serve them.

Some indications are: Guests who study the menu at great length are usually not good tippers. The waiters believe—and they are usually right—that the man would probably prefer a steak, or a roast or a roasted chicken right off, but he studies the menu because he is more interested in price than in complete satisfaction of his appetite. And, if he is cautious about what he spends on what he eats, he will also be cautious about what he gives the waiter for serving. The best tippers, as far as the menu test goes, are those who tell the captain or the waiter in general what food and wines they would like, and leave the details up to him.

The sort of necktie a man wears is an excellent criterion of what sort of tipper he is. The suit doesn't mean too much, in the waiters' judgment, but if the guest is wearing an inexpensive tie, the waiter never expects much from him. Waiters' thinking here is that if a man is not fastidious enough to wear a good type of neckwear, he either hasn't been around enough to know what he is expected to tip—and people who tip by instinct almost always tip below standard—or else he doesn't care particularly what people, including waiters, think of him.

The type of shirt he is wearing has a strong bearing. Those who wear white shirts tip better ordinarily than those with colored shirts. Of all colored-shirt wearers, those who wear shirts with stripes are, in the waiters' judgment, the lowest form.

Another strong indication as to tipping type is the sort of drink the guest orders. As a general rule of all drinkers around New York, those who prefer rye with ginger ale are the worst. Waiters grind their teeth when they hear that hated order given. A rye-and-water drinker is better, a bourbon-and-water drinker is better still, a bourbon-and-soda drinker is another improvement, and a Scotch-and-water man is excellent. But no tipper is as bad as a rye-and-ginger man, with the possible exception of the party that orders beer all around as soon as it is seated.

Another type generally "stiffish" are pipe smokers. Waiters figure one reason for this is that pipes are cheaper to operate than cigarettes are to buy, and most men who smoke pipes are more inclined to count their pennies. Pipe smokers are likely also to be more of the nonconformist type in most things, and if there is anybody for whom waiters have no patience it is the nonconformist.

Sometimes when a notoriously bad tipper comes to dine, waiters will set about to "break" him, which means to smother him with service. They will swarm about his table, lighting cigarettes as soon as he or one of his guests produces one, and empty the ash trays as soon as the first ash comes to rest. Glasses are refilled after every sip. The waiter will straighten each piece of china or silver the instant it is moved ever so slightly out of line, and bring a new napkin almost as soon as anybody at that table touches the napkin he has to his lips. Each dish is served with a flourish resembling a magician producing the missing lady. There is so much service that it becomes ridiculous and embarrassing to the victim, but there isn't much he can do except leave a big tip when the travesty is finished.

The responsibility of seeing that waiters do not behave in this unseemly manner and to guide smoothly all other operations of the dining room is that of the headwaiter, a strange and difficult profession. To fulfill his function properly, a headwaiter must have intelligence, organizational ability, diplomacy, a sense of justice, a splendid memory, a touch of snobbery, a suave bearing, a bit of the mailed-fist-in-the-velvet-glove, a dash of dignity and lots and lots of the good old oil.

The largest dining room in the Statler organization is the Café Rouge of the New York house, which, on a busy Saturday night, will have as many as 600 people dining at the same time. The largest crowd in recent years was 915 one Saturday evening to hear Charlie Spivak there. Ordinarily, about forty waiters, four captains, and twenty bus boys handle the crowd under John Banchero, headwaiter in that room since 1920. He has been on the job so long that he fulfills it almost automatically, but on a busy evening, John has got to see that the following does, or does not, happen:

That guests do not get too much to drink and insult other guests. . . . That unattached men do not become too chummy with parties containing ladies. . . . That dancers, fired by the gyrations of the band, do not go out of control upon the dance floor and tread on or maim, other dancers, less agile . . . That guests do not succeed in their efforts to lead the band. . . . That people do not become too enraged when soup is spilled down their necks. . . . That they are given fresh clothes, when such an event happens, and that their spoiled things are cleaned, if possible, before they leave. . . . That female diners, inspired by alcohol, do not disrobe in public. . . . That groups do not join in song. . . . That gentlemen do not pinch the backsides of passing ladies. . . . That couples do not confuse the dance floor with the boudoir. . . . That everybody enjoys his food. . . . That waiters do not insult guests, and that guests don't kill waiters. And, above all, that these duties are carried out in a graceful and inconspicuous way, so that nobody, besides those directly concerned, is aware that anything untoward is taking place.

Besides the qualities already enumerated that all good headwaiters should have, most of them are elevated from the ranks because they excel in some particular. John, for instance, was probably made a headwaiter because of his tranquil, benevolent disposition, which tends to soothe difficult situations before they develop. Furthermore, he was trained well in his profession since boyhood, first in hotels in Italy, where he was born, and, since 1905, in the best hotels in New York.

On the other hand, a headwaiter such as Eddie Laughlin, of the St. Louis Statler, was not trained in Europe, but in his home town, East St. Louis, Illinois. He started there as a waiter at seventeen, then graduated to the St. Louis hotels, where he won a reputation of being particularly patient in handling superdifficult guests. He may have won his headwaiter's spurs at the Mayfair Hotel, in his pre-Statler days, because he was known as the only waiter in St. Louis, who could, with any degree of self-control, serve a certain now-deceased millionaire. It was this man's custom to dine frequently, with his large family, at hotels where Eddie worked, and his idea of a waiter's tip for serving him and his whole family was twenty-five cents.

Then there is Kurt Moss, headwaiter in the swank Embassy Room of the Washington Statler. He is a suave, earnest and highly polished apple. The quality of headwaitership which he possesses in greatest abundance might best be described by telling about the bronze star that he won during the last war, and how he came to be decorated by General Eisenhower himself during one of the General's frequent sojourns at Statler's Washington hotel.

The decoration dates back to the time Kurt was an army cook. He'd been chef at the Hickory House in Miami before enlisting, but he won his greatest laurels with the army in Africa, where he conjured up mysteriously strawberry and peach shortcakes for the officers in the middle of the desert. He boasted that he could produce in the midst of all that sand any dish that an officer might fancy. One officer, thinking to stump him, said one day he had a yen for tuna fish.

Now, this segment of the army was being partly supplied with food dropped by parachute. The supplies occasionally included a sackful of beef hearts, which most of the soldiers regarded so unenthusiastically that these were never cooked for the mess, but given away to passing Bedouins.

Yet, Kurt relied chiefly on beef hearts to produce his tuna. Secretly he boiled a large potful all night. Then he ground them up with olive oil, celery and various spices. In a couple of roasting pans he shaped this conglomeration to look like fish. He baked

them so that they had an outside crust, stuck lemons where their
mouths were supposed to be, and announced to the officers' mess
that here was tuna fish.

The officers, whose brains may have been addled somewhat by
the desert sun, pronounced it the finest tuna they had ever eaten,
and did away with all of it. They were so impressed that Kurt's
commanding officer called him in, and asked how he had produced
tuna fish in the middle of the desert. He said it was a military
secret. In a couple of days the commanding general called him up,
and made it an order. When Kurt had told him, this general was
so impressed that he had Kurt placed in charge of the kitchen of
the Hotel Alpino on the Swiss border in Europe that the Army was
about to open as an officers' recreation spot.

It is from these achievements that Kurt's decoration stemmed.
Now, obviously any man who can make some old beef hearts into
something he feeds to people under the name of tuna fish, and wins
a bronze star doing it—instead of getting shot—is wasting his
time being anything except a headwaiter, which is what Kurt became at the Washington Statler.

Despite his prestige, the headwaiter does not benefit from tips,
in ordinary times, as much as most people think. A regular waiter
is paid from twenty to maybe thirty-five dollars a week by the
hotel, depending upon the union rate in that city. An ordinary
waiter around New York probably makes eighty-five to a hundred
dollars a week in tips, while an exceptional waiter might make
almost twice that. Most people tip the waiter at least something,
under the impression that this tip is apportioned to all the dining-
room personnel. Only about one party out of four tips the headwaiter or the captains, who take the order and have charge of
serving.

The headwaiter and the captains share their tips, while the regular waiter gives up only ten per cent of his tips, to his bus boy.
Probably even fewer guests would tip the headwaiter and captains,
if it were not for one powerful asset that all good headwaiters
possess, namely the ability to remember guests' names. When a
guest comes into the dining room with a party for the first time in
six months, and the headwaiter calls him by name, gives him a
good table, and recalls what he likes to eat and drink, that man

can find nothing wrong with the dinner, and usually gives the headwaiter a good tip. There is a saying among headwaiters: "When you call a guest by name, you have got him licked."

John Banchero, in the New York Cafe Rougé, can probably call a couple or so thousand guests by name, and remember what they like to eat. He can retain this information without seeing the guest for as long as six months to a year. Most headwaiters have a system for remembering names by associations, often based on the appearance and mannerisms of individual guests. These associations are sometimes unflattering to the guest, if he only knew. Many headwaiters remember certain guests because they recall various inhabitants of the forest, stream or barnyard.

There was a guest named Mr. Lake, whom one headwaiter never had difficulty remembering because this Mr. Lake walked, in the headwaiter's view, like a duck. It was easy to associate duck with lake.

Most headwaiters in hotels did very well for themselves during the last war, when on most nights there was a long line waiting at the velvet ropes to get into most dining rooms. There was such a frenzy to get tables that people pushed money in large quantities upon the headwaiter at the door. The ordinary waiters did well themselves. Some waiters now own expensive homes and apartment buildings from their savings from wartime tips. Headwaiters take a dim view of this. They often say that the war ruined a lot of waiters, because they feel a waiter who is financially well off is no longer concerned enough with pleasing the guests, but is inclined to be independent, surly, and generally no good.

The group that takes perhaps the darkest of all views on waiters as a class are the hotel food-checkers, who sit at a desk between the kitchen and the dining room, check prices on each item the waiters bring out, and stamp the price on the guest's check. In some large formal dining rooms, their desk may be seen in a remote corner back of a potted palm, where the checkers preside over their adding machines like a couple of sour school marms, viewing the waiters coming and going with a hostile eye. It is the opinion of many checkers that practically all waiters constantly plot the financial ruin of the hotel and robbery of the guests through bamboozling the checkers in various low ways.

In formal dining rooms, each waiter generally has three or four tables. When guests are seated at one of his tables, the food checkers issue the waiter a check, which contains a serial number and for which the waiter signs. Each time he brings an order of food or drink to that table, he passes the checker, who takes the check from his tray, adds to the charges the price of the new items, and gives it back to the waiter.

When the guests at that table are ready to leave, the waiter takes the check to the checker, who totals it. Then he presents it to the guest, who pays the waiter, who takes the check and the money to the checker. She takes the money, gives the waiter the proper change, keeps the check and cancels out the name of the waiter as being any longer responsible for that check.

If, after a waiter has been issued a check, he should lose it or not be able to produce it when his guests are ready to leave, the checkers react as Tower of London guards might be expected to behave if they couldn't find the crown jewels. This almost never happens, but Miss Georgia Graham, senior checker in the Statler Company, recalls bitterly such an instance that happened once when she was working at the Cleveland Statler. Four checks disappeared mysteriously, and each checker was required to memorize the serial numbers of the four, and glance at the number of every check she stamped for weeks thereafter to see if it was one of those missing.

When this case was finally solved, it turned out that a waiter had applied for a job at the Statler, and was hired by the headwaiter, issued a uniform, a badge and four checks. He never used these, but slipped down to his locker, changed into his street clothes and disappeared from the Statler forever. At a boarding house, where some waiters lived, he sold the four checks for ten dollars each to some regular Statler dining-room waiters.

The idea was that a waiter who had one of the fraudulent checks would keep it until an opportune time, when the dining room was crowded, and he was serving a table of guests who were spending lots of money. He would have their bill stamped upon the check he had bought, but which the checkers didn't know he had. Then, when the guests paid their bill, he would simply keep the money.

Since the check was not signed out to him, there would be no way for the hotel to know unless one of the checkers remembered the serial numbers of the missing checks, and recognized it when he brought out his order. That is what Miss Graham did. She called the house officers, and they watched the waiter until after the guests paid him and left. When he didn't turn in the money to the checker's desk, they had him arrested.

Since that time, Miss Graham has looked with suspicion upon waiters. She started the Statler system of checkers writing the total of the customer's bill in red ink, so the waiters could not up it—a practice she believes many waiters stand ready to do. She quotes horrendous examples of inexperienced checkers working at busy bar checkers' desks who have been shortchanged by crafty waiters, and of parties of guests in bars who innocently pay checks other and larger than their own. She has her checking crew of eleven women and five men make every bar waiter while he is in front of the bar checker, count the number of drinks on his tray, and compare them with the number listed on the guest's check. This is to forestall waiters from cadging drinks for themselves. On a few notable occasions, she has been known to descend from her check desk, grab a waiter by the throat, and shake him, like a terrier with a mole, after hearing him mention that some customer was "stiffing" him, and he thought he'd just make this up by adding a five-dollar tip for himself on the bill, which the customer probably wouldn't glance at.

Miss Graham's view is undoubtedly prejudiced, but she is haunted by the fact that if one of her checker's accounting for an entire meal in a restaurant is as far off balance as $1.50, she will be called up by the auditor. Besides that, she is one of the old-time employees, whose loyalty to the late E. M. Statler remains fiery and intense. She went to work for the Old Man in his Cleveland house in 1912, and has opened all the hotels the company has built since, serving as head checker at each until this difficult function was running well. She has known thousands of waiters, good and bad, but she remembers mainly the bad ones and the less flattering phases of their profession.

"I can spot a waiter as far as I can see one, whether he is in the dining room in uniform and carrying a tray, or whether he is in street clothes on the subway," she was remarking the other day.

"I see them on the subway all the time—these old waiters. I don't know a lot of them personally, but I can recognize them all right. They're standing there holding hard onto the strap to rest their old, flat feet, and their shoulders are stooped. They're wearing some tired old shoes they've blacked up to work in. Beneath the skirts of their overcoat you will probably see that they're wearing their old formal trousers, with a frayed satin stripe down the side, and you know they're on their way to work somewhere.

"I'm talking about these old-timers who serve hotel banquets. They have had good jobs in their time, a lot of them . . . head-waiters, maître d's. But they have drunk so much whisky and played the horses all their lives, and they haven't got a dime at their stage of life, when they ought to be resting and taking it easy in a little house of their own somewhere out in the country.

"Some of them shake so hard they can hardly hold a plate. Why we had an old extra around some time ago who was actually ninety years old. What's more, he could run circles around some of the others who were ten, or twenty or thirty years younger than he was. I asked him how he did it, and he said he drank a pint of gin every morning for breakfast instead of coffee."

The world of the extra waiter is a sort of limbo where waiters go eventually who are old and broke, or unfortunate or who have been bad. There are about 1,200 of them registered with the union in New York.

It should be said that there are many good waiters—in spite of what some food checkers might think—who are honorable, and honest, and who save their money, and work hard and provide for their families. But they have regular jobs in hotel dining rooms or in room service or in restaurants. Or else they are "regular extras." They report regularly at a certain hotel every day and usually handle the private parties, up to 200 guests. As many as are available are sent to help serve at banquets, which are dinners of from 200 guests up.

But the straight extras are the scrapings of the barrel, who report each day to the union office. They are assigned strictly through rotation of their numbers, and hotels, under their union contracts, must accept whatever waiters are sent, regardless of their age, appearance or ability. A waiter can be refused by a hotel only if he is drinking on the job, or refuses to work overtime in an emergency, or if he is caught in a dishonest act.

To serve a dinner, an extra waiter gets five dollars a night from New York hotels. He serves a table of ten guests, and receives a tip amounting to twelve per cent of the price per plate for his ten diners. This tip is figured in by the hotel when it sets the price for the banquet. The most popular banquet-type dinner at the New York Statler is turkey entree at five dollars per plate. This means that the waiter receives a six-dollar tip, plus his five dollars, or a total of eleven dollars for the evening.

Extra waiters prefer to serve a gay banquet, which gives them the opportunity to fetch drinks for the guests at their table. They get extra tips for that. Furthermore, some old waiters enjoy drinking the leavings from the glasses. They often carry a bottle, into which they pour remains of manhattans, martinis, bourbons and Scotches to form a hideous brew, with which they refresh themselves from time to time.

Another habit of extras, which the hotels do what they can to curb, at least in the dining room, is to take choice leftovers from the plates, which they eat either in a corner of the kitchen, or take home. In some cities, extra waiters know that most guests are not aware that their tips have been figured in with the price of the dinner so they will quietly start passing a plate, in some of the less prominent parts of the room, for their own private tip collection.

The banquet plates are served by the hotel's regular employees in the kitchen, and the waiters act as a sort of conveyor belt from the kitchen to the tables in the dining room. Most of the extras could no more handle the deft French service than they could perform sleight of hand. When they hold a dish or a tray, their grip is uncertain, and they often drop things.

When it is time for them to go into the dining room with another course or to clear tables, they are summoned to action by the banquet headwaiter and his captains, splendid in immaculate dinner clothes. They shout at the extras, like cattle drovers, in an effort to squeeze from them some semblance of spirit and snap.

Anyone who watches the service in a hotel banquet kitchen will quickly realize why hotel managements have been so concerned in recent times about the increasing shortage of waiters. Some hotels have abandoned waiters for banquets, among them the Detroit Statler, which uses waitresses.

A number of plans for remedying the waiter shortage, some highly improbable, have been advanced by various thinkers on that subject. These include one man who has been trying to interest the Statler organization for years in his "invention"—a system whereby tables would be served in a kitchen immediately below the dining room. The tables would then pop up mechanically, already served, into the dining room through openings in the floor, like quick-growing mushrooms.

The reason for the waiter shortage is that the old waiters are dying out and retiring, except those unfortunate ones who must cling on with the tattered fringe of extras, and they too are dying out fast. Very few new waiters have been able to come to this country since the tightening of immigration restrictions almost thirty years ago, and even fewer Americans have aspirations to be waiters. That profession has never become a high art among native Americans, as it has long been with Europeans.

Any American youngster who enters the food department of a hotel, in any position from dishwasher up does not set his goal at being a waiter in a fine dining room. According to René Black, manager of restaurants at the Waldorf-Astoria: "Your American is more interested in becoming some day the president of the company that operates the hotel than in whether or not Madame has the proper fork for her fish, or whether Monsieur is served his consommé at the proper temperature for his fullest enjoyment."

23

How to Build a Hotel

Since the days of the Tower of Babel, few construction projects have aroused more local comment than the new Hotel Statler did in Los Angeles, California, during the two years it was being built between the summers of 1950 and 1952.

Department-store owners and proprietors of other large businesses located in the downtown area, who had been worried about the spread of the city's shopping centers away from downtown and out into the fringes of the desert country, greeted the announcement of the new hotel with outcries of unqualified joy. A proposed four-million-dollar civic-sponsored downtown parking garage under Pershing Square, which had been discussed for years, went forward immediately under the impetus of enthusiasm inspired by commencement of the new Statler.

"If the smartest hotel operators in the world figure that downtown Los Angeles is a good place to do business," the executive secretary of the Downtown Business Men's Association told his membership, "I think we who are already in business here have nothing to worry about."

Construction began, after the Statler was announced, on a number of downtown office and other business buildings, whose owners or backers had been delaying because of doubts as to the future of downtown Los Angeles. Property values in the vicinity of the new project tripled within months after the hotel-office building had begun. The Statler Company's lawyers had to get busy discouraging motels and various undistinguished hostelries in and around Los Angeles from changing their names to "Statler" or reasonable facsimiles thereof.

A. Arthur Nickman, representative on the job for architects Holabird & Root & Burgee, of Chicago, during the period of construction, received constant requests to address local civic, social and fraternal bodies on details of the new project, which contains twenty-five acres of floor space, and has the distinction of being the largest of only four sizable hotels to be built in the United States between the boom days of the 1920's and the opening of the latter half of the twentieth century.

According to Nickman, more interest was shown by architects, engineers and builders from all parts of the world in the Los Angeles Statler than in any project with which he had been connected over the past twenty-five years, including the atomic-bomb plant at Oak Ridge, Tennessee. Almost every week, builders from as far away as Australia, Sweden, Denmark and England showed up on the job, and asked to be shown through.

Local newspapers, enthusiastic over the new hotel, once reported that oil had been struck on the site and again that a gold mine had been discovered there. Both reports were in error. As soon as definite plans for the hotel were announced, would-be guests, anxious to stay there, began shipping trunks and other luggage to the Los Angeles Statler, under the misapprehension that the place was already operating. Baggage, in varying amounts, continued to arrive every week at the construction project during the entire two years the hotel was in building.

Los Angeles taxicab drivers, piloting their fares about the lonely reaches of downtown, which becomes relatively deserted after sundown, would assure their fares: "Just wait until that new Statler opens. Downtown will have some life at night then."

Local civic leaders attributed all this interest to the prestige of the

Statler name and to the fact that Los Angeles was going to get its first important downtown hotel since the Los Angeles Biltmore was built in 1923.

Through the atmosphere they generate and the life that clusters around them, a city's important hotels, more than any other of its enterprises, breathe the personality of that city. It is because of its many imposing hotels, in great part, that Midtown Manhattan is regarded by many people as the most exciting urban spot in the world, especially after dark. Lower Manhattan, which has no hotels, is as deserted as a dead city, once the sun has gone down.

The Los Angeles Biltmore alone was not enough to create a definite center in that sprawling city. The reason Los Angeles had only this important hotel was that most of the city's growth had come since hotel building ceased almost entirely at the close of the 1920's. Since the war, when its greatest growth has taken place, Los Angeles had not gotten a new hotel because most operators had been convinced that large, fine hotels could not be built, in these times of towering building costs, that would make money, or even break even.

With the idea of more effectively lifting property values and increasing the desirability of the section for blocks around its holdings, the Statler Company decided to accompany its hotel with an office building and garage—like a miniature Rockefeller Center—which would be called "Statler Center."

The proportion of store space for rental in the Los Angeles hotel is larger than in any of the other Statlers. The idea of renting hotel space to shops appears to have been hit upon by accident by Cesar Ritz, just before the turn of the century, when an addition was built to the Paris Ritz. The addition was connected with the main part of the hotel by a long corridor, which impressed Ritz as being gloomy and dull. In order to brighten it, he invited some Paris modistes and jewelers to rent display space there.

Mr. Statler, when he first began to build hotels, was a trifle slow in taking full advantage of Ritz's idea. His houses in Cleveland and Detroit had very little store-rental space, until some years after his death, when the present management enlarged shop space in these two older houses. However, by the time he built his Boston hotel, Mr. Statler had become so enthusiastic about store rentals in hotels that he erected an office building with his hotel. Until the Los Angeles house came along, the Boston Statler was the only hotel in the world with an office building adjoining.

The Boston Statler office-building operation has turned out to be so satisfactory that the present Statler management will probably build an office building as a part of each of its future hotel enterprises of 1,000 rooms or more. Besides the rentals from the office buildings, the Statler Company manages to get office-building tenants, such as advertising or other firms that do considerable entertaining and are good customers for the hotel's restaurants and bars. The office-building space in the Los Angeles Statler was almost 100 per cent rented a year before the building was completed.

In calculating its expenses and profit in Los Angeles, Robert L. Sussieck, vice-president and treasurer of the company, figures—on the basis of Boston and Washington experience—a return of 16.7 per cent on the $10,925,000 of the company's own money that is its equity in the enterprise.

In conceiving its Los Angeles hotel, the Statler Company had two principal problems, which will confront any operator who contemplates building a new hotel in these times: First, a type of construction had to be designed that would not cost so much that the operation would be defeated financially before it began. Second, the company had to conceive innovations that would make the average guest prefer to stay in its new hotel, in spite of smaller rooms and other space limitations, made necessary by high building costs, as compared with older hotels.

In the actual construction principal savings in the Los Angeles hotel were effected by making the walls of concrete instead of masonry. Concrete walls not only are cheaper to construct, but, being thinner than masonry, conserve interior space. Lighter than usual concrete was used in the walls, allowing a lighter steel frame and less extensive foundations than are usual even with regular concrete walls. A new type of thinner than usual partitions were built between rooms, principally to save space. The expense of plastering the ceilings was eliminated by painting directly upon the concrete.

A disadvantage of concrete walls is that they look bare and blank, compared with masonry. To break the flat monotony and give the exterior an interesting, modern appearance, the Los Angeles Statler planners had built a new type of aluminum window frame that extends about three inches outward from the exterior walls, like window boxes, instead of being set into the walls in the usual way.

The concrete for the walls was poured into forms made with indentations, or creases, so that when the walls had set, they gave the appearance of being made of oblong blocks of stone. The purpose here was twofold: to give the walls a more attractive surface and to prevent joints from being noticeable in the concrete where the pouring stopped for one day and was commenced the next. This was the first time, so far as the architects know, that a plan was worked out in advance for pouring the concrete so that the joints would be thus concealed.

For room partitions the company is using a steel wire netting that carries a two-inch thickness of solid plaster. This two-inch wall contrasts with the five-inch wall of gypsum blocks coated with plaster in ordinary modern construction. The company's main concern here was that the thin walls might transmit too much noise from room to room. So the executives in New York had the partitions between their offices made like the proposed room partitions for the Los Angeles hotel, and harkened to their own office-to-office noises for two years to test how the new walls worked.

The executives concluded that the new-type partitions excluded about as much sound from next door as the old type did. Actually, the new-type walls reduce the sounds from next door by about thirty-nine decibels, as compared with a forty-two decibel reduction by old type wall. However, the company decided that the difference was not great enough to surrender the great saving in interior space of three inches per room that the new partitions made possible.

Besides the savings in actual construction of the building, the Los Angeles hotel is arranged for more economical operation of departments—the kitchens, for instance. Most hotels of this size have from five to ten kitchens for serving guest meals, or else waiters have to operate from the kitchen to several floor levels. The Los Angeles Statler has only two kitchens: a main kitchen on the main floor and a banquet kitchen immediately above it.

Each opens directly into the rooms it must serve, an arrangement made possible by the large building site, which gave the architects room to play around with arrangements. The company estimates that its Los Angeles kitchens can serve about twenty-five per cent more people in a given time than most other hotel kitchens of similar size. Of course, this means twenty-five per cent more income when business is at capacity. Furthermore, the Los Angeles kitchens can be operated with fifteen to twenty-five per cent fewer employees than most other hotel kitchens serving the same number of guests.

As originally conceived, the average size of each room of the Los Angeles hotel was 8,000 cubic feet—that is lumping all rooms together, guest rooms, dining rooms, kitchens, public spaces and dividing by the total number of rooms in the building. The company decided in 1947 it could not afford to build that much space, and turned the plans over to one of its young architects, William B. Tabler, to cut the cubic footage down to 6,000 per room, if possible. Tabler was able to do this largely by taking a cold-blooded and scientific attitude on what the size of each of the hotel's departments should be. He had learned that in hotels, as in most places, department heads are interested in getting the most possible space for their departments.

When he surveyed the department space in existing Statler hotels, he found that the size of the same departments varied widely from hotel to hotel. For instance, the banquet kitchen of the 1000-room Detroit Statler, built in 1915, contained 4500 square feet, while the banquet kitchen of the 1300-room Boston Statler, built in 1928, contained 11,000 square feet. The Detroit Statler's cigar stand occupied 182 square feet, while that of the Boston Statler took up 595 square feet.

He began questioning department heads and employees as to the specific use made of various sections of their department space. Tabler was thus able to revise the size of the Los Angeles departments considerably downward. This was the first time in the history of the hotel business, so far as is known, when an architect took this approach in determining department sizes.

The average-size guest room in the Los Angeles Statler is 164 square feet. This is slightly smaller than rooms in the Washington Statler, and they are regarded as small in comparison with the older hotels. It is simple enough to save costs by building small rooms. The trick is to make the small rooms more attractive to guests than larger ones in older hotels. The Statler people managed this admirably in their Washington house, where one of the attractions that offsets a room's smallness is air-conditioning.

The St. Louis Statler, in 1935, became the first completely air-conditioned hotel in the world, although the reason for air-conditioning there was the heavy heat of that city and had nothing to do with smallness of rooms.

The Carrier Corporation developed, especially for the Los Angeles Statler, a completely new "high velocity, high pressure," type of air-conditioning, which is expected to have an important effect upon all future air-conditioning because it is cheaper to install and provides a more positive type of air-conditioning. This system chills all air for the building at a central point to a temperature of fifty-five degrees. It forces the cold air through the building under high pressure through two-inch diameter pipes. These pipes are only about half as large as the smallest air-conditioning ducts used in the past, and one of the advantages is the saving of space in the building.

The air enters each guest room through a vent built into the wall just above the doorway leading into the entrance alcove. Back of the vent is built a boxlike "air-mixer," into which a hot-air duct is built as well as a cold-air pipe. The guest regulates the room temperature by mixing hot air into the cold air. This is the most positive type of air-conditioning ever developed, because one room can be kept as cold as fifty-five degrees, while the room next door can be made as warm as eighty-five or ninety degrees.

One of the principal advantages of this system is that it allows the Statler Company, in its new hotel, to avoid the expense of building regular steam-heating pipes throughout the building, and installing radiators and connecting pipes around the walls in each room. This innovation was one of the most important of the Statler answers to high costs of hotel building.

Guest-room windows in the Los Angeles Statler are unusually large, and, like those in the Washington house, are horizontal instead of vertical. The architects arrived at the horizontal-type window when building the Washington house. Because of Washington's building height restrictions, the company lowered its ceilings by about nine inches from normal height to get an extra floor into its building. With lowered ceilings, the ordinary-type windows, running up and down, looked peculiar. So the architects designed horizontal windows, which not only looked in better proportion, but gave the rooms the illusion of having more light, made them look larger and allowed the guest to see out of a greater portion of his window.

In some of the smaller Los Angeles rooms, a mirror is built on the wall at right angles to the window so that it reflects the view from the window. This gives the illusion of greater size and of being on a corner. The Los Angeles building, incidentally, is built with guest-room wings going off in oblique directions so that every room is an outside room. There are no courts, which is one of the few times a large hotel has been built without a court since the Middle Ages.

Most of the rooms have studio beds, which conserve the room's usable space. In some of the smaller rooms, the bed lamp is built into a picture frame above the head of the disguised bed to further conceal the fact that the room is used for sleeping. Some lamps, which are not concealed or camouflaged, are made so that half a lamp looks like a whole lamp. These lamps, made especially for the new hotel, look like regular dressing-table lamps that have been sawed in two from top to bottom. They are mounted on a dressing table, or at least the Los Angeles Statler's version of a dressing table, flush against the mirrored wall. The lamps take up only half as much space as lamps of their apparent size would, and their reflection in the mirror to the rear makes them look like regular whole lamps.

The color theme throughout most of the hotel's guest rooms and public rooms is cinnamon, willow green and tangerine, which are the company decorators' interpretation of the general atmosphere of Southern California set to color. Specially designed furniture is intended both to give the rooms a streamlined, contemporary look and to save space. Instead of the old chest-of-drawers, bureau, dressing table and desk, these furniture functions have been consolidated into one large combination piece that serves as all four. Extra drawers have been built into one end of the clothes closets. The closets are also arranged so they may be used as dressing rooms, which further increases the guest rooms' function as a living room.

The most striking portions of the building are the public parts— lobby, dining rooms, entrances, lobby-floor corridors, terraces and bars. The land surrounding the building is carefully manicured to give the impression of a resort hotel. A kidney-shaped swimming pool at the end of an outdoor cocktail terrace, which opens out of one end of the lobby, adds to this effect. The two principal sides of the lobby are almost entirely of glass, which allows sunlight to penetrate into the lobby all day, and give the interior what the architects conceive as the atmospheric mood of Southern California.

The hotel has three types of entrances. One is the so-called "silk hat" entrance for persons patronizing the hotel's restaurants, bars and the supper club. It opens off Wilshire Boulevard, and leads conveniently in the direction of those parts where the music is playing and drinking is being done.

Most interesting of the entrances is the one for tourists, off the Francisco Street side and one floor below street level. A motor concourse is located there, where tourists may park while unloading their automobiles before the cars are taken into the hotel's garage in the basement. A special registration desk is located near the motor concourse, and there is a special elevator that will take tourists, stained and battered from their travels, to their rooms without the necessity of going through the lobby at all. This is the first real effort made by a large commercial hotel in a city to recapture the tourist business, which motels have been gradually taking from regular hotels for years.

The third entrance, off Seventh Street, is principally to receive guests who arrive by taxicab. It is equipped with a luggage conveyor, like an endless chain, that takes baggage from the street immediately into the lobby in front of the registration desk. This is the first time in hotel history that such a conveyor has been installed. It is the most important innovation in handling arriving luggage since the Statler Company built its motor entrance into the rear of its Washington hotel.

Another idea for saving steps, but in an entirely different direction, has been the construction of a ladies' rest room in the supper club. This was an idea of Mrs. William Marcy, wife of the chairman of the Statler board of directors, who had observed that few night clubs or hotel supper rooms have this important adjunct. Ladies usually have to walk great distances when they have to go to the rest room, and, on nights when considerable drinking is being done, these trips are often frequent.

The main ballroom of the Los Angeles Statler is the first one ever completely equipped for telecasting. Furthermore, the balcony on one side of the room has been arranged with ports, through which newspaper or newsreel cameramen may photograph the speakers and other activities taking place at important banquets without going into the ballroom. Still another new idea in the ballroom is a stage that rises out of the floor by mechanical means, or which can be lowered to floor level and used as a regular part of the room for seating guests. This does not require the services of stage hands, who are expensive.

The ballroom has a permanent stage at one end. There is a special room built under the stairway outside the ballroom and near the supper room, where musicians and entertainers take their meals. In practically every hotel that has entertainment, members of the orchestra eat in the kitchen, getting in everybody's way. The ballroom is also equipped with a special rest room for VIP guests. The need for such a room became apparent at the Washington Statler, where the President and other distinguished guests, when attending important dinners there, have to walk halfway across the hotel every time they want to go to the toilet. A new one was built there recently.

One of the most novel ideas in the entire hotel is the lighting and decoration of the elevator lobbies on guest-room floors. With the idea of getting away from the dormitory atmosphere of guest floors in some hotels, the Statler people have arranged the elevator lobbies on the upper floors like miniatures of the main lobby, and have lighted them with cold cathode. The halls are also lighted with cathode, and these lights gradually grow dimmer the further a person progresses along the hall away from the elevator lobby.

The idea here is for the dimming lights to give the guest the idea that he is nearing a place of rest as he approaches his room. On the other hand, when he leaves his room to go downstairs, walking along the gradually brightening halls to the flashy elevator lobby is calculated to prepare him properly for his descent into the main lobby and all the goings-on down there.

The Statler Company has been giving thought to an idea of painting doors of its guest rooms in a different color for each wing.

One wing, for example, would have blue doors, another red, another green, another yellow. This would add gaiety to the building, and would probably solve also a problem that has bothered guests ever since big hotels have been in existence. This is the problem of remembering the wing in which their room is located. A guest shouldn't have much trouble remembering that his room is in the wing with the green doors.

There are two principal reasons why the Los Angeles Statler has been endowed with all its innovations, gadgets and ideas. One, already mentioned, is they make less obvious to the guest the painful efficiency and cost-saving that must be built into a new hotel in order for it to survive and prosper in these expensive times. The other reason is to build a sort of island of light and gaiety among the innocuous collection of buildings that is downtown Los Angeles.

By creating a bright spot in downtown Los Angeles, the Statler Company has in mind capturing the choice business of that city from the somber Los Angeles Biltmore, an immense, sprawling hotel with vast reaches of carved, beamed ceilings, massive and meaningless expanses of galleries and an exasperating atmosphere of established complacency. The new Statler has no carved ceilings or fancy woodwork or overabundance of space. What it has is color, brightness and stainless steel. It represents not only concessions to an age that has relegated fine craftsmanship to the museums; it is also the Statler Company's interpretation of a new era of changed tastes in which, the company believes, people are no longer so much concerned with how a thing is made as in how well it works.

The Los Angeles Statler may be more than a pioneering venture into a new type of hotel construction. It might be considered as an introduction of big-city ways into a frontier country town. For, in its way, Los Angeles is a frontier town, as San Francisco was a frontier, gold-hungry town a hundred years ago. But, in a hundred years, San Francisco has attained a handsome cosmopolitan polish that includes a number of fine hotels.

Los Angeles is still growing and groping. It has sunshine, which may be a greater attraction than gold. It has become the ideal and goal of millions looking for an escape from the steamy poverty in the Southeast, for those seeking a place to rest after the hard work and awful dreary sameness of Iowa and Kansas and for people who come looking for glamour and stay to praise the climate. And with them have come immense factories to take advantage of the hands of all these millions.

Los Angeles is already immense. Someday it may become a great city. It is the Statler people's idea to grow and prosper with this potentially great community. In the meantime, the Los Angeles Statler shouldn't have very much trouble outglamorizing Hollywood, which is eight miles away and is an unimpressive, disappointing and unglamorous place, in spite of all those things Louella Parsons writes.

24

The Statler of the Sticks
and Other Stories

The Statler Company has long been aware that in the hotel business, as in most other enterprises, there is at least one drawback to a chain operation, namely: local pride.

This chain organization, therefore, goes to great pains and expense to offset the situation that—except in Buffalo, where it started, and in New York, where nobody cares about such things—some local people might resent the fact that the Statler hotel in their community is run by an out-of-town corporation. Statler combats this by purchasing supplies and equipment locally, whenever feasible, by participating in local affairs, contributing to local charities and providing services for its guests that many of its local competitors never think of.

One such service is "taking on" over children of guests, on the theory, which politicians have followed for generations, that the shortest way to the heart of any family is to kiss the baby. The company does not actually require its managers to go around kissing youngsters, but their hotels cater to them. The kitchens are geared to prepare all sorts of formulas and children's diets, and are stocked with colorful children's menus and with dishes and crockery decorated with picture characters from Andersen, Grimm and Mother Goose. In the dining rooms, the headwaiter and his captains hover solicitously over child diners, handing out balloons and animal crackers.

Back during the 1930's, when the hotel business was not as rushed as it is nowadays, the Statler hotels decided to take in free all the children who stopped there with their parents during the slow months of July and August. Consequently, during July and August, Statler hotels became the objective of some of the largest families traveling in North America. Broods of from a dozen to eighteen children were constantly showing up, and moving in, with only Mama and Papa paying. One fond father insisted— and won his point—that the Boston Statler accept free as a guest his twenty-eight-year-old son. After all, the man pointed out, the boy *was* his child.

Statler officials still have a sneaking suspicion that a good lot of the large families were planted in their hotels by rival operators, who had taken an extremely pale view of the child-free policy as a dangerous precedent. "We got approximately every large family on the continent that was financially and physically able to travel," one Statler official has recalled, "except Papa Dionne. If we had kept our policy much longer, we'd have probably gotten them, too."

When a new manager is appointed for a Statler hotel, the company expects him to fling himself into local community affairs with abandon, and condition himself to local customs and peculiarities so that he quickly comes to be regarded as an old-line citizen and prominent civic leader. Even so, new managers sometimes find themselves in ridiculous situations because they do not thoroughly understand certain local customs, including modes of speech and conduct. Such a situation occurred to Donald M. Mumford shortly after he was promoted from executive assistant manager of the New York Statler to manager of the St. Louis Statler several years back.

The company often starts off a new manager in its St. Louis house, smallest in the original chain. Besides that, St. Louis is an exceptionally folksy and friendly place for a large city. This gives a new manager some excellent ground upon which to cultivate the art of being civic-minded.

About the time of Mumford's arrival as manager in St. Louis, there had occurred in the kitchens of that hotel a minor imbroglio between two Negro bus boys, in which one boy had cut the other with a razor. He was fired, and the hotel sent the other boy to a hospital to recover. A brief report of this encounter crossed the new manager's desk, but he failed to notice that the two given names of the boy who had wielded the razor were "Governor Smith." It is a custom of some families, particularly Negroes, in Missouri and points further south to name their children for great men. Apparently this boy had been named in honor of the late Governor Alfred E. Smith, of New York.

It so happened that the Governor of Missouri at the time was named Forrest Smith, a fact of which Mumford was aware, along with the knowledge that the Governor often stopped at the Statler when visiting St. Louis. One afternoon when Mumford answered his telephone, a voice said: "Hello, Mr. Mumford. This is Governor Smith."

Mumford had never met the Governor of Missouri, nor had he ever heard the sound of his voice, but he addressed the voice on the wire with enthusiasm. "How-do-you-do Governor," Mumford shouted in his heartiest tone. "It is a privilege and a pleasure to hear from you, Governor. What can I do for you, sir?"

Mumford was so involved in being solicitous that he failed to note a faint element of surprise in the voice at the other end of the wire at the warmth of this salutation. After a short pause, the voice went on: "I was calling you, Mr. Mumford, about a little trouble I had at your hotel two or three weeks ago."

"What! Trouble! Why, Governor!" Mumford exclaimed in a shocked tone. "I can scarcely credit such a thing. Of course, we regret whatever happened more than I can tell you. But I would like to say before we go any further with this conversation: Please be assured that, not only what I can do personally, but the attention of the entire Statler organization will be turned to rectifying any inconvenience that you may have experienced."

"Well, Mr. Mumford," the voice continued with growing confidence, "I had a little trouble with a bus boy in your Terrace Room."

"Oh, Governor!" Mumford's voice was tragic. "One of our employees! This is horrible! Oh my goodness! I don't know how to apologize. I can only say that your slightest wish is our command in this matter, if you will please give me all the details."

"I'm glad to hear that you feel that way, Mr. Mumford," the voice said, "because I was calling to see if you would give me my job back. That ole switch-bladed razor of mine didn't hurt that ole boy much, and I won't cut him no more. . . ."

As far as possible within limits of Statler's standardization, the company likes for each of its houses to fit its personality into the traditional atmosphere of its city. Probably the Boston Statler has more atmosphere to fit itself into than the others, Boston being the way it is. Typical of the high-collar functions at the Boston Statler are the Morning Musicals, held half a dozen times a season, and attended by the most blue-blooded of Back Bay's dowagers, matrons, maiden ladies and other female representatives of old families. They munch cake, sip tea and listen critically to the restrained recitations of concert stars or to the gentle strains of chamber music.

So sacred are these occasions that, while they are going on, not an elevator is allowed to operate in that part of the building. No telephone is allowed to ring on that floor. Special officers are stationed in the kitchens to warn the help not to bang pots and pans together, and to handle dishes and glasses with a delicate touch, while in the street below the ballroom windows, other officers keep traffic noises politely subdued.

Since history and tradition are held in high esteem in Boston, the Statler there is fast becoming as traditional as the Old North Church. One of its traditions is an annual cocktail party and buffet commemorating the great East Coast hurricane of 1938. This is a good example of smart hotel promotion in converting an upheaval of nature into favorable publicity for the house. Each year, on the anniversary night of the hurricane, all of the prominent Bostonians who happened to be in the Statler when the hurricane struck are invited to a dinner commemorating the event, and a goodly number of them it is.

On that fateful night in 1938, the flower of Boston's business and social life had been invited to the Statler for the joint opening of the new Lounge Bar and the dancing season in the Terrace Room. When the big wind hit, a number of unscheduled events took place in the Statler, which the majority of the guests probably do not know about to this day.

The late Louis Rorimer, then Statler's head decorator, became seasick in his suite when he thought the wind caused the walls to sway. In another suite, John Hevenor, now vice-president of the company, was trapped when his window blew out. This produced a suction in his room so that he could not open the door into the corridor. He had to wait out the storm alone and remote from the comforts of the new bar.

A trio of Mexican musicians, who had been employed for the Lounge Bar, were busy in their room sorting through their library of sheet music. They had several trunkfuls of it stacked on the beds, on tables, in chairs and on the floor, when the window blew in. The Mexicans managed to wrench open their door into the corridor, and fled, followed by their entire library of sheet music.

Down in the Terrace Room, Clyde Lucas and his orchestra were tuning up to start the fall dancing season. There were some electrical guitars in the band, but the hotel's electricians were too busy plugging up windows that were blowing in to bother with plugging the band's electrical instruments into wall sockets. The musicians finally made the connections themselves, which was unfortunate, since they plugged into the direct current, instead of the alternating outlets. The instruments blew up with loud reports and small acrid puffs of smoke.

Meanwhile, some members of a conventioning ladies' organization, the Daughters of ——, were creating considerable interest in the bar. Perhaps the ladies had taken an extra cocktail or so against the inclement weather, for they had seen fit to adorn their busts with some circular strips of paper, an inch wide and about two feet in diameter that they had removed from the toilet seats in their bathrooms. It is a Statler policy, when a room is vacated, to sterilize the toilet seats before the next guest comes in, and to leave one of these strips around the seats to inform the new guest that such a service has been done.

Thus, the ladies caused raised eyebrows among the proper Bostonians present when they appeared in the bar with their bosoms emblazoned with the words: "Sterilized for Your Protection."

In times of crisis, such as the New England hurricane, the Statler people feel that their employees are more efficient and loyal than most, because they often make a lifetime career with the company. Around nine per cent of the company's more than 8,000 employees have been with Statler twenty-five years or longer. More than thirty years ago, Statler became the first hotel company to start vacations with pay and free insurance for all employees. Nowadays, recreational councils in each house sponsor dances for employees, card parties, golf and softball tournaments, and an annual bowling tournament is held between teams representing all the houses in the chain. Employees in each hotel give musical shows for their own and their families' entertainment once or twice a year, and at Christmastime, employee choruses serenade guests with caroling in the lobby.

Once a year, at a dinner given in each house, employees who are completing their twenty-fifth year with the company are given a certificate and a $100 U.S. bond. All other employees who have already completed their twenty-five years and received their recognition are invited to the feast, featuring *filet mignon* and baked Alaska.

At these occasions, employees like to recall some of their strange experiences in hotel work, such as the case of the old lady from California who had come to Boston for medical treatment, and was stopping at the Statler. She had explained to the headwaiter that her food must be prepared very simply, and asked for someone to wait on her regularly. She was assigned an old captain of waiters, whose feet were giving out and who was about ready for retirement.

The old captain looked after the old lady's wants in the dining room for three or four weeks; then she went home. Six months later, a representative from a law firm came to the hotel looking for this captain of waiters, but his feet had finally collapsed, and he had been forced to quit. He didn't have much to live on, because a lot of old ladies, like the one from California, forget to tip old waiters. But it seems the old lady in California had died and had left the old waiter $10,000 as her one tip.

In Washington a few Christmases ago, a waiter named Constantine Collins had resolved to give all his tips for one day to the Christ Child Society, which operates a convalescent home near

Rockville, Maryland. Collins' ten-year-old son had been a patient there, and had recovered from a critical operation. So the waiter felt grateful.

On the day Collins had selected to give the society his tips, he received one for fifty dollars from an open-handed room-service patron, who handed him the bill, and said "Merry Christmas." In thanking him, the waiter explained to the guest his intention of giving the money to the Christ Child Society. The guest, a textile manufacturer and philanthropist, Allen L. Goldfine, of New York, was so impressed that he eventually made a contribution of $18,000 to the society, which used the money to complete the cardiac wing to its hospital.

The company's monthly house organ, *The Statler News,* edited by J. P. Richardson, Statler's advertising manager, makes great use of items of this nature. Quite often such stories get much wider circulation in the national and international press and radio, because the Statler people have an advanced approach to publicity. They are probably the most successful of all hotel companies in getting the names of their hotels bandied about favorably before the reading and listening public.

Each of the Statlers has either a full-time or a part-time publicity representative, with offices and a press room in the hotel. The company prints a book of instructions and principles to guide its publicity people.

The book warns publicity men not to try to place articles that are trivial and not newsworthy. "Editors' confidence in your judgment would be impaired." They are encouraged to invite newspaper and radio people to the hotel for cocktails, luncheon or dinner, and to create in their pressrooms a "press club" atmosphere. They are cautioned against favoritism in breaking news releases with one newspaper or radio station.

When news breaks that is unfavorable to the hotel—a suicide or theft or an accident—the Statler representative is firmly instructed:

Do not attempt to conceal from the press the fact that the occurrence did take place. You, in fact, are expected to go further, to report the occurrence to the papers immediately, before it is picked up elsewhere.

Give them all the facts. Try not to leave any loose ends. If a story is cleaned up in one day, so much the better. The material will be lacking to revive it the next day.

The company has found that this straightforward approach is appreciated by editors, who are more inclined to play down the hotel's name in these cases than if the company had tried to hide the facts.

On stories favorable to the company, however, the publicity people are instructed, above all, to

look for the unusual angle. . . . When something unusual, something cute, something funny, something extraordinarily moving happens in your house, if you think the occurrence merits wide coverage, *pick up the phone, and call the executive offices in New York.* A good feature is best when it is fresh. Network news commentators are looking for the light, uplifting human interest material. A cute anecdote enables them to end the broadcast, concerned for the most part with heavy material, on a bright note. Besides, your good features can be used in many other ways. . . .

A good example of what the book is talking about here is a story that became known as "The Statler of the Sticks" during the fall of 1950 when versions of it were published in practically all the daily newspapers in America. It was remarked upon by most of the better-known radio commentators, and hit television and the newsreels. It became, in fact, one of the outstanding national feature stories of the year.

The story concerned one John K. Hill, proprietor of the Center Ossipee Inn, in the wilds of New Hampshire, who had adopted as the slogan for his inn "The Statler of the Sticks." He had printed this slogan upon the paper napkins used in his dining room, on his stationery and at various places about his property. The fun began one day when Mr. Hill received a letter from the law firm in New York, of Root, Ballantine, Harlan, Bushby & Palmer, which said:

Dear Mr. Hill: It has come to the attention of our client, Hotels Statler, Inc., that you are using for your inn the term, "The Statler of the Sticks." While the Statler Company realizes that you operate a very reputable and well-run inn, it is contrary to the policy of the Statler Company to permit the use of its name except by hotels owned and operated by the company. In fact, we have been obliged to take steps in different parts of the country to prevent unauthorized use of the Statler name. We should appreciate it very much, therefore, if you would discontinue your use of the Statler name. Will you kindly advise us accordingly, and oblige. . . .

Now, Mr. Hill is a wiry, tough, sawed-off craggy-faced salty New Englander, and the letter from the big legal firm struck him as pretty stuffy. He chewed on his lead pencil, scratched his head, and composed a reply, couched in the idiom of Abe Martin and Chick Sale, which said in part:

Gentlemen: I have at hand your letter asking me to cease and desist from using the name of Statler in my advertising. . . . If I do not stop using the name, I suppose you will write and say you will make trouble for me. That will be an awfully hard thing for you to do for several reasons, viz, as follows and to wit:

My wife left me, getting tired of me and this town, and when she left, did dump into my lap—or rather, left underneath the blotter—about $1,000 worth of bills, which I am paying off. Two of my daughters have recently got married to young fellows, who may or may not come to live off me with or without any sundry offsprings, which may or may not be on the way.

There is a substantial mortgage on this place. I do not keep any checking account, holding my cash in my left and right pants pockets, and keeping my accounts on a clear pine board, which I burn March 16. . . . My legal advisors are two of the justices of the New Hampshire Superior Court, the Chief Justice of the Supreme Court of New Hampshire, also our County Judge Probate, our County Solicitor, our Municipal Court Justice, our High Sheriff and our local troop of State Police. All these gentlemen help themselves to coffee and doughnuts in my kitchen when the spirit moves them, which seems to be about every day.

I have taken your letter up with each and every one of them, who say that the action begun by you is damned mean, as the type of house I have conducted for nearly forty years brings honor to the name of Statler, and, if anything, the Statler folks owe me money for boosting them, instead of stopping me from using their name on my letterhead. . . .

In fact, I have always given, and do now give, a level of personal service far beyond any offered by the Statler organization to its guests. For instance, I always furnish the guest with a rat trap for his room free of charge. No charge is made for cheese for same. Of course, if the guest requests Camembert, Gruyere or Roquefort, a nominal charge is made. . . .

I run a clean and moral house. I ain't had but one regular guest hung for murder, and that was Fred Small, who was dropped back in 1918 over at Concord. Since he did not have a good suit for his final public appearance, I made a special trip to Concord, and gave him my suit. And that is a damn lot better service to the guest than your client, the Statler people, have in the past, or will in the foreseeable future, render a guest.

Now you might send a representative up here to talk this over. As I intimated, I have a gallery of notables patronizing my kitchen. . . . The best way to settle this matter is for you to send up a clean, sober and quiet representative of your firm around November 1, when our deer season opens. If he is a right guy, I will let him out into my kitchen, and he can state his case to the notables there assembled. . . . Cordially, (signed) John K. Hill.

Mr. Hill enclosed with his letter a cardboard poster, which proclaimed itself to be: "The Ten Commandments of the Statler of the Sticks." This document commanded the guests not to wear hobnailed boots in bed, or leave valuables at the desk for safekeeping.

Our safe has been cracked three times, and has not been replaced [it said]. If you cannot look after your own watch and money, that is distinctly not the fault of the management. . . .

No meals are served in rooms. If a guest is too sick to get down to the dining room, he should either stay in bed or go to a hospital. Guests must not criticize the cooking. If you do not like it, you are at perfect liberty to go out to the kitchen and try to do better. . . .

In case of disagreement regarding cards or politics, please refrain from fighting or calling the Sheriff. . . . In case of fire, please do not call the Fire Department. Our local department usually does more damage than the fire. . . .

It is true that some eyebrows were raised when these remarkable documents arrived at the sedate offices of Root, Ballantine, Harlan, Bushby & Palmer on Nassau Street in New York. But this distinguished firm had served the Statler Company long enough to realize that here might be a publicity coup for that organization, and Hill's letter was passed along to Statler's public relations offices.

Here, they were quick to see, was a story with perfect appeal— the little country innkeeper, with a sense of humor, fighting the rich hotel organization in New York. The story's popularity with readers was assured, but Statler went to some pains to be shown in a favorable light instead of as a heartless commercial tyrant. The Young & Rubicam advertising agency, which represents Statler, was also representing the radio network program, "We the People." So Statler, through its advertising agents, tipped off Dan Seymour, producer of "We the People," about Hill, and Seymour invited him to New York to appear on that program.

As soon as he had accepted, the Statler people invited the proprietor of the Center Ossipee Inn to be their guest in the biggest suite in their hotel during his stay in New York. Mr. Hill accepted that also, and Statler began to set up press conferences and give attention to possible photographic angles in his rooms, as though preparing for the reception of a visiting prime minister from abroad. Practically all the press and radio represented in the New York area, including *House and Garden* and *The Voice of America,* were invited to meet and interview Mr. Hill.

Mr. Hill arrived as scheduled, and his sojourn was a success to all parties concerned. The newspapers, news services, radio, etc., got a good story. Statler garnered more good publicity than any other hotel company received that year. And, when he got back home to Center Ossipee, Mr. Hill's inn was overflowing with curious guests, who had heard about all these goings-on, and wished to view Mr. Hill and his hotel first hand.

The high point of his stay in New York occurred when Mr. Hill and Arthur F. Douglas shook hands and exchanged pleasantries; Mr. Hill promised to abandon his slogan, and Mr. Douglas said "Thank you." The two then buried a hatchet in a mound of earth that had been brought into the suite, while a large portion of the nation's newspapers, wire services, radio networks, television networks and newsreel companies recorded these ceremonies for the enlightenment of people everywhere. At year's end, the United Press editors voted the "Statler of the Sticks" incident the fifth best news story that happened in New England in 1950 and the funniest anywhere in the land.

Another example of Statler publicity's being on the ball happened in the summer of 1951 when General Douglas MacArthur returned to this country, and was accorded one of the greatest

ovations in history and one of the largest coverages of newspaper
space and radio time. The Washington Statler, which anticipated
this as soon as it understood the General was returning—and wishing to get into the act—sent cables inviting him to stay at the
Statler while in Washington.

The General accepted. Not only did the Statler reap all sorts of
publicity while he was in Washington, when every breath he took
was news. But for several days before his arrival, photographs of
the Statler's Presidential suite, where the General and his family
were to stay, were appearing on the front pages of newspapers all
over the country. Earle P. Brown, the Washington house's publicity man, arranged, among other gimmicks, for a piano tuner to
come up and be photographed getting the grand piano in the suite
in proper tone for young Arthur MacArthur to practice his music
lessons—an attention that instrument had not received since the
elevation of a certain musician to the high office in the land for
which the suite is named.

A good many other Washington hotels may or may not have extended invitations to the General. What probably helped the Statler
to nab him was that the Statler sent its invitations—not to the General—but to his aide, Lieutenant Colonel Sidney Huff. The Statler
knew that it is usually a General's aide who attends to such details.
Furthermore, a cable addressed to General MacArthur would probably have become mixed in the thousands of messages he was
receiving at the moment, and might have been lost in the shuffle.

Perhaps Statler's greatest publicity stroke of all time involved
another military figure. He was a certain Captain Frank L. Lillyman,
of the parachute troops in Europe. Through the eager abetment of
the Statler Company, Captain Lillyman became, for a while in
1945, the articulate voice of most of the men overseas in uniform
talking about the comforts back home.

This all began one wet night shortly after the end of the war
when Captain Lillyman, a native of Syracuse, New York, found
himself in a shell-torn hut not far from the French-German border
—alone, except for a couple of bottles of French wine and a portable typewriter. He sat there all night in the cold. And, as the candle
became spilled wax and the wine melted to dregs, Captain Lillyman
wrote a long letter.

He had been in Europe for more than a year at the time, and in the whole period he had not eaten a real egg or seen a real bottle of milk. Nor had he tasted any luxury. So he put into his letter all the things to eat that he had yearned for while relegated to the dismal continent from which he wrote. He mailed it to the manager of the Statler Company's Pennsylvania Hotel in New York, and this is what his letter said:

Dear Sir: Inasmuch as I have not written a business letter in several years, I shall attempt to make this a personal letter to get my ideas across. I have noticed many of the magazines that reach us carry advertisements of the Statler Hotels that say they can meet all emergencies. This isn't exactly an emergency, but more of a problem, and I am asking you to help me with it.

Every man who has been overseas has had certain dreams, plans, or what-have-you that he is going to do when he gets back to the States. I have had mine, and I will outline them to you, and when it is all through, ask you three questions: (1) Can you do it? (2) How much will it cost? and (3) How much advance notice will you require?

First of all, allow me to introduce myself—it may help you to make a decision and to assure you that I am not completely insane. Name: Lillyman, Frank L., a captain of parachute troops, now assigned to Intelligence Service and expected to arrive in October (late) or early November. Five combat operations, three hospitalizations and eight decorations.

I have written down during the past two years the things I want when I return to the States. I have a wife and daughter three and a half years old. When I arrive home, I desire to stay at a hotel like the Pennsylvania for approximately seven days. I desire a suite that will face east so the sun will wake me up in the morning.

Each morning I shall want a cup of English-made tea served to me in bed, and during the approximately seven days I shall reside there, I will want three meals a day, made up of dishes from the list that follows. I do not desire to know in advance what dishes will be served, but I do not want a dish repeated. I desire my breakfasts in the suite, with a suitable menu for my daughter; the noon meal likewise, but the evening meal available either in your dining room or in my suite.

During my stay at the Pennsylvania, I do not desire any employees to call me by my military rank, regardless of whether I am in uniform or not. The title, "Mister," will be music to my ears. I desire a maid to be available for my wife, who is capable of taking care of the child, and prefer her to be a large, gray-haired, motherly type wearing a black dress with a white apron and white cap.

Each morning, when breakfast is served in the suite, a fresh, appropriate bouquet of flowers to be delivered to my wife, with one of my cards. Each morning, when breakfast is served, a new doll or suitable toy to be delivered to my daughter. I would also like a suggested schedule for day's activities, including sightseeing, shopping, movies, theater and night clubs. At breakfast also, a copy of the Syracuse *Herald*, New York *News, Mirror* and Syracuse (NY) *Post-Standard.*

In the suite I would like a record player with any and all Strauss selections, especially Tales of the Vienna Woods, and such other records as you would suggest. I would also like a radio.

The daily menus can be made up from the following, and supplemental dishes, to assure a balanced diet, I will leave to your discretion: BREAKFAST: (in addition to the morning tea.) Orange juice, real juice not canned. Sliced bananas with cream, sliced fresh peaches with cream, Quaker's puffed-wheat with cream, warm shredded wheat with cream, raspberries, blueberries, or blackberries with cream; waffles with real maple syrup; light scrambled eggs made with real cream, melted butter, salt and pepper, two poached eggs on thin, buttered toast; three slices of fried, boiled ham, without fat, with a fried egg sunny-side-up but the yolk pink and the whites firm, fried in butter—two medium boiled eggs with fried little pork sausages; V-8 vegetable juice and fresh milk. Silex coffee brewed in the room, so I can smell it cooking.

LUNCHES: Tuna fish salad with quarter-sliced, hard-boiled eggs and long slices of real pimentos; lobster salad, chicken salad with celery, little pork sausages with melted Kraft cheese; creamed potatoes au gratin, a big baked potato, sliced cold tongue, Campbell's pork and beans, shrimp salad and shrimp cocktail; hot, homemade biscuits, fresh milk.

DINNER: Filet mignon with lots of mushrooms, planked steak with lots of mushrooms, T-bone steak (no fat) with lots of mushrooms, broiled lobster with butter and lemon sauce, broiled veal cutlet, escalloped potatoes, lobster à la Newburg, crêpes suzette, shrimp cocktail.

In addition to the three meals mentioned, I would like, preferably before retiring, the following to be made available: a banana split with cherry, vanilla and peach ice cream, chopped walnuts on which sliced peaches and sweet syrup would be covered with whipped cream, and a maraschino cherry on each scoop of ice cream; a sweet cantaloupe, a quarter of watermelon, a sweet honey dew melon, smoked herring and a big dill pickle.

For desserts to the mid-day meal and dinner, selections will be made from the following: whipped cream or custard puffs, éclairs, French pastry, strawberry shortcake with light warm shortcakes—the berries crushed and the cake covered with whipped cream and a whole strawberry on top.

If meals are served after dark in the suite, I would like tapers for table lighting. I desire a one-way telephone that is out-going only.

I am afraid my desires are a bit far-fetched, but there they are, and once again, I'll ask three questions:

(1) Can you do it? (If you can't, it is all right.—If you can, you can cite this case in your future advertisements.)

(2) How much will it cost? (I'm a captain, not a general.)

(3) How much advance notice will you require? (Guarantee to wire you the day I hit the States.)

Thanking you in advance for even taking the time to consider such an absurd letter, I remain

> Sincerely yours,
> Frank L. Lillyman,
> Sept. 26, 1945.

Well, the Statler Company took him up, and, of course, it was all on the house. The Pennsylvania's manager, James H. McCabe, wrote Captain Lillyman assuring him that all these things were possible: the bouquets, tea ("as English as we can make it,") the newspapers, the record player and Strauss waltzes, the menus, the lighted tapers, the "grey-haired, motherly type maid in a dark uniform." McCabe pointed out that employees of the house customarily addressed guests as "Sir," and asked, "Would this be permissible instead of 'Mister.' Please set us straight on that."

The hotel ended its letter with something as near a flourish of trumpets and a roll of drums as can be gotten on paper:

You ask what it costs, Not One Red Cent. We wish that all the men who have completed the grand job you have could receive the same recognition and hospitality. Obviously, this is not feasible, but the Hotel Pennsylvania can do this for one man, and that man is you. . . . In the name of those who, over the years, have been our guests and friends at Hotel Pennsylvania and throughout the Statler system, we welcome you.

The Lillyman story may have received more play than any feature ever developed by a hotel. Not only the newspapers, radio, newsreels, etc., set up press headquarters to cover the doings of the

Lillyman Family, but it was all recorded in *Time, Life, Look, Newsweek, The Readers Digest,* ad infinitum. Probably somewhere or other, records of these doings were buried in the cornerstone of a new post office.

After that, a good many other people tried with hotels and a good many hotels tried with other soldiers to imitate the Lillyman episode, but none of them worked. It was the kind of a story that is good for only once, because it was spontaneous and real. What made it that way was that it came at a time when several millions of American soldiers were in sight of home, and Captain Lillyman had expressed, in general, what most of them would like to have found when they got there.

That is the sort of feature the Statler publicity men pray for.

25

The Crumbling Palaces

Never, since the tavern ceased to be a community problem and became a community center, has the hotel industry fully appreciated the exalted prestige it has achieved. With some exceptions, outstanding of which is probably the Statler Company, the advance and progress of the hotel industry as a whole over the past twenty years has been halting, resisting and complaining. The hotel business may well be the most reluctant successful industry in the history of American enterprise.

It did not become the seventh largest industry in America so much because of its own enterprise and resourcefulness as because it occupies a position of glamour in the imaginations of most people, who are inclined to tolerate its ineptitudes and weaknesses and to wish it well. In spite of some guests' excessive and ridiculous demands of hotels, people by and large tend to overlook the bumblings in service and shortcomings in equipment and comforts of many hotels that claim to be first class. This is because people like to *think* they are getting attention and service, and the hotel is the only place they know to go to seek these things. The hotel is the common man's palace, and, as has been said, everybody has a basic need for a palace of some sort every now and then.

Whether or not it wishes to accept the responsibility, a community's leading hotel is as much a public institution as it is a private enterprise. This is a unique and enviable place for a private business to occupy, but a great many hotel owners are inclined to regard it as more of a burden than an opportunity.

Since the booming days of the 1920's when great numbers of hotels were built—often not as the result of a real need, but as an expression of the booster exuberance of that bounding era—many hotel operators have withdrawn into their shells. They have become impervious to suggestions that they make real improvements of their facilities or expansion of their properties, regardless of obvious needs. And a good example of this state of affairs existed until recently in Dallas, Texas, one of the fastest growing of American communities.

That city has two leading hotels, the Adolphus and the Baker. Since completion of the Baker in 1925, the population of Dallas has increased by 347,000, or 129 per cent, and 780 new manufacturers have started in business there. Late in 1951 there were seven more major office buildings under construction. Yet, in all this period and with all of that growth, the only expansion of the city's major hotel facilities has been the addition of 250 rooms to the Adolphus.

Now Dallas is the center of one of the richest and most promising areas in America. It is the financial center and the fashion capital of the Southwest. People come regularly from as far as 500 miles away to trade in Dallas. The football stadium there seats 75,320 persons, and football in Dallas is more of a unified, all-consuming community ceremony and fiesta than a mere sporting event. Tickets for big games go at from twenty-five to fifty dollars each. Practically every hotel room in Dallas is engaged far ahead of time, sometimes as long as a year or so in advance. Overflow crowds occupy most of the rentable rooms within a 100-mile radius.

The Dallas Chamber of Commerce sponsors four times a year the American Fashion Association shows, attended by some 5,000 retailers from seventeen states and by about 500 dealers from fashion manufacturing centers of the country. These exhibitors and their displays alone take up a large part of the hotel space. Retailers attending the shows bed down in motels, boarding houses and tourist camps all over that part of Texas. Those living within

100 miles of Dallas often drive in for the show each day, and go home at night.

There had been much gnashing of teeth in recent years by persons who wished to stay in Dallas hotels but could not get rooms, even when football and fashion occasions were not flooding the facilities. One of the city's leading merchants reported that he often received sarcastic replies when he wrote letters to out-of-city people, inviting them to come to Dallas to shop.

"You might as well stop inviting me to Dallas until you can get me a place to stay," many of the replies said, in effect. "I'm more certain of getting a room in Kansas City."

The largest ballroom in Dallas was the Baker Hotel's Crystal Room, which seats 800 persons, but the city leaders felt that Dallas needed a ballroom that seated from 1,200 to 1,400 persons for several occasions each year. The Chamber of Commerce had been urging the local hotel operators and others to erect a hotel with such facilities, and usually when the agitation became heated, the hotel managements would indicate that they were considering a new building. But pretty soon the agitation and new hotel talk would die down.

When John W. Carpenter, a utilities executive, was elected president of the Chamber of Commerce in January, 1949, he announced that Dallas was going to have a new hotel, if the Chamber of Commerce had to build it. That body formed a hotel committee, and invited representatives of the three leading hotel chains—Hilton, Statler and Sheraton—down to talk things over. It was the Chamber of Commerce's idea to lend whoever built the hotel some money at low interest rates, and to use its influence to throw as much business as possible in the direction of the new hotel.

The Statler Company was the one with whom the Chamber of Commerce committee came to an agreement: that Statler would build a 700-room hotel at a cost of approximately $11,000,000, of which the Chamber of Commerce would raise $1,500,000, and loan to Statler at two per cent interest per year for fifteen years. Conrad N. Hilton had asked the Dallas group to raise twice that amount, if he was to build the hotel. But the main reason the Dallas group wanted Statler, according to Robert Thornton, bank president and member of the hotel committee, was that the group was impressed by the Statler name and reputation, and desired a "class hotel, meaning the top in modern-type luxury hotels," which they felt Statler would build.

Now Mr. Hilton operates a number of hotels that are known as "class hotels." Among these is the elderly Plaza in New York, a dignified and charming old monument to the latter nineteenth century. But it is as dated as the hansom cabs that wait across the street to haul tourists through Central Park. Of course, it would be impossible to build such a hotel that would be profitable in these times, even if anyone should want to reproduce the Plaza. Furthermore, Mr. Hilton had not built a "class hotel," or any other sort of hotel in this country, since before the days of the depression, and the Dallas committee knew it. Like his other holdings, Mr. Hilton had bought the Plaza secondhand, after the Plaza had served a long and full life and when its chief charm lay in its senility.

But the Dallas group wouldn't have wanted anything like the Plaza even if they could have had it. They had in mind a hotel that would exude class in the modern manner, which would become the talk of the Southwest—something new and shining and modern. In fact, the Dallas committee's contract with the Statler Company specifies that the Dallas hotel shall be "of the same class and type" as the Statler Hotel in Washington.

The Dallas hotel people should not be too much censured for not responding to public outcries to build new hotels there. Probably the same thing happens, in some degree, in all cities that need a new hotel. For the facts are that hotel building is a risky and highly technical business, as has been shown by wholesale collapses of hotels in the past, and very few hotel owners or operators know much about building a hotel. They never had the opportunity to learn.

Back in the days when the old Waldorf-Astoria was setting the fashion in fine hotels, most of the famous houses were not built for any very logical reason, but usually because of loyalty, or pride, or passion.

Sometimes hotels were built because some wealthy man got mad at an existing hotel. The Philadelphia Ritz-Carlton was conceived in 1910 by George Widener, a member of that prominent Philadelphia family of wealthy sportsmen, because he was miffed at the Bellevue-

Stratford. He had asked for a certain dining room for a dinner party and didn't get it. So Widener, with a true hotel builder's logic of that era, announced he was going to build a hotel that would drive the Bellevue-Stratford out of business. He put up the money for the hotel, and signed a management contract with the Ritz Development Company, which managed the house from the time of its completion in 1911 until 1918. However, Widener did not live to see his hotel completed. He was returning from Paris to the United States with plans for the building, and took passage on the *Titanic*.

Then there were a good many wealthy men who built monuments to themselves in the form of a hotel, and the old Waldorf-Astoria itself is a good example of that. The Waldorf was conceived by William Waldorf Astor, after his neighbors along Fifth Avenue had voted the Democratic ticket, probably for the first time in their lives, to defeat Astor when he ran as a Republican for Congress from that silk-stocking district. Astor, concluding that he was not appreciated at home, moved away to England, where he became a viscount and the first of the line of English Astors, who at present have as their most illustrious representative Lady Nancy Astor, M.P.

Before he left to become a Briton, however, William Waldorf Astor announced his intention of building a memorial to himself on the site of his home, the southern half of the block west of Fifth Avenue between Thirty-third and Thirty-fourth streets. All the neighborhood was agog to learn whether this edifice would be a fine church or maybe a library.

They were horrified when they learned that it was to be a hotel, as hotels were held in low esteem in those days. Most enraged of all was John Jacob Astor, IV, a cousin of the hotel builder, whose home occupied the northern half of the same block.

The Waldorf Hotel opened in 1893, and, because it was such a splendid building and because of the managerial and promotional genius of its lessor, George C. Boldt, the Waldorf became a famous sight along Fifth Avenue instead of a problem and an eyesore. It did more to elevate the prestige of hotels than any other hotel that ever existed.

Cousin John Jacob Astor was impressed, but he still did not like to live next door to a hotel. So he had his home torn down, and he built the Astoria Hotel that connected with the Waldorf. It was opened in 1896. The two hotels, which were operated as one, became such a stamping ground for wealthy society and the sporting set that the Waldorf-Astoria's fame need not be dwelt upon further here. Its passing was mourned by its patrons as though for the death of a great and loved man. Even now, a good many people who do not know any better like to say that hotels of the old Waldorf type should never have been allowed to die. This is about as silly as pining for the return of the sedan chair as a means of transportation.

The Waldorf and the Astoria hotels were built as near together as possible, and connected with large archways. But, unknown to most patrons, there were heavy steel doors that slid into the walls. The purpose of these was to separate the two structures so that they could be operated separately in case relations between the Cousins Astor, which were not too happy, should ever become too strained.

Such foolishness as this characterized the conception and building of a great many of this country's famous hotels late in the last century and early in this one. The only reason why hotels conceived under such ridiculous circumstances were able to survive— let alone become rich and famous—was that they had little competition; there was plenty of money among the upper classes, few taxes and low building and help costs.

The old Waldorf-Astoria and other hotels of its ilk were more European than American in concept and conduct. Like old art treasures, they were imported into this country by American millionaires from their culture-seeking junkets on the Continent, and were never truly American at all. A few of them hung around for many years, and contributed much to American folklore. It was only as recently as 1951 that the final remnant of this nostalgic hotel culture choked its life away among the clouds of mortar dust that attended the wrecking of the Ritz-Carlton on Madison Avenue in New York.

Regarded in a cold and unromantic light, these old palaces did more harm than good to the American hotel industry; they tended to be more confusing than constructive to Americans who wished to enter the hotel business. Most of these men were content to copy the type of hotel invented by E. M. Statler. They were on sound enough ground there, but they seemed to have the idea, perhaps inspired by the successes of the illogically inspired hotels of the old Waldorf epoch, that just because they chose to build a hotel, it was bound to succeed.

And so arrived the wild hotel-building era of the 1920's, when most of the present leading hotels were built. Many resulted from wild stock-selling schemes, such as the Madison Hotel in New York, a $3,300,000 structure on paper. It was built by a syndicate that put only $100,000 worth of equity into the structure and sold bonds to innocent investors for the remainder. Hotels were built all over the country with stock so watered that the buildings often did not represent more than half the value of the bonds.

Other hotels were honest buildings, but were erected as a result of community pride and enthusiasm when and where no hotel was needed. A good example of this is the new Waldorf-Astoria. After the old Waldorf was sold and wrecked, a dozen New York millionaires decided to sponsor a new $40,000,000 Waldorf, with assistance of the New York Central and the New York, New Haven & Hartford railroads, upon whose property the big new project was to be built. New York had no real use for this magnificent hotel at the time. Far too many hotels had been built already, but the new Waldorf was conceived as a piece of sentiment, based upon the premise that any hotel with that name in New York could not but succeed.

And so the millionaires deposited their part of the financing on a Monday in October, 1929. The next day, as it turned out, was "Black Tuesday" on the New York Stock Exchange. But the plans were not abandoned, because a Waldorf could not fail. The building went bravely ahead as the depression darkened and to the accompaniment of the distant crashes of hotel financial structures tumbling here and there about the land.

Then one day in 1931 the splendid new Waldorf-Astoria had its grand opening. Thirty thousand people came to cheer and admire and to make off with every ash tray in the house as souvenirs. President Hoover made a speech, and the bright lights blazed that night from every window at Park Avenue and Fiftieth Street. And then, within six weeks, the fine new hotel was two-thirds empty, and the

Waldorf proceeded to lose an average of $4,000 every day for the next seven years.

The same sort of thing happened to thousands of other hotels, under less dramatic circumstances and on a smaller scale. By the time the hotel industry began to recover with the war boom of the early 1940's, four-fifths of the American hotels had been through the wringer. The parties who ended up owning the wrung-out hotel properties had adopted the cautious policy of "hold-on-to-what-you've-got-and-avoid-expansion-at-all-costs"—an attitude that persists with a good many hotel ownerships to this good day.

And throughout all these adventures, peaks and depths experienced by the hotel industry, the average hotel operator or owner never did learn many sound ideas about how to build a hotel—except, perhaps, not to try. The 27,987 hotels listed by the U. S. Department of Commerce in 1939 had dwindled to 24,448 by 1948, and this decline took place over a period of unparalleled good business enjoyed by American hotels.

Undoubtedly a good many hotel owners or would-be owners would have liked to build new houses before now, but know-how is lacking on how to translate traditional hotel functions into a building that can be practical in the postwar economy. Persons wishing to build a hotel of 300 to 500 rooms in these times for a city of maybe 450,000 population have to build spacious ballrooms and public spaces to handle large community occasions, if they expect to fulfill the traditional duties of leading hotels. And so far, no workable plan has been devised that will allow these facilities to be built and carried financially by such a hotel in these times of high building costs.

Another stumbling block to new hotel construction has been the reluctance of investors to lend money on new hotels. Investors, such as insurance companies, learned a bitter lesson during the 1920's, and have been inclined to take a low view of hotel investments generally ever since. The glaring exception here is the Statler Company. Investors, impressed with the operations of that firm, have been making large loans at low rates to Statler ever since the war.

Because of the desire of large investors to lend money on its operations, it may be the Statler Company that will solve for the hotel industry the problem of how to build medium-sized hotels, as it was the late Mr. Statler who invented the pattern for large hotels about forty years ago. With a 450-room hotel planned to start in Hartford, Connecticut, in 1952, the Statler Company is entering the medium-sized hotel field for the first time.

The Aetna Insurance Company, which had lent Statler money for other projects, became interested in getting Statler to build a new hotel in Hartford, which had not had a new one in many years. The insurance people made such an attractive proposition that Statler prepared to enter the medium-sized hotel field, even though the founder was strictly a big-hotel man. The Aetna and Travelers insurance companies put up $5,000,000 jointly. Statler's share was $900,000 to provide the furnishings.

Before starting to work on its Hartford plans, the Statler Company architects got some experience in smaller-hotel design in creating the thirty-six-room "practice inn" for the Department of Hotel Administration at Cornell University, Ithaca, New York. This practice hotel contains, on a reduced scale, all of a large hotel's facilities. The building, which cost $2,500,000, was made possible through the Statler Foundation, and is called "Statler Hall." The Foundation was set up in the late Mr. Statler's will for the further-ance of knowledge of hotel operations in America.

Cornell and Michigan State universities are the two most prominent of a dozen institutions that now offer courses in hotel manage-ment. Until Cornell opened its department in 1922, no definite courses of instruction on how to run hotels were offered anywhere in this country. Such knowledge was picked up directly and in-formally, by working in hotels, but most of this know-how was based upon the ideas of the late Mr. Statler.

Now that the training plant of the country's largest and oldest hotel school has been designed by Statler architects according to Statler ideas and furnished with Statler-type equipment, the gen-eration of rising young hotel men are bound to be more than ever imbued with the tenets of the one-time bellboy of the old McLure House at Wheeling. This will probably have a healthy and stabi-lizing effect upon the conception, building and operation of hotels, which in the past has often been unrestrained, highly individualistic and often completely senseless.

Plans for the Hartford Statler have been drawn by William Tabler. If the Hartford Statler is anywhere nearly as successful as estimates indicate it will be, it will probably serve as a pattern for similar hotels the company may construct in such cities as Denver, Kansas City or Indianapolis.

The Hartford Statler will be a modernistic building, with sixty-six per cent of its guest rooms looking out over the Statehouse park in the Connecticut capital. The building's exterior will probably be of metal or glass framed with aluminum. The hotel will contain most of the cost-saving ideas and many of the innovations found in the Los Angeles Statler. There are several radical departures, however, from the Los Angeles plan in the interest of flexibility of operations in a smaller hotel.

An important feature of the Hartford plan is that it contains only one kitchen. By way of contrast, the Washington Statler, which is twice the size of Hartford and has the name of being one of the most efficient commercial hotels ever built, has four kitchens. The Hartford kitchen has been arranged on the same floor with and to serve directly the coffee shop, lounge bar, ballroom and main dining room and supper club.

One of the biggest overheads carried by leading hotels has always been the ballroom, a large space that is used only occasionally. The Hartford insurance companies and civic leaders felt that the new Statler should have a ballroom that seated as many as 1,300, but a ballroom of that size would be used only a few times a year. The rest of the time it would merely deteriorate.

Tabler, however, has devised a plan which allows the ballroom space to be used daily as private dining or meeting rooms, separated from one another by double sliding doors. These are made of a new type of plastic intended to deaden sound. They will slide into the walls when the entire space is needed as a ballroom for a big occasion. The company has installed some of these doors in its private dining rooms at Boston to test their resistance to sound. If they succeed in blocking sound transmission properly—as indications are that they will—the Hartford Statler will become the world's first hotel that uses its grand ballroom space every day.

The Dallas Statler, which will be almost twice the size of the Hartford house, will have a regular ballroom, seating 1,400, but an interesting idea has been planned for enlarging the supper club for Saturday nights and on occasions of football weekends and other celebrations. Normally the supper club is a modest-sized room to handle regular crowds. But it is built next to the coffee shop, which may be thrown into the supper room, by means of sliding doors, on big nights. The coffee shop is designed to fit in with the decor of the entertainment room, and screens will conceal the coffee-shop counters, along the far wall, when the coffee shop is performing as a glamour spot.

One reason why the Dallas civic leaders wanted a "luxury" hotel was to appeal to the oil men who are the nearest thing to the steel and railroad millionaires of the latter 1890's and early 1900's, who made such hotels as the old Waldorf rich and famous. They tell in Dallas about one oil man who, after a four-day stay at the Baker Hotel, tipped the bellboy who waited on his suite a $1,000 thoroughbred Hereford bull. Stanley Marcus, president of the famous Neiman-Marcus store in Dallas, tells of one man who bought from him a $25,000 diamond one Saturday morning, but refused to leave the store until he had also bought three mink coats—one for his wife, one for his sister and one for his mother-in-law.

The fact that the Dallas Chamber of Commerce looked to the Statler Company to bring that booming city its first "luxury hotel" is interesting in itself. Until the last few years, the company had always been regarded as strictly a commercial operator—the best in its field, but still entirely commercial. However, times, conditions and ideas about what luxuries are change. The Statler Company has suddenly found itself operating in a "luxury hotel" field for two principal reasons: No longer can any hotel afford three servants for each room, as the old Ritz once did. And so, with rows of bowing flunkies out of the picture, the type of hotel service conceived originally by Mr. Statler—and understood best by his company—has become unquestionably the best in the hotel field. The other reason—and perhaps the more important—is that the Statler is the only company that has been going forward with new ideas in designing and operating hotels.

The innovations, gadgets and conveniences to be found in the new Statlers represent to most people a de luxe hotel just as marble stairways, rococo, mahogany, and plush meant a luxury hotel to the society of millionaires and gallants that once disported in the old Waldorf-Astoria.

"We could go out and buy up a lot of old hotels, and sit back and talk about how big we were, and probably make a lot more money than we are now," Arthur Douglas was saying not long ago. "But that seems pointless to us. Certainly it is not in the Statler tradition. We are doing all right financially, and we want to spend what money and energy we have to spare in creating some new and worth-while things in the hotel industry. Of course, we want to make some money for ourselves doing it. The Old Man's spirit would probably come up and haunt us if we did something in his name that didn't show a profit."

The Statler organization is pioneering now in the modern era as E. M. Statler was pioneering when he built the first hotel in the world with a bath in every room. That was very advanced then and very impressive. But in recent years, the comforts and conveniences found in many homes are ahead of those in hotels. The Statler notion is that the main reason for stopping in hotels in the first place, outside of sheer necessity, is that people think they can get in hotels things to which they are not accustomed at home. Which, essentially, is why people travel in the first place.

John W. Root, of the architectural firm of Holabird & Root & Burgee, who personally contributed a great deal to the designs of both the Washington and Los Angeles Statlers, has said, "I suppose you might say the architectural thing the Statler crowd is hitting at is something like this:

"You take the New York Statler, or any of those big older hotels that have been around a long time. Here is a big cavern of a lobby that is impressive in its way, with columns and balconies, but no daylight ever gets into the place. The lights are always burning, and it looks the same whether it is six o'clock on a rainy morning, or high noon on a beautiful day or midnight with a storm outside.

"On the other hand, take the Statler down at Washington. With all those glass walls, a lot of light gets in, and the lobby, restaurants and lounges reflect the moods of the weather and the hours of the day. In the late afternoon, along about cocktail time, the sun is going down, and dark is coming on. A kind of lush, romantic glow comes over the place, emphasized by the lights and soft walls.

"People get to thinking about cocktails and a nice dinner. A guy in a dress suit begins to feel he is really somebody. And women put on their low-cut dresses, and strut up and down those attractive stairways, feeling like some picture they saw in a fashion magazine. Women love walking about on stairways, somehow.

"I guess you might say what that hotel has got is sex appeal. It makes some of those old-style houses in the classic tradition, with their carved woodwork and columns, look stuffy and dull. It is the original concept of the hotel of the future. The ideas originally implanted there are the hope of the hotel business of the future."